JUSTICE AND LEGITIMACY IN UPBRINGING

Justice and Legitimacy in Upbringing

MATTHEW CLAYTON

OXFORD
UNIVERSITY PRESS

This book has been printed digitally and produced in a standard specification in order to ensure its continuing availability

OXFORD
UNIVERSITY PRESS

Great Clarendon Street, Oxford OX2 6DP

Oxford University Press is a department of the University of Oxford. It furthers the University's objective of excellence in research, scholarship, and education by publishing worldwide in

Oxford New York

Auckland Cape Town Dar es Salaam Hong Kong Karachi Kuala Lumpur Madrid Melbourne Mexico City Nairobi New Delhi Shanghai Taipei Toronto

With offices in

Argentina Austria Brazil Chile Czech Republic France Greece Guatemala Hungary Italy Japan South Korea Poland Portugal Singapore Switzerland Thailand Turkey Ukraine Vietnam

Oxford is a registered trade mark of Oxford University Press in the UK and in certain other countries

Published in the United States by Oxford University Press Inc., New York

Reprinted 2009

ISBN 978-0-19-926894-8

For my mother
and in memory of my father
passionate educators, brilliant parents

Contents

Acknowledgements

In developing the arguments set out in this book I have benefited from the criticisms and suggestions of many people. Earlier versions of certain arguments were presented at various institutions: the Institute of Education, University of London; the Department of Politics and International Relations, University of Nottingham; the Department of Sociology, University of Oxford; the Philosophy of Education Society of Great Britain Annual Conference; the Political Theory Research Seminar, University of Warwick. I am grateful to the audiences at all of the above for their comments.

The ideas in this book have developed over a number of years. Many friends, teachers, and colleagues have provided help in the form of written comments on papers or stimulating conversations about various issues. They include Harry Brighouse, Justine Burley, Simon Caney, Paula Casal, Tak Wing Chan, Thomas Christiano, Daniel Clayton, G. A. Cohen, John Cunliffe, Marc Fleurbaey, Michael Freeman, Susan Hurley, Crispin Jenkinson, Hussein Kassim, David Knott, Meira Levinson, Deborah Mabbett, Andrew Mason, David Miller, Andres Moles, Fabienne Peter, Thomas Pogge, Andrew Reeve, the late Keith Smalley, Will Smith, David Stevens, Adam Swift, John Turner, Richard Wagland, John White, Patricia White, and Martin Wilkinson. I should also like to register my thanks to Dominic Byatt and Claire Croft at Oxford University Press for their encouragement and considerable patience.

I am especially indebted to two people. Many years ago Mark Philp was my doctoral supervisor and, since that time, he has been an invaluable source of encouragement and advice. Even though his primary interests lie in different areas of political theory, I have benefited from his uncanny ability to help me clarify my thoughts and structure them in a more helpful way. I have learnt most about political philosophy from Andrew Williams whose inspiration, insight, criticism, and enthusiasm have made an enormous difference. Because of his influence, this book is significantly less dreary than it otherwise would have been.

This book was completed in 2004–5 during research leave from the University of Warwick, which was partly funded by a grant from the Arts and Humanities Research Council. I am grateful to the AHRC for its generous support.

Sections 2–4 contain material originally published in 'Political Liberalism, Disagreement, and Sectarianism', *Polis: Revista de Stiinte Politice*, 6 (1999), 71–92. I am grateful to IMAS-SA for permission to use this material.

This book is about the ideals of justice and legitimacy and their implications for the upbringing of children. After having presented an earlier version of Chapter 3 at a seminar in London, I was approached by a member of the audience who insisted that my views would be different if I raised children myself. Once I explained that I was already raising two children, she was dismayed. I thank my family—Katherine, Joe, and Hannah—for their love, support, and countless helpful and enjoyable conversations about the issues I discuss in this book. For the sake of Joe and Hannah, I hope my conception of liberal parenting is not too misguided.

I dedicate this book to my parents, June and Graham Clayton, who made me appreciate the importance of politics, philosophy, and education and the need to think seriously about them, and who have supported me in every way. I regret that my father did not live to read this book, for his reaction to it would have been something to behold. He would have disagreed with some of the positions I defend. But I like to think that he and my mother would endorse the fundamental ideals that animate this work.

Introduction

QUESTIONS OF UPBRINGING

Many, perhaps most, issues concerning the upbringing of children are strategic in nature. Parents seek guidance on how to help their children acquire necessary mental and physical skills and develop in other ways. Teachers aspire to fashion a stimulating and enriching curriculum for their pupils and apply it to meet the particular needs of different children. And the community, represented by the government, aims to make efficient budgetary decisions with respect to different kinds of educational provision. Nevertheless, apart from wanting to provide an upbringing that serves the interests of children in an efficient, stimulating, and enriching manner, we also aspire to treat children legitimately and justly. My aim in this work is to develop and defend an account of these two liberal ideals—justice and legitimacy—that is tailored to address certain important issues concerning the upbringing of children. The questions I discuss concern the *content* of a child's upbringing and the *distribution* of rights and resources that are related to it. Thus, I examine issues such as the legitimacy of parents or public officials shaping children's beliefs and desires, and the permissibility of enrolling children into controversial ethical practices. In addition, I address certain issues related to how rights to raise children should be allocated and the circumstances under which social resources should be directed to support a child's upbringing. And, finally, I consider particular questions concerning the age at which individuals should qualify for rights normally enjoyed by adults, such as the right to vote.

The account I offer rests on a particular liberal conception of political morality that is indebted to Rawls. As I explain in Chapter 1, however, Rawls would reject some of the ideals with which I operate, in particular, my account of the value of autonomy. It is not my aim to offer a faithful rendition of his conception of liberal justice and then extend it to deal with questions of upbringing. I simply take from Rawls and other philosophers those ideals and arguments that strike me as plausible and then work them into a conception that provides a distinctive and attractive account of upbringing. The foundational ideal that animates the conception I develop is the ideal of fair social cooperation between free and equal persons. Such persons have an interest in acting from a sense of justice and in leading autonomous lives. Thus, my central task is to assess the implications of these interests in justice and autonomy for educational policy and the conduct of parents.

In Chapter 2, I address two matters concerning the rights of children and parents. First, which principles should guide the allocation of childrearing rights? I contrast child-centred approaches to this question with a dual interest view in which the allocation of custody over children should be sensitive to the interests of both children and parents. Defending the latter, I then turn to address how social resources should be distributed for the purposes of childrearing, given the unequal distribution of luck that exists between families. Through no fault of theirs, some are born into families that are less well equipped to provide for their education. In the liberal view I affirm, the effects of bad luck should be shared, but to what extent? Following Dworkin, I develop a hypothetical insurance model for theorizing justice in the distribution of childrearing resources.

Having set out a conception of the rights enjoyed by parents and children respectively, in Chapters 3 and 4 I turn to certain issues concerning the content of children's upbringing. To what extent, if at all, can parents or others legitimately enrol children into particular beliefs and practices? One prominent liberal view is that the ideal of personal autonomy sets a limit to what parents can do to or for their children. On this view parents are permitted to impart particular religious beliefs, say, to their children, or include them in their religious ceremonies, provided that they allow the children to be educated in a manner that will enable them to lead autonomous lives as adults. Many have claimed that this liberal view *condemns* too much, for it effectively forbids communities from acting to preserve their own religious practices by preventing their children from being attracted to other ways of life available within society. In Chapter 3, I argue for the opposite position, namely, that the received liberal view *permits* too much. Parents, like governments, I argue, should be governed by the ideal of public reason, which requires them to bring their children up according to principles that do not depend upon controversial beliefs about religion.

If children cannot legitimately be enrolled into controversial ethical conceptions, is it similarly wrong to impart to them a desire to lead just lives? Some have argued that it is, on the grounds that the legitimacy of the liberal state depends upon the free and unmanipulated consent of the governed. Chapter 4 challenges this claim and presents a conception of political legitimacy that requires the development of a sense of justice in children. It also sets out the contours of that sense with a discussion of various liberal virtues, including civility and reciprocity, and an assessment of the relevance of nationality in political education.

In the final chapter we return to questions concerning the allocation of legal rights, this time addressing justice in the acquisition of rights that are normally held by adults but denied to children. Are age-based restrictions on the enjoyment of legal rights justifiable and, if so, where should we set the age of majority? Focusing on the issue of the age of electoral majority, Chapter 5 offers an argument in favour of a minimum voting age and itemizes the considerations that should determine at which age it should be set.

The conception of upbringing I present is neither complete nor fully defended. It is incomplete because there are many important issues that I do not consider. With respect to distributive matters, for example, I do not discuss whether it is just for parents to buy expensive private schooling for their children in order to provide them with a competitive educational advantage over their peers, and I do not engage with debates over affirmative action or the funding of further and higher education. And it is not fully defended, because although in Chapter 2 I set out a conception of justice for the distribution of educational resources and defend that conception against various objections, I do not establish that it is preferable to alternative accounts of educational justice, such as those that attach priority to the elimination of class-based inequalities.[1] My aim, however, is not to offer a critical survey of alternative conceptions that have been articulated by others, but to develop and defend a positive account of justice in upbringing.

Many liberal accounts of upbringing are primarily concerned with articulating principles to guide the educational policies pursued by governments. Thus, they ask questions concerning whether, and under what conditions, faith schools should be subsidized by public funds, what kind of political education, if any, should be offered to children in schools, whether the availability of expensive private schooling is consistent with distributive justice, and how school budgets should be set in the light of the significant inequalities that exist between different regions or neighbourhoods. Such accounts operate with a distinction between political and personal morality. While we have duties to treat others justly these can be externalized in the social, economic, and legal institutions that constrain us. So our duty to reduce social and economic inequality, for example, might be accommodated by economic arrangements that tax income or expenditure and transfer resources according to individuals' entitlements from the point of view of justice. This moral division of labour is appealing, it is claimed, because if we can fashion such arrangements that fulfil our duties of justice, we can get on with pursuing our personal goals and relationships in the knowledge that by complying with these institutional requirements we are conforming to the demands of justice.[2]

The standing challenge to this moral division of labour is summed up in the slogan that advertises the position of certain feminists and egalitarians: 'the personal is political'. A conception of justice is incomplete, they claim, if its purview does not include the personal choices people make about family or occupation. Justice is denied if inequality is exacerbated by the economic bargaining of the talented rich, not just in virtue of the prevalence of unfair tax and benefit arrangements. And some argue that while justice between the sexes requires various reforms of the workplace and childcare policy, it is also served by spouses observing an equal division of both paid and unpaid work in their daily lives. Thus, a conception of justice should evaluate the conduct of economic agents or spouses, for example, even if the option of enforcing these requirements of justice through the mechanisms of the state is unavailable or unattractive.

This is a powerful challenge that invites liberal theorists to re-examine the contours of the distinction between political and personal morality. In some cases, liberals might seek to defend themselves by insisting that the costs of abandoning or revising the moral division of labour are too great. But they might also consider extending the reach of their ideals of freedom and equality to evaluate certain kinds of personal conduct that they have traditionally been loath to discuss. One of the distinctive features of the conception I propose is that it follows the second strategy. As I explain in Chapter 3, the 'parental' is in various relevant respects 'political' and, therefore, parents should regard themselves as duty-bound to respect their children's autonomy by not enrolling them into ethical practices the worth of which is disputed by reasonable persons. That argument questions the conduct of millions of parents. But there is no embarrassment in that. As Dworkin observes: '[I]n past centuries liberal ideals were not at all boring; they excited passions and fuelled revolutions. Liberalism was not seen, then, as a wise and cautious formula for citizens tired of ideological wars, but as a new and exhilarating way for people to live together in political community.'[3] My hope is that the conception of upbringing I develop will contribute to the renewal of liberalism as a challenging and reforming political doctrine.

NOTES

1. I propose to discuss these matters in another book. For some initial thoughts on whether the purchase of private schooling is just, see Clayton and Stevens, 'School Choice and the Burdens of Justice', *Theory and Research in Education*, 2 (2004), 111–26. That paper is a critical commentary on Swift's book-length treatment of the subject, *How Not to Be a Hypocrite: School Choice for the Morally Perplexed Parent* (London: Routledge, 2003). For my critique of a conception of educational justice that prioritizes the elimination of class-based inequalities, see Clayton, 'Rawls and Natural Aristocracy', *Croatian Journal of Philosophy*, 1 (2001), 239–59.
2. The idea that liberalism rests on a moral division of labour is developed by Nagel, *Equality and Partiality* (New York: Oxford University Press, 1991).
3. Dworkin, 'Foundations of Liberal Equality', in Grethe Peterson (ed.), *The Tanner Lectures on Human Values*, vol. XI (Salt Lake City, UT: University of Utah Press, 1990), 6.

1

Liberal Foundations

1.1 RAWLS ON JUSTICE AND LEGITIMACY

In this chapter I sketch a liberal account of political morality, which I shall later develop and deploy in the context of issues of upbringing. The account I describe is eclectic, in the sense that it draws upon the work of a number of different liberal theorists, principally Rawls and Dworkin. I begin by outlining Rawls's conception of liberalism, justice as fairness viewed as a political conception of justice, which rests on the ideal of social cooperation between free and equal persons. Noting certain problems with Rawls's account, I introduce certain ideals made popular by other liberal thinkers in the hope of describing an anti-perfectionist liberal conception of political morality.

Here, I shall provide only a brief and rough outline of the position Rawls defends in his two most important works, *A Theory of Justice* and *Political Liberalism.*[1] A detailed examination of some of the key claims and arguments that are relevant to upbringing will follow in subsequent chapters. Let us begin, then, with his conception of justice, justice as fairness. The fundamental ideal from which Rawls's conception develops is the ideal of fair social cooperation between free and equal persons. His ambition is to render coherent our considered convictions related to that ideal.

The basic aim of a conception of justice is to identify principles that ought to govern the major social, economic, and political institutions of society, the basic structure of society, such that there is a fair distribution of the benefits and burdens produced by social cooperation. Responding to this requirement, Rawls offers an account of the basic structure, the goods that individuals have an interest in obtaining, and a way of judging whether a particular distribution of such goods is just. With respect to the first, the characterization of the basic structure, he limits his focus to the major institutions of society that significantly affect our life prospects and self-understandings and under which, in the usual case, we live from birth to death. Thus, his fundamental concern is to describe public principles for the regulation of these institutions. Principles of social justice that apply to *individuals* do so in a way that makes essential reference to the basic structure so understood. As free and equal individuals, we have an interest in developing and exercising our sense of justice, such that we promote and comply with just social institutions. Rawls's restricted focus on the basic structure is highly controversial but it is a key element in the conception of upbringing that I shall develop (sec. 1.5).

Justice as fairness proposes two principles of justice to regulate the basic structure. The first, the basic liberties principle, secures for everyone an equal entitlement to the familiar civil and political rights of a constitutional democracy. The second, subordinate, principle, which regulates the distribution of social and economic goods, asserts that inequalities in such goods must be regulated through property law, and tax and benefit policies, so that they maximally benefit the least advantaged, subject to everyone enjoying fair equality of opportunity to occupy positions of advantage. Rawls defends the view that these two principles are just, because they would be preferred over utilitarian and certain other principles by parties who are asked to choose principles to govern the basic structure within a choice situation which guarantees that whichever principles are chosen are fair. In his thought experiment of the original position, representative parties are asked to choose principles for the distribution of primary social goods that everyone has an interest in obtaining—liberty, rights, opportunity, wealth and income, and the social bases of self-respect—without any knowledge of the particular features that characterize the individuals they represent. The parties do not know, for example, the sex, race, class, level of productivity, or religion of their clients, and are charged with the task of promoting their interests, understood in terms of the possession of primary social goods. Not knowing whether their clients are more or less capable of wealth generation, devout or atheist, black or white, Rawls argues that representatives in the original position would adopt the two principles of justice, giving priority to the first basic liberties principle. These principles are just, then, because they serve the interests of individuals, understood as free and equal persons, and are adopted via a fair procedure that eliminates the influence of natural or social luck on the agreement made.[2] The principles are also presented as an attractive way of bringing into reflective equilibrium the convictions we hold about justice at various levels of abstraction.[3]

As Rawls himself acknowledges, a number of problems beset his account of justice in *A Theory of Justice*. One defect in his initial exposition of justice as fairness is the lack of sustained justification of the choice of primary social goods as the appropriate metric for making interpersonal comparisons from the point of view of justice. Another concerns an ambiguity with respect to the extent to which his conception of justice depends upon controversial views about religion or ethics. In his later work, Rawls addresses these and other issues with respect to justice and legitimacy.

Defending his adoption of primary social goods as the appropriate conception of advantage, Rawls deepens his conception of social cooperation by offering an account of the interests of individuals as free and equal persons. In particular, he claims that such individuals have two highest order interests in developing and deploying two moral powers: the capacity to understand and comply with norms of justice, and the capacity to form, revise, and rationally to pursue a conception of the good life. In addition to these interests, individuals should be regarded as having an interest in pursuing their respective conceptions of the good: the distinctive religious, ethical, aesthetic commitments they hold. On the basis of this conception of our interests as free and equal persons, Rawls defends, among others things, various liberal and democratic freedoms—including rights to freedom of conscience, religion, association, and expression—and their priority over social and economic provision, on the basis that they serve us in the acquisition and exercise of the two moral powers and are important means though which we may pursue our different conceptions of the good.[4]

The second, perhaps most notable, revision of justice as fairness is that Rawls came to present his account as a conception of *political*, rather than *comprehensive*, liberalism. At the heart of Rawls's political liberalism is a striking claim about the kind of theorizing appropriate for political philosophers of constitutional democracies. Rawls claims that such theorists should articulate political, rather than comprehensive or metaphysical, conceptions of political morality. A political conception is marked by (*a*) a distinctive subject matter; (*b*) its avoidance of particular modes of justification; and (*c*) its reliance on other kinds of justification. Let me briefly review these three features of political liberalism.

First, Rawls retains his focus on the basic structure, insisting that a political conception of justice is 'a moral conception worked out for a specific kind of subject, namely, for political, social, and economic institutions'.[5] It involves a set of claims about how this structure should operate: the principles by which it should be guided, the ideals that justify the adoption of these principles, and the forms of reasoning which should guide political agents. It is a conception that establishes principles to regulate the distribution of political authority in society, and to guide the decisions of individuals in positions of such authority, as well as citizens in choosing between rival political platforms. Political conceptions are distinguished from *general* moral conceptions that seek to guide *non-political* conduct, which relates, for example, to one's choice of occupation, religion, or associative group.

Second, a conception is political only if the presentation and justification of its principles of justice does not rely on claims about the soundness of particular comprehensive doctrines.[6] Such doctrines are defined by the *content* of the beliefs that constitute them. As examples, Rawls mentions various conceptions of ethical value: beliefs about personal character and the kinds of activities, interpersonal relationships, and virtues that a life should embody or that individuals ought to pursue. In addition, comprehensive doctrines might include beliefs about impersonal goods as specified by religious conceptions: conceptions of the meaning of life or arguments concerning the existence of a god, for example. To be sure, political conceptions rely on particular values and have their own conceptions of (political) virtue. Nevertheless, unlike comprehensive doctrines, they are not constituted, or informed, by the specific kinds of ideals outlined above.[7]

Third, while a political conception eschews appeal to controversial general and comprehensive doctrines, Rawls claims that its content is derived from ideals concerning political morality which are implicit in the tradition of democratic thought that has developed over the last few centuries.[8] In particular, the tradition can be interpreted as centrally involved with the meaning and importance of the political ideals of freedom and equality.[9] Thus, a political conception must elaborate an ideal of political association that embodies these ideals and gives each its due weight.

From the three features of political liberalism outlined above the contrast between it and conceptions of ethical liberalism as expounded by Mill and Kant is evident. In different ways these thinkers articulate controversial comprehensive doctrines of well-being or practical reason. Their views remain liberal because they claim that their comprehensive concerns support limitations on the extent to which the state is morally permitted to enforce particular religious doctrines, for example. However, according to Rawls, if liberalism is defended by appeal to comprehensive doctrines, it is just another sectarian doctrine, because conceptions of the good will or practical reason as formulated by Kant, or of qualitative hedonism or individuality as theorized by Mill, are not widely shared in democratic societies. He believes that *political* conceptions of justice are more attractive, since they alone are non-sectarian and are capable of eliciting the agreement of reasonable people. They fulfil the requirement that a conception of justice should look across the divide between comprehensive liberals and, for example, certain Christians who reject, say, Mill's conception of qualitative hedonism.

Thus, Rawls came to expound justice as fairness as a political conception that provides 'a publicly recognised point of view from which all citizens can examine before one another whether their political and social institutions are just'.[10] As such, it derives principles of justice to regulate the basic structure from the fundamental ideal of fair social cooperation between citizens regarded as free and equal.[11] The conception is political in the three respects outlined above. First, its subject matter is restricted to the issue of which principles should regulate the basic structure. Second, it involves the ideal of a *well-ordered* society, which requires the articulation of a conception that is free-standing from particular comprehensive doctrines. And, third, in working with the ideal of citizens as free and equal, it addresses the question of justice by reference to certain enduring ideals within the democratic political culture.

1.2 INDIVIDUAL AUTONOMY AND ANTI-PERFECTIONISM

A fundamental ideal that animates Rawls's political liberalism, as well as other liberal conceptions, is the ideal of individual autonomy or self-determination. There is a genuine issue concerning whether this ideal must be construed as part of a comprehensive doctrine if it is adequately to serve as a basis for liberal politics and education. I discuss that issue in Section 1.3. Here, bracketing that question, I offer an account of individual autonomy that will form the basis of certain positions I shall adopt in later chapters.

For an individual to determine, or to be the author of, her own life there must be the right kind of relationship between her and the goals, projects, and relationships she pursues; and her adoption of such goals, projects, and relationships must have the right kind of history. With respect to the first requirement, an autonomous life is one in which the individual concerned identifies with, or endorses, the ideals or goals that guide her conduct. It is easy to see how this might be thwarted. An atheist who is forced or cajoled into religious worship lacks autonomy, since her conduct goes against her conviction that such worship is pointless. Moreover, she lacks autonomy even if her atheism is mistaken. The ideal of autonomy is not about the worth of one's ends, or the truth of one's convictions, but, in part, about whether one's life coheres with one's ends and convictions.[12]

The life of an autonomous individual, then, has a shape that reflects her convictions. Yet this is not sufficient for autonomy. A life lived fully in accordance with one's beliefs remains non-autonomous if the beliefs and desires that motivate it are affirmed without the right kind of deliberation, or in the absence of an autonomy-supporting context. Let us call these two dimensions of individual autonomy the *intrapersonal* and *environmental* conditions of autonomy. Consider the intrapersonal condition first. An individual who leads an autonomous life is one who exercises her capacity to form, revise, and pursue her ethical convictions.[13] Thus, the capacity for autonomy involves the possession of a number of mental and physical powers that enable an individual to deliberate rationally and critically about the various goals and relationships that are available to her; to revise her existing goals on the basis of new opportunities, fresh evidence, and the like; to nest her various commitments in an appropriate hierarchical structure, such that her fundamental aims are served by the more immediate goals she pursues; and to pursue her different projects in a rational manner, by adopting the appropriate means to achieve her ends, in the light of an appreciation of the probabilities relevant to her decisions.

The environmental dimension of autonomy is nicely illustrated by Raz's imaginary example of the man in the pit. In this case, a man has fallen into a pit from which he cannot escape, but which affords sufficient nourishment for him to live, such that his life is without pain, but he lacks any meaningful opportunities. He can eat now or later, sleep now or later, and has other similar choices to make. But the harsh environment in which he lives effectively prevents him from being the author of his life, on any plausible description of that ideal.[14]

The *ethical* environment required for individual autonomy might be described as *meaningful ethical pluralism.* As Raz insists, the man in the pit faces certain choices—when to eat and sleep, for example—which are essential for an autonomous life. Nevertheless, he lacks options with respect to the range of overarching projects that typically give life meaning: options with respect to different kinds of relationship he might be part of, and options to pursue a variety of long-term projects or commitments that determine the shape of one's life.[15] Moreover, the options available must offer genuine variety. One cannot be an autonomous eater if, despite a plethora of restaurants, burger and chips is the only available dish.

The environmental conditions of autonomy are also partly *political* in nature. If an individual is to follow her religious convictions, for example, she must enjoy freedom of religion and of association, so that she may worship the particular god she affirms, perhaps in common with others. Similarly, if she is to form and revise her conception of the good life, then she must be able rationally and critically to evaluate alternative conceptions, and to tailor her preferred conception to her particular life. The protection of liberal freedoms of religion, association, and expression are important here as well, since the inevitable effect of different individuals exercising these freedoms is ethical pluralism and ethical discussion, which enable one to develop and exercise one's evaluative powers.[16] This ethical pluralism may also provide the meaningful pluralism mentioned above, which is an essential condition of autonomy. Thus, the maintenance of familiar liberal legal rights is beneficial in terms of meeting the various requirements of individual autonomy: that an individual's life reflects the convictions she has formed as a product of the right kind of reflection in an appropriate ethical context.[17]

I turn now to the political dimension of autonomy directly. Discussion of this dimension goes beyond the issues concerning the political aspects of the environmental conditions of autonomy, important though these are. It brings into focus the prominent idea of *anti-perfectionism* as an essential element of liberalism premised on the ideal of individual autonomy. First, notice that from the *partial* description offered above autonomy seems consistent with the perfectionist view that there are no principled reasons which limit the state's appeal to the intrinsic merits of particular comprehensive doctrines when deciding law or policy. An autonomy-supporting policy, so understood, affords individuals the right kind of intellectual powers critically to reflect upon their ethical lives, and an environment in which they face meaningful ethical pluralism and are permitted to pursue their particular comprehensive conceptions. But this is consistent with the government favouring certain comprehensive doctrines on the grounds that people live better lives by affirming and following these doctrines. To be sure, autonomy tells against certain *means* of favouring these doctrines or discouraging people from following others. For example, as is well known, the use of the criminal law will often be a clumsy tool in discouraging people from pursuing unworthy goals or projects, because imprisonment or significant fines for pursuing unworthy goals will prevent individuals from pursuing *valuable* goals as well and, therefore, may not improve their lives. But less invasive means are available to political authorities. For example, they may deploy their tax revenue to subsidize the advertisement and pursuit of worthwhile goals, activities, and relationships. Suppose that atheism is detrimental to well-being. Judging this correctly, but also recognizing the ideal of autonomy as stated above, a government would extend the liberal freedoms of conscience, expression, and association to atheists and the devout alike. But it might also subsidize religious institutions in a variety of ways, or offer opportunities to individuals that ease their transition from atheism to belief.[18]

Now, political liberalism as described above eschews an appeal to the intrinsic merits of competing comprehensive doctrines. It accommodates the anti-perfectionist view that there are principled reasons of political morality to limit the extent to which government assesses and acts on the intrinsic merits of alternative comprehensive doctrines. These reasons include the good of maintaining an overlapping consensus between reasonable individuals. Such anti-perfectionism is implied by a *fuller* account of the ideal of individual autonomy in the following way. We have established that individual autonomy is the ideal of each individual being the author of her own life. The fundamental political question, which Rousseau identified, is how to reconcile this ideal with the constraints that are necessary for effective and just social cooperation.[19] In other domains of our lives, such as which, if any, religious group we affiliate to, we are subject to rules and sanctions, but these constraints are ones we choose to accept. In contrast, the political domain is marked by a distinctive relationship between state and citizen which is (*a*) involuntary, (*b*) lifelong, and (*c*) which has a significant effect on the life prospects, aims, and self-conceptions of citizens.[20] These features are sufficient to require principles of justice that regulate the basic structure to be publicly justifiable. As Rawls says, in brief:

> [O]ur exercise of political power is fully proper only when it is exercised in accordance with a constitution the essentials of which all citizens as free and equal may reasonably be expected to endorse in the light of principles and ideals acceptable to their common human reason. This is the liberal principle of legitimacy.[21]

Further elaborating liberal legitimacy through *the publicity condition*, Rawls distinguishes between three elements of publicity:

1. There is a common knowledge that everyone accepts that the basic structure is regulated by principles of justice that everyone accepts.
2. The principles of justice are accepted on the basis of beliefs which are publicly accepted, and on uncontroversial methods of reasoning, e.g. general beliefs about social psychology and basic structural institutions which are uncontroversial, and shared methods of inquiry and reason.
3. The full justification of the principles of justice is publicly known or, at least, publicly available.[22]

In justification of this ideal, Rawls refers to the ideals of full autonomy and mutual respect.[23] Full autonomy is a condition achieved only if citizens freely identify with the constraints that they face, in the sense that they understand the content and justificatory bases of the constraints, and freely accept them.[24] Under conditions in which social cooperation is both possible and necessary, we must articulate an ideal of social cooperation which, while recognizing our need for principles of justice that constrain the activities of individuals in order to facilitate the appropriate kind of social cooperation, ensures that each regards her constraints as legitimate given her reasonable, but particular, interests and ethical concerns. In this way, individual freedom is reconciled with the necessity of political constraints, and the self-government of citizens is secured, because individuals comply with their own wills.

Second, the publicity condition involves a norm of mutual respect. Reflecting on the distinction between treating persons as means or ends, Larmore claims:

> To respect another person as an end is to insist that coercive or political principles be as justifiable to that person as they are to us. Equal respect involves treating all persons, to which such principles apply, in this way.[25]

Larmore's thought is that respect involves acknowledging the freedom and equality of others by recognizing the importance of them affirming the constraints that they face on the basis of their own moral powers. To force a person to abide by constraints that she reasonably rejects, even if the constraints are premised on true beliefs, is to regard her exercise of her sense of justice and rational powers as insufficient for her view to count equally in the determination of political principles and policies. This is a form of disrespect.[26]

We might regard these two explanations of the appeal of the publicity condition as related in the following way. It is Rawls's view that individuals should be politically autonomous, or self-governing, which requires principles of justice that are acceptable to each free and equal person. And mutual respect is an ideal of how one's fellow citizens should be treated, which recognizes the importance of acknowledging their autonomy.[27]

A fuller account of autonomy, then, involves the ideal that the constraints into which one is born should be ones that satisfy the publicity condition, which consists in individuals identifying with the principles and rules that constrain them. The final stage in the autonomy-based argument for political liberalism is to show how the publicity condition supports its anti-perfectionism. Rawls's argument might be reconstructed roughly as follows:

1. Free and equal persons have an interest in developing and exercising two important powers: the capacity for a sense of justice and for a conception of the good.
2. Political institutions that guarantee the familiar civil and political liberties—the freedoms of conscience, expression, association, and the right to participate in the political process—represent some of the social and political conditions of the satisfaction of these interests.
3. The exercise of human theoretical and practical reason under such conditions of freedom inevitably produces a diversity of comprehensive doctrines (due to the burdens of judgement), even among persons who do not err due to prejudice or ignorance.
4. Society is fully legitimate, or well-ordered, only if it satisfies the publicity requirement, which requires consensus among reasonable persons on its principles of justice and their justification.
5. Thus, two fundamental components of justice as fairness—its conception of citizens as free and equal and of a well-ordered society—when understood in light of certain enduring facts about the human condition (the burdens of judgement), require justice as fairness to be articulated as a political conception which is free-standing of claims about the truth and falsity of competing comprehensive doctrines.

Let us examine the argument in more detail. Rawls suggests that free and equal persons have two moral powers and interests in developing and deploying these powers. First, they have an interest in having a sense of justice. Second, free and equal persons have a capacity for a conception of the good.[28] Granted that individuals have an interest of some kind in realizing and exercising their capacity for a sense of justice and for a conception of the good, what are the conditions for its satisfaction? Answering this question, Rawls appeals to his (revised) account of primary social goods that specifies the goods—rights and liberties, powers and opportunities, material resources, and so forth—which are necessary or all-purpose means for the realization of free and equal personality, and the ability to pursue one's comprehensive conception.[29] In particular, he argues in some detail that the realization of a sense of justice and a capacity for a conception of the good requires freedom of expression, association, and other familiar liberties.[30] This derivation of civil and political liberties from a conception of the interests of individuals, though controversial, appears straightforward in a liberal conception.

A significant consequence of free institutions is the fact of reasonable comprehensive pluralism. Prior to explaining the inevitability of such disagreement a few remarks about Rawls's understanding of reasonableness are in order. We can distinguish between two specifications of reasonableness that operate within Rawls's view.[31] First, there is, what I shall call, *political* reasonableness, which has two basic aspects:

> The first basic aspect of the reasonable . . . is the willingness to propose fair terms of cooperation and to abide by them provided others do. The second basic aspect . . . is the willingness to recognize the burdens of judgement and to accept their consequences for the use of public reason in directing the legitimate exercise of political power in a constitutional regime.[32]

The two aspects of reasonableness cited here are moral virtues that relate to the basic structure, which is why I call them, jointly, political reasonableness. They consist of (*a*) a desire conditionally to cooperate with others on fair terms and (*b*) a desire to achieve a system of social cooperation guided by principles of justice that are acceptable to every reasonable person.

The second specification of reasonableness, which can be found in Rawls's view, might be called epistemological (or, for short, *epistemic*) reasonableness. This is a notion that is employed in characterizing the nature of people's beliefs. In this sense, one's view is reasonable if one possesses the requisite powers of theoretical and practical reason and one's beliefs are the product of one's employment of these powers under conditions of freedom. These powers consist in the ability to weigh evidence appropriately, draw inferences, balance competing considerations, and so on. On the other hand, one's view is epistemically unreasonable if it is the product of practical or theoretical irrationalities, or bias due to the social and political conditions in which one deliberates.[33]

Rawls argues that humans are beset by various burdens of judgements, such that the exercise of our theoretical, practical, and moral faculties under conditions of freedom inevitably gives rise to a plurality of comprehensive doctrines. Moreover, since this pluralism is a product of the free activity of persons who are epistemically reasonable, we should regard it as a permanent feature of free democratic societies, rather than a product of ignorance or prejudice that may be overcome.[34] The argument for this conclusion rests on a series of relatively uncontroversial theoretical and empirical claims concerning the situation of different people from the point of view of evaluating arguments and empirical evidence. In particular, Rawls identifies several obstacles to the generation of agreement. These include problems in the assessment of empirical evidence, difficulties in the interpretation and employment of concepts, the fact that the position from which different individuals tackle matters is relevantly different, the lack, sometimes, of a clearly decisive argument on one side of the issue, and the presence of incommensurability.[35]

Much more might be said about this matter. Nevertheless, it is relatively uncontroversial that, for these reasons, if individuals employ their theoretical and practical powers under conditions of freedom, a plurality of comprehensive doctrines will be the inevitable product. Free and equal persons who have an interest in engaging in fair social cooperation, and in exercising their capacities rationally to form, revise, and pursue a conception of the good, require free institutions. Under these conditions, due to the burdens of judgement, individuals will inevitably align themselves to different comprehensive doctrines. This pluralism is epistemically reasonable in virtue of it being an alignment of free and equal persons under conditions of freedom. This part of the argument discusses the inevitable consequences of the recognition of two important interests that citizens have. Rawls adds to this the ideal of a politically reasonable response to the burdens of judgement that involves the ideal of publicity. A conception of justice should ideally be accepted publicly in the sense that every citizen should accept the same principles of justice and their justification, and this acceptance should be understood publicly. If we accept this ideal of publicity in conjunction with the ideals of freedom and equality and their inevitable consequences, an anti-perfectionist conception becomes the only kind of conception of justice capable of satisfying it. This is the case, because any conception of justice that is premised on a particular comprehensive doctrine will inevitably and reasonably be rejected by some section of the citizenry. Thus, such conceptions cannot generate public acceptance and facilitate the political autonomy of every citizen. Only if a conception of justice is anti-perfectionist, and justified on the basis of commonly shared political beliefs among free and equal persons, can the appropriate kind of public acceptance prevail.

Ethical pluralism, then, is the inevitable product of free and equal individuals exercising their capacity to adopt, revise, and pursue particular comprehensive doctrines within free institutions. If, in addition, we want our political world to respect our interest in being politically autonomous, and thereby identify with the constraints it places upon us, the principles that govern it must satisfy the publicity condition, which requires principles to be acceptable to all free and equal persons. The conjunction of reasonable pluralism and the need for publicly justifiable political institutions, supports anti-perfectionist liberalism: liberal institutions that respect the interests we have as free and equal persons, but that are not moved by the soundness of further ideals of human flourishing to promote controversial comprehensive doctrines.

1.3 TWO OBJECTIONS TO POLITICAL LIBERALISM CONSIDERED

The nature of social justice and liberal legitimacy, and the status of the ideal of individual autonomy, can be further clarified by considering two objections that are sometimes raised against political liberalism. The first questions the apparent optimism political liberals exhibit with respect to the possibility of establishing a consensus on the basis of a particular account of justice. The second challenges the political liberal's anti-perfectionism by claiming that its commitment to autonomy is, in effect, an appeal to a particular, controversial, comprehensive doctrine. Let us address these objections in turn.

1.3.1 Disagreements over Justice

The first objection claims that Rawls is too sanguine about the possibility of achieving consensus on principles of justice, even in an idealized society of free and equal persons. Political reasonableness involves a willingness to cooperate on fair terms with others and to propose principles of justice that all can share. Yet it does not follow from this that everyone has the same view of fair cooperation. A criticism of political liberalism that rests on the reasonableness of disagreement about justice can be put as follows. Granted that people disagree as much about considerations of fairness as they do about comprehensive doctrines, if the central aim of political liberalism is to present a conception of political morality which does not rely on controversial ideals that divide reasonable people, it should put to one side controversial claims about socio-economic justice: only by avoiding such issues can political liberals achieve the social unity, defined in terms of the publicity condition, which they value.[36]

This objection, which notes the similarity between disagreements about comprehensive doctrines and disputes over conceptions of justice, can be elaborated in one of two ways. First, perfectionists might argue that even though people disagree about both sets of issues, political agents may still consider the soundness of particular comprehensive doctrines or conceptions of justice when deciding how political institutions should be arranged, or what the law should be.[37] By contrast, proceduralists about political morality argue that since disagreements about justice as fairness, and, in particular, its provisions for socio-economic justice, are as permanent a feature of democratic culture as disagreements about comprehensive doctrines, we should devise political arrangements that mediate both kinds of disagreement in a way that can elicit the agreement of the disputants. Typically, they elaborate such arrangements in terms of democratic procedures and some kind of majoritarian principle.

The common claim of these perfectionist and proceduralist critiques is that the distinction between conceptions of justice and comprehensive doctrines does not match the distinction between issues that can and cannot elicit agreement within democratic societies. Consequently, Rawls, for example, faces a dilemma between (*a*) maintaining his commitment to social unity on the basis of the publicity condition, in which case he must admit that a well-ordered society cannot insist on justice as fairness, but only a more modest set of political arrangements that can elicit public agreement, and (*b*) maintaining his belief in the appropriateness of enforcing justice as fairness, thereby weakening the requirement of public agreement, in which case sound comprehensive doctrines might legitimately be enforced as well.

Rawls's answer to such a dilemma is to reiterate the overriding nature of *political* reasonableness and the importance this notion attaches to fair terms of cooperation and agreement respectively. In particular, on the basis of his specification of reasonableness, he claims that certain moral reasons apply to us: some of these concern the provision of certain political and civil rights and other social primary goods; others involve constraints on the exercise of political power for the sake of legitimacy.

Recall that political reasonableness involves two related ideas: reciprocity and eliciting the agreement of other reasonable people. Crudely stated, reciprocity involves the idea that the advantage of each person who participates in social cooperation should be promoted in an appropriate way. As Rawls interprets it, this rules out certain libertarian views that do not regard the goods which are the product of social cooperation as available for distribution according to a principle that exhibits a concern for the advantage of each individual. Or, at least, if they do, they interpret advantage implausibly in terms of property rights rather than the primary goods of liberty, opportunity, wealth and income, and so on. Thus, in assessing the reasonableness of libertarian conceptions, which prescribe the protection of property rights and free markets, an appropriate test is whether they satisfy the criteria specified by the ideal of fair attention to each participant's advantage, and Rawls plausibly claims that such conceptions fail to satisfy them. In fact, he claims that only liberal conceptions of justice, specified in terms of three conditions, can satisfy the requirement of reciprocity which is partly constitutive of political reasonableness. These conditions are principles that (*a*) protect basic liberties and opportunities; (*b*) attach a special priority to their protection over the promotion of other aspects of individuals' advantage; and (*c*) require 'measures assuring all citizens, whatever their social position, adequate all-purpose means to make intelligent and effective use of their liberties and opportunities'.[38] In addition, Rawls believes that various provisions are necessary to implement these principles, including the public financing of elections, equality of opportunity, a decent distribution of income, society acting as the employer of last resort, and basic health care for all citizens.[39]

This part of the idea of reasonableness adopts an abstract characterization of reciprocity that justifies a broadly liberal conception of justice.

Rawls's specific conception of justice, justice as fairness, can be viewed as a particular interpretation of reciprocity which yields particular liberal principles and social institutions. As such, it is one of many liberal conceptions of justice, but one which Rawls argues is *more* reasonable in virtue of the more plausible way in which it interprets reciprocity and defends its principles on the basis of an attractive ideal of social cooperation. The details of this argument are set out primarily in *A Theory of Justice* and need not detain at present.[40]

From this characterization of the first aspect of reasonableness it is clear that certain disagreements about justice do not threaten the ideal of a well-ordered society of reasonable people. Since many political conflicts within contemporary democracies are not disputes between reasonable people, the fact of these disagreements is not sufficient to worry political liberals so far as their ideal is concerned.[41] More importantly, political liberalism is not threatened by the likelihood of *epistemically* reasonable people endorsing libertarian views in a society regulated by, say, justice as fairness. That there may exist epistemically reasonable, but politically unreasonable, people is, perhaps, a permanent fact of social life and one which politically reasonable people should guard against. But provided we regard social unity as premised on the agreement of politically reasonable persons, we need not revise justice as fairness to accommodate, say, libertarian values, for the sake of social unity.

In addition to the requirement of reciprocity, the idea of political reasonableness invokes the notion of reasonable agreement and recognition of the fact of reasonable disagreements given the burdens of judgement. We need not rehearse the characterization of these burdens. It suffices to reiterate that people who are reasonable (in both epistemic and political senses of the term) will inevitably disagree about comprehensive matters and, as Rawls explains, the exercise of political power is legitimate only if people who are reasonable in these senses endorse the conception and principles that guide the use of that power. Consequently, since comprehensive disagreement between reasonable people is inevitable, perfectionist uses of political power are illegitimate.

With this more precise account of reasonableness on hand, we can reply to the dilemma stated above which arises if we concede the fact of disagreement on matters of justice in a democratic society. The second horn of the dilemma says that if Rawls maintains that, despite the existence of disagreement, justice as fairness can legitimately be enforced, then he cannot use the fact of disagreement as an argument for taking an anti-perfectionist stance with respect to comprehensive ethical issues, such as the nature of personal well-being. A Rawlsian response to this might be to stress that the value of reconciling disagreement is conditional upon that disagreement existing between *reasonable* persons who, by hypothesis, agree on an abstract, partially described but still controversial, conception of justice. Thus, the right distinction between justice and comprehensive doctrines might yet be defended. Critics of justice as fairness—even those who are epistemically reasonable and live in a democratic society—need not be accommodated by revisions to the conception of justice, if they are politically unreasonable. By contrast, since an adequate political morality requires the endorsement of fully reasonable persons who inevitably disagree about comprehensive issues, political morality should avoid taking a stand with respect to these issues.

A similar response is available to those who stress the first horn of the dilemma. The criticism here is that if Rawls persists in valuing social unity, he cannot also insist on enforcing justice as fairness, because people will disagree over its soundness. Rawls's response might be that disagreement as such does not matter, but only disagreement between reasonable people who, by hypothesis, endorse the reciprocity requirement. Since most actual disagreement about justice is not of this kind, it does not render the enforcement of justice as fairness illegitimate.[42]

The response above leaves one prominent question open: what if reasonable people disagree about *which* of the reasonable conceptions of justice is most attractive? Recall that political reasonableness does not require an acceptance of justice as fairness. It is a threshold requirement that a person satisfies if he or she endorses the two conditions mentioned above: the requirement of reciprocity and an acknowledgement of the burdens of judgement. No doubt, some who reach the threshold will be more reasonable than others. But political liberalism treats everyone who meets the threshold as enjoying equal status as a citizen. Now, due to the burdens of judgement, it is likely that reasonable people will disagree over certain questions of justice. For example, even those who affirm principles that guarantee the protection and priority of the basic liberties, and an adequate provision of the means which make possession of these liberties worthwhile, might disagree about the precise principles and institutions that are required to fill in the details of such a conception of justice. Rawls himself cites the dispute that exists between reasonable people over the justice of the difference principle as a case in point.[43]

Rawls expects such reasonable disagreement to exist and claims that while he believes that justice as fairness is the most reasonable conception of justice, because it incorporates the most attractive interpretation of the two basic aspects of reasonableness, social unity might be obtained on the basis of liberal conceptions of justice other than justice as fairness. Here, Rawls envisages possible trade-offs between the justice of principles and their legitimacy.[44] Moreover, this is always a possibility within justice as fairness, since it regards some kind of majoritarian principle to be legitimate in cases in which a decision must be made (see Section 4.2 for further discussion of this issue).

I conclude, therefore, that these criticisms of political liberalism that relate to disagreements about justice are misplaced. Rawls has offered sound reasons why political arrangements may enforce a particular conception of justice in the face of disagreement, while they should remain anti-perfectionist in dealing with disagreements about comprehensive matters. No doubt more can be said about this matter, but at least the structure of political liberalism's response to this issue is clear.

1.3.2 Individual Autonomy, Political Liberalism, and Anti-Perfectionism

A more threatening objection to political liberalism is that it collapses into comprehensive liberalism. As I have articulated it, political liberalism seeks an overlapping consensus between reasonable people who disagree over questions concerning personal well-being, and impersonal issues such as the nature of the universe, the existence of a benevolent god, and the meaning of life. But in the course of defending liberal social and political institutions, and the need for an overlapping consensus, I appealed to the interests of free and equal persons in leading autonomous lives. Some have claimed that this simply smuggles a controversial comprehensive doctrine in through the back door.[45] In assessing this challenge, let me consider and criticize Rawls's response and, thereafter, explain how a more modest anti-perfectionist liberalism can be retained while conceding some of the force of the objection.

Rawls's reply to the challenge draws a distinction between an individual's public, or institutional, identity, and her moral, or non-institutional, identity. In the former sense, as a citizen, an individual can accept that she has an interest in developing and exercising her capacity for a conception of the good, which motivates a concern for the liberal rights that support that capacity. However, in her non-institutional life, as a member of a church, for example, she may hold a different view. There, she may think it inconceivable that her view of religion will change, or that it is *against* her interest to have or to exercise the capacity rationally to revise her religious convictions. As a citizen, she will favour the freedoms of religion, association, and expression; as a member of a church, she may take steps to ensure that she do not step back from, and reflect on, the value of her deepest religious commitments. Rawls employs the distinction to argue that even if an individual who loses her faith, or converts to another religion, may be believed non-institutionally to have become a different person, her public, institutional, identity remains unaffected, and she retains all the citizenship rights she enjoyed beforehand.[46]

In Rawls's conception, then, it is possible to describe a purely political conception of an individual's interests that involves a description of her interests when viewed as a citizen. It is a conception that applies only when we consider which ideals and principles should regulate the basic structure, and it makes no claims whatsoever about the nature of personal well-being, the meaning of life, or other comprehensive matters. This conception of the person, he insists, is a possible point of consensus for individuals who are moved by very different comprehensive convictions, some of whom treat autonomy as central to well-being, while others regard unswerving, unreflective loyalty as ethically required.

The central criticism of this strategy concedes that Rawls's conception of the person as free and equal is a *possible* basis for an overlapping consensus. Nevertheless, it is unclear why those who reject the comprehensive claim that they have an interest in being able rationally to reflect on, and revise, their conception of the good should accept that they have such an interest as citizens. If a person, thinking non-institutionally, believes that loss of faith is the equivalent of death, and that this is a conclusive reason to bind herself to the mast of an unreflective life so as to avoid such a loss of faith, then it is not obvious why she should refrain from acting on this reason in the public domain.[47]

A more modest, but more plausible, reply to the objection that the ideal of autonomy is just another comprehensive doctrine accepts that a liberal conception must rest on some controversial ethical claims, but rejects the view that we must, therefore, abandon the idea of anti-perfectionist liberalism. To set the scene for this reply, we must note certain important distinctions. First, let us note Rawls's distinction between *fully* and *partially* comprehensive doctrines: 'A conception is fully comprehensive if it includes all recognized values and virtues of human life . . . partially comprehensive when it comprises a number of, but by no means all, non-political values and virtues and is rather loosely articulated.'[48] As we have established, Rawls's political liberalism is free-standing of even partially comprehensive doctrines, in the sense that no appeal is made to the validity of particular claims about non-political value. If political liberalism is construed in these terms, the considerations above suggest that it should be rejected in favour of a partially comprehensive liberalism, in which the good of individual autonomy is a fundamental value.

But we might instead draw a rather different, perhaps more illuminating, distinction between *perfectionist* and *anti-perfectionist* liberals. Perfectionism is the view that there are *no principled limits* to the extent to which government may appeal to the intrinsic merits of alternative comprehensive doctrines.[49] In contrast, anti-perfectionists claim that there are sound reasons of political morality that justify drawing a limit to the extent to which government may appeal to such information. In their view, even if government may appeal to some of the truth about non-political value, it may not appeal to the whole truth.[50]

Political and partially comprehensive liberals can share the anti-perfectionist label, and distinguish themselves from perfectionists who appeal to fully comprehensive doctrines within political morality. For our purposes, let us accept that the ideal of individual autonomy invokes certain controversial non-political claims, such as the idea that individuals ought to reflect their central ethical convictions, and should exercise, from time to time, their rational faculties to revise and pursue a particular view of well-being or religion. It does not follow from this that our political morality is perfectionist. As we established in Section 1.2, the intrapersonal and environmental dimensions of autonomy are *compatible* with a further appeal to ethical value. Perfectionists take this route, and seek to describe the political conditions under which people can be encouraged, through various means that do not threaten these dimensions of autonomy, to jettison their misguided goals in favour of goals that are more worthy of pursuit. In contrast, anti-perfectionists argue against this further appeal, because it would jeopardize the maintenance of publicly justifiable political institutions, which is necessary for *political* autonomy, given reasonable comprehensive pluralism. Thus, once the *political* dimension of autonomy, which is overlooked or rejected by perfectionists, is introduced, there is a principled basis for limiting the extent to which comprehensive ideals can legitimately be invoked.[51]

Notice that I say partially comprehensive liberals *can* share the anti-perfectionist camp, rather than that they necessarily *do*, because we need to know a little more about why partially comprehensive liberals do not appeal to full information about comprehensive matters to establish that they do, in fact, share it. Only if their refusal so to appeal is motivated by the recognition that there are reasons to put aside certain valid claims about ethics for political purposes do they count as anti-perfectionist. If, in contrast, they simply refuse to articulate a fully comprehensive doctrine because, for example, it is unnecessary to justify the particular conclusion they aim to defend, then this is compatible with them invoking a fully comprehensive doctrine as and when that is necessary to defend other conclusions. If the latter is the basis of their partially comprehensive liberalism, then, plainly, they disagree fundamentally with anti-perfectionists.[52]

Let me summarize this reply. Rawls has provided a way of resisting the collapse of political liberalism into comprehensive liberalism, but we have seen that this reply is implausible, because the institutional/non-institutional distinction on which it rests lacks adequate motivation. The more plausible response accepts that liberal political morality rests on certain controversial claims concerning the value of an autonomous life, just as it invokes a disputed conception of justice, but insists that it remains anti-perfectionist. It does so, because it cites the *political* dimension of autonomy as a reason to limit the extent to which government can legitimately appeal to controversial comprehensive doctrines. Thus, an autonomy-based anti-perfectionist political morality is both possible and attractive.[53]

1.4 A LIBERAL CONCEPTION OF ADVANTAGE

Having set out the fundamental liberal ideals that form the basis of my account of upbringing, I turn to two particular questions, the resolution of which will set the terms for the argument to come. The first asks for a conception of advantage by reference to which we can judge whether justice is achieved. The second asks for a more precise characterization of the types of institution or conduct that are to be evaluated from the point of view of justice and legitimacy (Section 1.5).

A theory of upbringing must address questions concerning the characterization and importance of children's interests: How many resources should be devoted to the lives and education of children? How should such resources be distributed between differently placed children and parents? And, how should we characterize the goods that an upbringing should ideally deliver to a child? In the following chapters I discuss certain aspects of these questions. Here, I offer an initial orientation to them by outlining a general liberal conception of advantage that can be used and refined in subsequent chapters in the context of specific issues related to the status and interest of children. I do so by outlining two conceptions of advantage that have considerable plausibility given the anti-perfectionist political morality described above. The first, articulated by Rawls, is an *interest-based* account, which theorizes advantage in terms of the possession of primary social goods and a particular set of basic capabilities. The second, advanced by Dworkin, is an *ambition-sensitive* account, which makes reference to how suitably situated individuals invoking their own distinctive aims and values would make trade-offs between different sets of goods. I hope to offer a hybrid conception of advantage that embodies the attractive features of these two accounts.

Ideally, our conception of advantage should be acceptable to free and equal persons who hold different and possibly competing comprehensive convictions. Rawls claims that his primary goods metric satisfies this requirement. He defines these goods as follows:

> These are various social conditions and all-purpose means that are generally necessary to enable citizens adequately to develop and fully exercise their two moral powers, and to pursue their determinate conceptions of the good.[54]

Rawls distinguishes between a number of different primary social goods, including basic rights and freedoms, political, educational and occupational opportunity, income and wealth, and the social bases of self-respect. His two principles of justice propose particular arrangements for the distribution of these goods: equal basic liberties, fair equality of opportunity that aims to reduce class-based inequalities in education and employment, and the difference principle that attaches priority to raising the wealth and income of the group with least wealth and income.

Rawls's account is interest-based because the primary goods metric is justified by reference to the interests of free and equal persons in developing and exercising (*a*) their sense of justice and (*b*) their capacity for a conception of the good, and (*c*) in obtaining the means to pursue the particular conceptions of the good they affirm. It rests, therefore, on a conception of our needs rather than an appeal to our preferences. However, it retains its liberal status, because its conception of our interests does not rest on particular claims concerning the details of human well-being, but rather on a restricted account of the needs of free and equal persons.

Now, Rawls accepts that the primary goods he lists do not represent a complete conception of advantage for the purposes of justice. Rather, the list is offered against background simplifying assumptions that are made to limit the questions addressed. In particular, it is assumed that citizens are sufficiently similar to one another in their possession of basic capabilities, for example, their being in good health, well nourished, and able to do certain things, such as care for themselves, move around freely, pursue an occupation, and take part in social and political life. If we assume that all individuals enjoy basic capabilities that are sufficient to be 'normal, fully cooperating members of society', then, Rawls insists, primary goods are a suitable metric of interpersonal comparison for purposes of justice.[55]

However, as Rawls acknowledges, we must make adjustments to the account of advantage to deal with inequalities in capability, and he addresses two instances in this regard. In the first, while there are inequalities in capability due to differences in natural luck, for example, no one falls below the capability level to be normal cooperating citizens. Here, Rawls says that justice as fairness makes no adjustment to the distribution of primary goods, such as income, to rectify or compensate for capability inequality above the threshold for normal cooperation. In the second, certain individuals fall below the relevant capability threshold due to illness or accident, for example. Addressing this possibility, Rawls suggests that justice requires the provision of medical care, the extent and distribution of which must be determined by legislative deliberation under the guidance of the two principles of justice and the capability threshold. Representatives must consider the nature of citizens' needs, the opportunity costs of various levels of medical care in terms of the provision of other goods, and strike an appropriate balance that serves the interests of citizens over a complete life.[56]

Various objections might be levelled against Rawls's position on capability inequality. With respect to the first case, the invoking of a minimum above which capability inequality is not a concern of justice, it is unclear how such a threshold can be defended. For, intuitively, it seems that inequalities in health, for example, remain morally relevant even when they do not inhibit people's cooperation within society. Furthermore, if *these* inequalities do not matter above a threshold, how can Rawls plausibly remain committed to the difference principle, which arranges inequalities of earning potential between normal cooperators so that they work to everyone's advantage?

The second case concerning individuals who fall below the threshold presents a deeper problem for the interest-based conception of advantage. The problem is that the account offers little guidance on how to balance the different interests at stake. Rawls cites the following as examples of items that must be weighed in the balance: our interest in having a productive workforce, receiving an education, investing for the future, and having a pension, as well as in defence and pursuing a just foreign policy. No doubt this is an accurate itemization of some key interests that compete with our interest in being healthy. In addition, the ideal of individuals being normal cooperating free and equal citizens offers some guidance as to how trade-offs might be made. For example, Rawls rightly claims that cosmetic medicine cannot plausibly be considered an urgent need from the point of view of justice. Nevertheless, when we choose how many resources should be devoted to expensive medical provision, such as transplant surgery that saves the lives of a few, compared to less expensive health care that significantly improves the functioning of many, such as treatment to mollify the effects of lung disease, it is difficult to see how an appeal to our interest being normal cooperating members is sufficiently fine-grained to offer the right kind of guidance. Such problems are at least as great if we compare how many resources to devote to different kinds of health care compared to education, unemployment benefit, or pensions. Compare the treatment of lung conditions with extra educational provision for pupils with special needs. It is unclear how we are to attach weights to these very different interests.

In many cases, then, it is unclear how an appeal to our interests as normal cooperating free and equal citizens can supply sufficiently determinate guidance on questions of social choice between various goods. When this is the case, legislative representatives will need to look for a rather different account of advantage to supplement Rawls's interest-based conception. One possible way of overcoming the indeterminacy problem that besets the interest-based account in these cases is to use information concerning suitably situated individuals' preferences for different goods in the manner envisaged by Dworkin.

Dworkin's resource egalitarianism has two key components: the so-called envy test, which is a test for equality between individuals in their enjoyment of impersonal resources, such as land and monetary resources; and a hypothetical insurance scheme, which deals with inequalities in people's enjoyment of personal resources, such as differences in health or natural talent. Employing the envy test, Dworkin proposes that a distribution of impersonal resources is equal only if no one prefers anyone else's bundle of resources to her own.[57] The test provides an attractive characterization of liberal equality, for it accounts for the egalitarian intuition that inequalities in circumstances are unjust. If Ailsa and Ben hold the same values and aims, but Ailsa possesses more natural resources, then both would prefer to be in her position and, therefore, the distribution of resources fails the test. Thus, the envy test correctly identifies inequalities that are problematic from the point of view of equality. It also identifies inequalities that are not unjust. Sometimes, a difference in wealth might be explained by a difference of ambition, rather than of circumstance. Imagine David and Dan are equally placed so far as their abilities and other circumstances are concerned, but David pursues a career for monetary gain while Dan prefers to teach geography, which commands lower monetary remuneration in the market. In this case, there is a difference of wealth, but no unjust inequality, because it is not the case that Dan would prefer to have David's bundle of occupation and income.

As Dworkin explains, equality of resources 'allows us to cite, as disadvantages and handicaps, only what we treat in the same way in our own ethical life'.[58] His conception is attractive from a liberal point of view because it avoids appealing to a controversial account of the good life. If the state must avoid using a standard of interpersonal comparison that can be rejected by reasonable individuals, one way of doing this is to fashion a conception that allows individuals to bring their own convictions to the egalitarian table, which is what the envy test does.[59] In this way, the different ambitions and convictions of individuals are accommodated, because each is permitted to express her claim for compensation by citing a lack of items that *she* regards as helpful to the realization of her aims.

In dealing with differences in personal resources—the presence or absence of mental or physical disabilities, or inequalities of wealth-producing talent—Dworkin proposes a hypothetical insurance scheme to judge the demands of justice. Consider the medical case once more.[60] Ideally, we want a conception of justice that gives us guidance on the size and distribution of the health care budget. Dworkin's ambition-sensitive solution is to ask what insurance policies would be bought by suitably situated individuals. The medical insurance decisions of individuals in *existing* capitalist societies are not a sound guide for addressing justice in health care, because they are made against a background of imperfect knowledge, an unjust distribution of wealth and income, and are taken in the knowledge of the particular medical problems each individual faces. Dworkin insists that if we are to judge the justice of health care by appeal to individuals' insurance decisions, then these sources of unfairness must be eliminated. Thus, he asks us to consider what insurance decisions rational individuals would take with respect to health care if they had perfect information about the costs and benefits of different treatments and policies, enjoyed a fair share of wealth and income, and lacked information about their individual probabilities of having or developing different medical conditions. Under Dworkin's veil of ignorance the insuring parties do retain information about the *average* probability of having or developing certain conditions. Nevertheless, no one knows whether her own probability of developing a condition is higher or lower than the average.

The hypothetical insurance scheme places the insuring parties in a position such that the medical risks they face are equal, their choice is perfectly informed, and none of them enjoys more or less than a fair share of income with which to insure. Now, Dworkin asks us to speculate what insurance policies with respect to health care individuals would purchase in such a scenario. The scheme is ambition-sensitive because the insuring parties consult their own preferences and aims in life and, in particular, they ask themselves how much they value good health compared to other goods, such as wealth and income, education, pensions, and so on. In addition, they attach higher priority to certain kinds of health care over others. For example, many would value expensive life-saving treatment for conditions that affect them earlier in life more highly than similarly expensive life-saving treatment for conditions that affect them towards the end of their lives. Thus, insuring parties would purchase insurance packages that protect their health to a particular extent, and they would buy greater protection against certain health risks compared to others.

Dworkin holds that justice demands that whatever insurance decisions individuals would make concerning medical care in this idealized context should be matched by social policies in our own society. The upshot of his thought experiment is a case for a health service that is funded out of progressive taxation and free at the point of delivery. In addition, the size of the budget for that health service and how that budget is distributed across different kinds of medical provision should be determined by the insurance scheme. For instance, Dworkin argues that it is highly unlikely that the medical insurance decisions of equally situated individuals would match the current distribution of medical services in the USA, in which some 40 per cent of the health care budget is spent on people in the last six months of their lives. Insurers would not, he suggests, buy policies to provide life support in the event of lapsing into a permanent vegetative state or expensive medical treatment when in the late stages of Alzheimer's. The resources that might be used to purchase such medical provision would be better spent, he claims, pursuing other goods earlier in life.[61]

One obvious objection to the hypothetical insurance scheme is that it is impossible to determine with confidence which policies individuals would purchase if they enjoyed an equal share of resources and lacked knowledge of their own particular good or bad fortune in life. This is the case because one's ambitions are, in part, affected by the circumstances in which one lives, including the resources at one's disposal. If current conditions are changed, then, for all we know, indviduals' ambitions might be significantly different. Thus the promised ambition sensitivity, it might be argued, is illusory since the necessary counterfactual identification of individuals' preferences is impossible.

Dworkin accepts this objection in so far as he concedes the impossibility of an *individualized* hypothetical insurance scheme, which would tailor each person's entitlements to match the insurance decisions she would have made were she equally placed. Nevertheless, a more modest scheme is possible, which demands that society match what people would *on average* purchase in such a context. Here, we may look to the actual insurance decisions of average income earners for some, albeit imperfect, guidance on the question of what society would on average choose if everyone had an equal share of impersonal resources.[62] At the very least, the hypothetical insurance scheme provides a structure for thinking about a just response to capability equality that displays some concern to accommodate the ambitions people have. In the absence of a determinate interest-based solution, such a conception has its attractions from a liberal point of view.

Other objections to the resourcist conception of advantage are available. I postpone a discussion of them until after I have deployed the approach to deal with certain issues concerning upbringing (Section 2.5). Here, I merely want to state the conception of advantage that emerges from the two conceptions discussed above. A plausible liberal conception of advantage will, in the first instance, rest on a conception of our status as free and equal persons with interests in pursuing justice, autonomy, and a particular conception of the good life. In many cases, we need look no further than these interests to resolve the issue at hand. However, in some cases, such as those concerning health care, an appeal to our interests as free and equal persons will not offer sufficient guidance on policy. In these cases, a liberal conception must describe an appropriate way of deciding policy that accommodates people's ambitions and ethical convictions. Dworkin's ambition-sensitive conception of equality of resources, including his hypothetical insurance scheme, represents an approach to these questions that satisfies this requirement, at least when it is constrained by a prior commitment to satisfy our interests as free and equal citizens.

1.5 THE SITE OF JUSTICE AND LEGITIMACY

I finish my characterization of the liberal conception of justice and legitimacy that forms the platform for the account of upbringing to come by making a few remarks about the *site* of justice and legitimacy. The 'site' question asks for a more precise delineation of the items that are our focus. It is tempting to say that many things can be evaluated from the point of view of justice. For example, some may say that an individual who is mean to, or dismissive of, children acts unjustly towards them, or is a less just person than she might be. However, an inquiry into the rightness or wrongness of individuals' conduct or the quality of their dispositions is a very different enterprise from an evaluation of an education policy pursued by a government. It is important, therefore, to establish which kinds of item are in view when we are applying a conception of justice or legitimacy to questions concerning the upbringing of children.

Given the liberal view outlined above, we have a natural answer to the question of the site of justice and legitimacy. Our focus is the basic structure of society. As already discussed, the basic structure consists of the major institutions of society that apply to individuals involuntarily, because they are born into and live under them for their entire lives. The other key feature of basic structural institutions is that they significantly affect citizens' life prospects and self-understandings. It is fitting for institutions having these properties to be subject to evaluation from the point of view of justice and legitimacy.

Now there remain two key questions that require further clarification in the light of the recent debate over the site of justice. The first, raised by G. A. Cohen, is whether an institution must operate through coercion to qualify as part of the basic structure. Now it is undeniable that many basic structural institutions are indeed coercive. To establish this we need only observe the criminal law and the sanctions it imposes on unlawful conduct. Nevertheless, the question is: If an institution does not operate through coercion, does it follow that it is not part of the basic structure, which is our focus from the point of view of justice? An alternative interpretation holds that to be part of the basic structure it is sufficient for an institution that applies to us without our free consent to be one that has a significant effect on our lives. Call this the *profound importance* account in contrast to the *coercion* account of what counts as a basic structural institution.

As Cohen has argued in the context of economic justice, conduct *within* the coercively enforced law can significantly affect individuals' life prospects. His central example is the widespread practice of the productive making their willingness to work harder, or to take socially desirable jobs, dependent on their receiving greater than average and, indeed, inequality-generating incentive payments. Cohen describes an alternative egalitarian ethos under which the productive recognize a duty to work harder for no more than an equal share of economic advantage. Cohen rightly claims that the choice between the egalitarian ethos and the ethos of permissible incentive-seeking has significant implications for citizens' life prospects, even though it is not essentially a choice between different *coercive* institutions.[63]

On the basis of these two accounts of the basic structure, Cohen insists that Rawlsians face a dilemma. Either they adopt the coercion account of the basic structure or the profound importance account. If they take the first option, then (*a*) their conception of the basic structure is inconsistent with other claims they make, particularly their inclusion of the family as part of the basic structure; and (*b*) the conception is implausible because it conflicts with the widely held and sound conviction that certain non-coercive practices are evaluable from the point of view of justice. Again, the example he offers concerns the family: 'a regular practice of favouring sons over daughters in the matter of providing higher education', though non-coercive, should be assessed on grounds of justice.[64] If, on the other hand, Rawlsians adopt the profound importance account of the basic structure, without insisting on the presence of coercion, then the ethi of individuals who act within the law fall within the purview of justice. Cohen maintains that this is a more plausible view, but its adoption signals the defeat of one of the most notable features of Rawlsian liberalism: its incentive-based defence of economic inequality. As is well known, the difference principle requires the tax and income structure of society to be arranged to the maximum benefit of the least advantaged. It does so by allowing inequality-generating payments to be given to the productive so as to induce a greater economic contribution from them. But it makes such payments against a background that takes for granted the permissibility of individuals making their daily economic choices in a purely self-interested manner. However, as Cohen has shown, this arrangement in which tax policy serves the least advantaged given the alleged permissible self-seeking conduct of individuals is significantly less beneficial to the least advantaged than his alternative egalitarian ethos in which individuals work according to their ability and, in return, enjoy an equal share of economic advantage.[65] Therefore, while more plausible, the profound importance account of the basic structure threatens one of the most prominent features of Rawlsian justice.

The case against the coercion account of the basic structure is compelling. No doubt, the presence or absence of coercion is often relevant from the point of view of justice, but it is surely not the only thing that is relevant. When we discuss justice, we are discussing how to arrange our social world so that individuals get their due. If justice is recipient-based, at least in part, then it is difficult to see why informal practices that are not coercive but that, nevertheless, have significant effects on people's life chances and self-understandings are not part of the site of justice.

Thus, in considering justice and legitimacy in upbringing our focus includes not only the different possible legal arrangements for the care and education of children but also other arrangements that affect children in significant ways, such as the customary practices with respect to how parents *use* their legal rights over children. Since families have a profound effect on the values that a child acquires and the life chances she enjoys, the conduct of parents is evaluable from the point of view of justice. Indeed, as I argue at greater length (see Section 3.3), there are sound reasons to regard parental conduct as subject to many of the restrictions of public reason that apply to public officials and citizens. In addition, there are other aspects of justice within the family that I do not discuss. For example, many feminists argue that a gendered division of labour within the family, which is the dominant practice of most societies, is significantly detrimental to the interests of women and to the development of a sense of justice in children. If that case is accepted, then justice requires a thoroughgoing review of the distribution of opportunity and resources between the sexes.[66] In these and other ways, then, the profound importance interpretation of the basic structure leads us to an assessment of the aims and conduct of parents in contrast to a narrow focus on education policy as pursued by governments.

I said there were two key questions concerning the basic structure. We have answered the first concerning the sufficient conditions for an item to fall within the purview of justice. Yet one issue left hanging concerns whether the profound importance interpretation of the basic structure remains consistent with a liberal account of justice that refuses to demand the adoption of an egalitarian ethos of the kind Cohen has in mind. Here our second question is relevant. The question is: What are the desirable properties of principles of justice to govern the basic structure? Now the desirability of certain properties is more or less obvious. One is that they must achieve a fair distribution of social benefits and burdens. In the Rawlsian view, (Pareto) efficiency is another desirable property of principles of justice.[67] And a third, which is significant for our purposes, is that we have reasons to prefer principles of justice to the extent that they are capable of producing rules that satisfy the publicity requirement. As noted above, this requirement has a number of dimensions. First given the burdens of judgement, publicly justifiable principles of justice will be ones that do not appeal to the whole truth about ethics. Given the inevitability of reasonable comprehensive pluralism, such an appeal would jeopardize the acceptability of the resulting principles. Second, as Williams emphasizes, justice must be seen to be done in the sense that it is desirable for the principles of justice to be such that the rules they issue can be seen to be implemented.[68] It is valuable for citizens to be able to appreciate that the rules that constrain their conduct realize justice and, therefore, it is preferable for principles of justice to be ones that generate rules that can be applied in a publicly verifiable manner. Both aspects of publicity are supported by the ideal of political autonomy discussed earlier, which values citizens' willing affirmation of the moral and legal constraints to which they are subject.[69]

Given the desirability of public principles of justice, Rawlsians might seek to retain their reluctance to embrace Cohen's egalitarian ethos on the grounds that it is incapable of generating a *public* set of economic rules. As Williams argues, because of the complex comparative judgements that must figure in an assessment of whether a person with a particular set of talents has worked hard enough or taken a sufficiently socially desirable job, it is highly unlikely that this person (or others) can establish with any confidence that she has complied with the egalitarian ethos. If such problems are insurmountable, then there are reasons of publicity to favour principles, like Rawls's difference principle, that are capable of supplying publicly verifiable economic rules.[70]

Whereas our discussion of the first question leads to the view that parental conduct falls within the purview of justice, our answer to the second supports the claim that the principles of justice and legitimacy through which we evaluate parental conduct should be ones that can be satisfied or violated in a publicly verifiable manner. Notice that this does not mean that the rules must be such that they cannot be flouted without other people knowing that they have been broken. Pretty much any set of social rules is susceptible to that problem. In framing public rules for an ideal world we stipulate that individuals recognize a duty to abide by the rules whatever they turn out to be. The problem that the ideal of political autonomy highlights is not the problem of rule-breaking by the unjust, but the problem of the rules being insufficiently determinate for the just to be confident that their conduct complies with them. Hence, it is desirable for the principles of justice we fashion for parents to be ones by which parents of good faith can live. For example, it is clear that a rule that requires parents to display equal concern for the fortune of their son and daughter is an appropriately verifiable rule, because it is just and provides sufficiently determinate guidance: it is broken, for example, if they finance their son through higher education but make their daughter pay for her own tuition. By contrast, a principle that asserts the injustice of parents displaying more concern for their children compared to the concern shown on average by other parents is problematic in a similar way to Cohen's egalitarian ethos. It is highly unlikely that faced with such a rule, parents would be able with any confidence to determine what level of concern they ought to show their own children. They would need to have a comparative understanding of the special needs of their own and other children, and a detailed appreciation of the multiple ways in which support can be offered—through providing monetary resources, a beneficial milieu, various kinds of effective parenting, and so on. It would be impossible for a parent to be confident that the concern she shows complies with the principle that children in different families should receive equal concern from their parents. This is not to say that other rules that limit the extent to which parents favour their own children cannot be publicly verified. A rule prohibiting the purchase of expensive advantageous education is a case in point. Such a rule, it might be argued, is fair on grounds of equal justice and publicly verifiable. And to take another example, we might review the general incidence of disability, special needs, or economic inequality and frame rules to supplement the income of parents in a way that compensates them or their children for the bad luck they suffer (Section 2.5). Compensatory policies of that kind are capable of operating as public rules that can facilitate political autonomy.

In conclusion, then, the upshot of the discussion of the site of justice is that it would be a mistake to restrict our attention merely to education and childcare policy as pursued by governments. Whilst an account of justice in upbringing must deal effectively with such policy issues, it must also attend to how parents and others act *within* the legal rules that constrain them; parents can act unjustly towards their children without breaking the law. Yet our acceptance of this truth must not overlook the fundamental liberal ideal that principles of justice should guide parents in a manner that facilitates their autonomy as self-governing individuals. If we must have principles of justice that constrain parents directly, they should be ones that are justified on the basis of the ideals of freedom and equality and that provide clear and determinate prescriptions.

NOTES

1. Rawls, *A Theory of Justice*, rev. edn. (Cambridge, MA: The Belknap Press of Harvard University Press, 1999); *Political Liberalism* (New York: Columbia University Press, 1996).
2. Rawls, *A Theory of Justice*, esp. secs. 3–4, 20–30.
3. Ibid. esp. secs. 9–17.
4. See, in particular, *Political Liberalism*, lecture VIII.
5. Rawls, *Political Liberalism*, p. 11.
6. Ibid. p. 12.

7. Strictly speaking, political liberalism avoids appeal to conceptions that are general or comprehensive. The generality of a doctrine is specified by the *range of subjects* to which it applies. A doctrine is political only if its subject matter is the political domain alone; it is general if it applies to non-political subjects as well. The comprehensiveness of a doctrine is indicated by the *content* of its ideal, as explained in the text. Even though generality and comprehensiveness normally go together, one can conceive of a doctrine that is non-general, applying only to the political domain, and yet relies upon comprehensive ideals. Political conceptions avoid both the generality and comprehensiveness that are characteristic of religious, philosophical, and moral doctrines. Rawls rightly claims that the more general a conception is, the more comprehensive its content must be: see ibid. p. 175. Indeed, when he discusses comprehensive doctrines Rawls has in mind comprehensive *and* general doctrines. For reasons of clarity I follow Rawls in this respect.
8. Ibid. pp. 13–14.
9. Ibid. pp. 4–5.
10. Ibid. p. 9.
11. Ibid. pp. 4, 15.
12. Dworkin, *Sovereign Virtue: The Theory and Practice of Equality* (Cambridge, MA: Harvard University Press, 2000), pp. 216–18, 267–74.
13. Rawls calls this moral power 'the capacity for a conception of the good'. See *Political Liberalism*, esp. pp. 310–15.
14. Raz, *The Morality of Freedom* (Oxford: Clarendon Press, 1986), pp. 373–4.
15. He also notes, in the case of the hounded woman who has a full range of options but must spend her entire life avoiding being killed by a beast, that one cannot live an autonomous life if every choice one takes is potentially a fatal one. See Raz, *The Morality of Freedom*, pp. 374–6.
16. Mill, *On Liberty*, ch. 3.
17. Here I follow Rawls's account. See *Political Liberalism*, pp. 310–15.
18. For more on this issue, see Raz, *The Morality of Freedom*, pp. 378–81 and ch. 15, and Clayton, 'Liberal Equality and Ethics', *Ethics*, 113 (2002), 8–22, and 'A Puzzle about Ethics, Justice, and the Sacred', in Justine Burley (ed.), *Dworkin and His Critics* (Oxford: Blackwell, 2004).
19. The task Rousseau sets himself is: 'To find a form of association that defends and protects the person and goods of each associate with all the common force, and by means of which each one, uniting with all, nevertheless obeys only himself and remains as free as before.' Rousseau, *On the Social Contract*, ed. Roger Masters, trans. Judith Masters (New York: St Martin's Press, 1978), p. 53.
20. Rawls, *Political Liberalism*, p. 68.

21. Rawls, *Political Liberalism*, p. 137; see also p. 217; 'Reply to Habermas', *The Journal of Philosophy*, 92 (1995), 146 ff; and 'The Idea of Public Reason Revisited', in *Collected Papers* (Cambridge, MA: Harvard University Press, 1999), pp. 577–8. Nagel claims that it is the element of coercion that imposes the special requirement that principles of justice must be ones that reasonable persons can share. See Nagel, 'Moral Conflict and Political Legitimacy', *Philosophy and Public Affairs*, 16 (1987), pp. 223–4, and n. 8.
22. Rawls, *Political Liberalism*, pp. 66–7.
23. The ideal of public justification might also be valuable instrumentally because it increases the probability of citizens conforming to principles of justice. On this kind of justification, see Joshua Cohen, 'A More Democratic Liberalism', *Michigan Law Review*, 92 (1994), 1516. See also Gray, *Mill on Liberty: A Defence* (London: Routledge, 1983), p. 66.
24. As Rawls and others emphasize, this is a familiar and attractive ideal, which is present in the political philosophies of Rousseau and Hegel. See Rawls, 'The Idea of an Overlapping Consensus', in *Collected Papers*, p. 426, n. 10; Joshua Cohen, 'Reflections on Rousseau: Autonomy and Democracy', *Philosophy and Public Affairs*, 15 (1986), esp. 274–88; 'Moral Pluralism and Political Consensus', in D. Copp et al. (eds.), *The Idea Of Democracy* (Cambridge: Cambridge University Press, 1993), pp. 274–6, and 'A More Democratic Liberalism', 1515–17.
25. Larmore, 'Political Liberalism', *Political Theory*, 18 (1990), 349. See also Nagel, 'Moral Conflict and Political Legitimacy', p. 223, n. 8, and *Equality and Partiality* (New York: Oxford University Press, 1991), p. 159.
26. Rawls, *Political Liberalism*, pp. 61–2.
27. A third way in which the publicity condition is attractive is that it facilitates the realization of a social, or communal, good. As Rawls argues:

    > [W]henever there is a shared final end, an end that requires the cooperation of many to achieve, the good realized is social: it is realized through citizens' joint activity in mutual dependence on the appropriate actions being taken by others. Thus, establishing and successfully conducting reasonably just (though of course always imperfect) democratic institutions over a long period of time... is a great social good and appreciated as such. (Rawls, *Political Liberalism*, p. 204)

    Now, the publicity requirement, alongside the maintenance of free institutions, is necessary for the production of such communal goods understood as the pursuit of shared final ends. Suppose that the activity of different individuals and groups are coordinated by principles that some regard as illegitimate. Such activity might produce a good that can be realized only through the activity of many. Nevertheless, what is attractive about communal goods is that the different individuals who cooperate to produce them do so *because* they share the same end. When such goods are produced under conditions in which the contributing parties freely identify with their production, the activity constitutes a valuable shared experience. Yet, given the inevitable comprehensive pluralism within a free society, such a shared experience is not possible if the goods pursued are *comprehensive* in Rawls's sense. For further discussion of the sense in which Rawls's argument can be considered communitarian, see Williams's unpublished paper 'John Rawls, Communitarian'; Mulhall and Swift, *Liberals and Communitarians*, 2nd edn. (Oxford: Blackwell, 1996), ch. 6, esp. pp. 198–205, 221–2; Doppelt, 'Is Rawls's Kantian Liberalism Coherent and Defensible?', *Ethics*, 99 (1989), 829–32 (and 832–9 for instructive criticism of certain communitarian objections to Rawls as set out in Sandel's *Liberalism and the Limits of Justice* (Cambridge: Cambridge University Press, 1982)); Ackerman, 'Political Liberalisms', *The Journal of Philosophy*, 91 (1994), 385–6; Joshua Cohen, 'Procedure and Substance in Deliberative Democracy', in Seyla Benhabib (ed.), *Democracy and Difference: Contesting the Boundaries of the Political* (Princeton, NJ: Princeton University Press, 1996).

28. Rawls, *Political Liberalism*, p. 19.
29. Ibid. pp. 178–90, and Lecture VIII.
30. This is not the only kind of argument for basic liberties. For example, Rawls also offers a defence of the freedoms of conscience and religion that appeals to the value of reasonable agreement. See ibid. p. 61.
31. Here I follow Waldron, 'Justice Revisited (A Review of *Political Liberalism*)', *The Times Literary Supplement*, 18 June 1993, 5–6.
32. Rawls, *Political Liberalism*, p. 54.
33. Compare Joshua Cohen: 'An understanding of value is fully reasonable just in case its adherents are stably disposed to affirm it as they acquire new information and subject it to critical reflection.' 'Moral Pluralism and Political Consensus', pp. 281–2.
34. This does not, of course, imply that such pluralism should be celebrated, or that ethical scepticism, which asserts that we cannot obtain knowledge about comprehensive matters, is sound.
35. For Rawls's elaboration of these explanations, see *Political Liberalism*, pp. 56–7.
36. For the criticism that disagreement about justice is as inevitable as disagreement about comprehensive doctrines, see Sandel, 'Review of *Political Liberalism*', *Harvard Law Review*, 107 (1994), 1782–9; Mulhall and Swift, *Liberals and Communitarians*, p. 234 ff; Caney, 'Anti-perfectionism and Rawlsian

Liberalism', *Political Studies*, 43 (1995), 257–8; Waldron, 'Justice Revisited', 5–6, and 'Disagreements about Justice', *Pacific Philosophical Quarterly*, 75 (1994), 372–87. These critics do not agree, however, on what is the most appropriate response to this fact.

37. Consider, for example, Sandel's rhetorical question: 'If government can affirm the justice of redistributive policies even in the face of disagreement by libertarians, why cannot government affirm in law, say the moral legitimacy of homosexuality, even in the face of disagreement by those who regard homosexuality as sin?' See Sandel, 'Review of *Political Liberalism*', 1788.
38. Rawls, *Political Liberalism*, p. xlviii.
39. Ibid. pp. lvii–lx. Below, I discuss the second aspect of reasonableness: reasonable agreement. However, I wish to dispel the impression some may have that the ideal of reasonable agreement does not figure in the ideal of fair terms of cooperation. In fact, the choice of primary goods as the metric for interpersonal comparison is motivated, in part, by the concern for public agreement on matters of justice (see Section 1.4).
40. See, in addition, Rawls, *Justice as Fairness: A Restatement* (Cambridge, MA: The Belknap Press of Harvard University Press, 2001).
41. Of course, such disagreements may worry political liberals for other reasons, such as the extent to which actual democracies can be transformed into well-ordered societies.
42. For an alternative internal critique of the proceduralist conception, see Joshua Cohen, 'Pluralism and Proceduralism', *Chicago-Kent Law Review*, 69 (1994), 589–618. For discussion of further Rawlsian arguments against proceduralism, see Joshua Cohen's 'For a Democratic Society', in Samuel Freeman (ed.), *The Cambridge Companion to Rawls* (Cambridge: Cambridge University Press, 2003).
43. Rawls, *Political Liberalism*, p. xlix.
44. Ibid. pp. 65–6.
45. Eamonn Callan defends the smuggling claim, but not in the context of the capacity for a conception of a good, which is what interests us here. His view is that taking the burdens of judgement seriously must affect the manner in which one relates to one's own comprehensive conception, which is itself a partially comprehensive matter. See Callan, *Creating Citizens: Political Education and Liberal Democracy* (Oxford: Clarendon Press, 1997), ch. 2, esp. pp. 28–42. I do not follow Callan's analysis, because I interpret the role of the burdens of judgement in Rawls's account of political liberalism differently. The role of the burdens of judgement is to support the claim that comprehensive pluralism is an inevitable consequence of free institutions. Accepting the burdens of judgement involves recognizing this fact and, in light of the

ideal of liberal legitimacy, respecting a duty not to appeal to controversial comprehensive conceptions when acting politically. On this interpretation, accepting the burdens of judgement does not require 'serious imaginative engagement' (*Creating Citizens*, p. 40) with comprehensive views one rejects. It is consistent with acceptance of the burdens to regard another view as unworthy of serious examination, while understanding the general human limitations that explain how such errors of reasoning arise. Thus, Rawls's account is not a disguised form of comprehensive liberalism in virtue of his conception of the burdens of judgement.

46. Rawls, *Political Liberalism*, pp. 30–2.
47. The criticism is made by Kymlicka, *Liberalism, Community and Culture* (Oxford: Clarendon Press, 1989), p. 58. See, in addition, Levinson, *The Demands of Liberal Education* (Oxford: Oxford University Press, 1999), pp. 18–21. Notice that the criticism is not that Rawls's political liberalism rests on a disguised comprehensive liberalism. There is no doubting the coherence of Rawls's view. It is its *plausibility* that is in question. One possible reply available to Rawls is that the good of political autonomy, which requires each individual to identify with the constraints she faces, generates a reason to adopt a conception of the person that does not derive from any particular comprehensive doctrine. But this does not supply a conclusive reason to regard the interest in rational revisability as the *only* possible political conception of our interests. The Ulysses believer, who wants to be bound to her faith, might present her desire as a political conception of our interests. To be sure, as Rawls notes, this would be a different political conception, which denies free and equal citizenship. True, but we remain in need of a justification for rejecting it in favour of one that cites an interest in rational revision.
48. Rawls, *Political Liberalism*, p. 13.
49. See, for example, Raz: '[I]n principle all moral reasons are fair game for governmental action. "Perfectionism" is merely a term used to indicate that there is no fundamental principled inhibition on governments acting for any valid moral reason.' 'Facing Up: A Reply', *Southern California Law Review*, 62 (1989), 1230.
50. Interestingly, Rawls sometimes presents his political conception of justice as not appealing to the whole truth, which is a more modest position than the claim that it avoids any appeal to even partially comprehensive ideals. See 'The Idea of Public Reason Revisited', pp. 574, 579.
51. I am indebted here to Williams's unpublished work, 'The Rejection of Perfectionism'.
52. Thus, the idea of a so-called 'weak perfectionism' is a misnomer. Either the view recognizes political ideals that generate reasons not to appeal to the

whole truth about ethics, in which case it is anti-perfectionist, or it does not, in which case it is perfectionist *tout court.*

53. Note also a further way in which autonomy-based liberalism might be anti-perfectionist. Even though it views autonomy as valuable in people's non-political lives, it need not be committed to any particular defence of that value. For example, the capacity for a conception of the good might be believed by some to be a central part of a successful life, or, by others, as an ethical duty that we must fulfil even if it causes us misery. We need not choose between these different accounts, provided they agree on the content and implications of our interest in developing and exercising this capacity.
54. Rawls, *Justice as Fairness: A Restatement* (Cambridge, MA: The Belknap Press of Harvard University Press, 2001), p. 57.
55. Ibid. pp. 169–70.
56. Ibid. pp. 170–6.
57. The envy test is a necessary condition of equality in the distribution of impersonal resources. Dworkin notes that certain kinds of arbitrariness that are compatible with satisfaction of the test are, nevertheless, contrary to the demands of justice, and must therefore be avoided. See Dworkin, *Sovereign Virtue*, pp. 67–8.
58. Ibid. p. 294. Dworkin's claim that an adequate account of advantage should be one that matches people's particular ethical judgements is a central part of his critique of equality of welfare and equality of access to welfare. Welfarist conceptions, like Dworkin's resourcist view, take into account the preferences of different people. But welfarists aim for equality of preference-satisfaction, which produces very different results compared to Dworkin's appeal to preferences in equality of resources. The basic problem for welfarists is that they are committed to asserting that if Dan's preference-satisfaction is lower than David's, then we ought to compensate Dan for this, even though Dan may believe that his life of geography is far superior to David's life pursuing money. It seems highly counter-intuitive for Dan to claim compensation from David when he believes his life is in no respect worse than David's. Yet welfarists seem committed to this counter-intuitive position. The debate over the resourcist and welfarist accounts of advantage is extensive. See *Sovereign Virtue*, chs. 1 and 7; Arneson, 'Liberalism, Distributive Subjectivism, and Equal Opportunity for Welfare', *Philosophy and Public Affairs*, 19 (1990), 77–93; G. A. Cohen, 'On the Currency of Egalitarian Justice', *Ethics*, 99 (1989), 906–44; G. A. Cohen, 'Expensive Taste Rides Again', in Justine Burley (ed.), *Dworkin and His Critics* (Oxford: Blackwell, 2004); and Dworkin, 'Ronald Dworkin Replies' in the same volume, pp. 339–50. For sympathetic discussion of Dworkin's critique of welfarist conceptions of advantage, see Williams, 'Equality for the

Ambitious', *The Philosophical Quarterly*, 52 (2002), 377–89, and Clayton, 'The Resources of Liberal Equality', *Imprints*, 9 (2000), 63–84.

59. Dworkin himself defends equality of resources on the basis of an account of ethics, the challenge model. See *Sovereign Virtue*, ch. 6; Clayton, 'Liberal Equality and Ethics'; and Dworkin, 'Sovereign Virtue Revisited', *Ethics*, 113 (2002), 140–3. However, he also appeals to the ideal of partnership democracy that 'insists that citizens be able to see themselves as joint authors of collective decisions', which appears similar to Rawls's account of liberal legitimacy. See *Sovereign Virtue*, p. 295 and Clayton, 'The Resources of Liberal Equality', 78–80.
60. In what follows I discuss Dworkin's account in 'Justice in the Distribution of Health Care', in Matthew Clayton and Andrew Williams (eds.), *The Ideal of Equality*, pp. 203–22. See, in addition, *Sovereign Virtue*, ch. 8.
61. Ibid. pp. 212–13.
62. That is, if they face a relatively open medical insurance market. Dworkin adds that the guidance would be improved if different medical insurance regimes were proposed and debated. See ibid. pp. 212–18.
63. See G. A. Cohen, 'Where the Action Is: On the Site of Distributive Justice', *Philosophy and Public Affairs*, 26 (1997), 3–30.
64. Ibid. 21.
65. For further discussion of the incentive argument for inequality, see G. A. Cohen, 'Incentives, Inequality, and Community', in Stephen Darwall (ed.), *Equal Freedom* (Ann Arbor, MI: University of Michigan Press, 1995); 'The Pareto Argument for Inequality', *Social Philosophy and Policy*, 12 (1995), 160–85; *If You're an Egalitarian, How Come You're So Rich?* (Cambridge, MA: Harvard University Press, 2000), pp. 1–6, 117–47. Notice that the egalitarian ethos is not subject to straightforward exploitation objections, which assert that it is unfair for the productive to be under a duty to work hard for the sake of the worst off, because it rests on an account of equality in which individuals are compensated for their labour burdens.
66. See Okin, *Justice, Gender, and the Family* (New York: Basic Books, 1989), esp. chs. 1, 5, 7–8.
67. This is not uncontroversial. For a critique of the view that principles of justice are a subset of Pareto efficient principles, see Temkin, 'Equality, Priority, and the Levelling Down Objection', in Clayton and Williams (eds.), *The Ideal of Equality*.
68. Williams, 'Incentives, Inequality, and Publicity', *Philosophy and Public Affairs*, 27 (1998), 225–47.
69. Ibid. 242–46. Williams cites further grounds for the desirability of principles satisfying the publicity requirement.
70. Ibid. esp. 235–42.

2

Childrearing Rights and Their Distribution

An account of justice in upbringing must address issues of fairness with respect to those who raise children as well as justice for children. So one of our central issues concerns the content and distribution of childrearing rights. How should we characterize the rights and duties of childrearers? What cluster of options, injunctions, and requirements does custody of children confer on parents from the point of view of justice? What are the conditions for the possession of such rights and duties? And what are the implications for the distribution of other resources, such as wealth and income, of our answers to these questions? Should the costs of upbringing be borne exclusively by parents, or should parents be subsidized in their childrearing by others in the community?

One influential conception of childrearing rights defended by a number of liberal thinkers in recent years is *child-centred.* It regards childrearing rights as derived solely from the interests of children. On this view the interests of parents that are independent of those of the child have no direct importance in the resolution of childrearing issues. In this chapter, I challenge that conception and articulate a *dual interest view* in which the interests of both children and parents count in the allocation of childrearing rights. If we embrace this view, we need an account of how to resolve the conflicts of interest that might arise between parents and children. Responding to this requirement, I employ and develop the hybrid liberal account of advantage described earlier (Section 1.4) to defend a particular conception of justice in the distribution of childrearing rights.

2.1 CHILDREARING INTERESTS AND ISSUES OF JUSTICE

The right to rear children is a term that can be used to describe a number of different clusters of more particular rights. At this point, prior to the development of a conception of justice for children and parents, it is premature to define in any detail a specific cluster of rights that falls under a plausible conception of the right to rear. To fix ideas, we might think of the right to rear as a set of claim rights protecting certain decisions a parent might take with respect to her child: decisions concerning what the child reads, hears, eats, or views, where he or she lives, how he or she spends the recreational time, and so on. The injunctions of such claim rights might take various forms, ranging from the wrongness of others interfering with such decisions to the wrongness of punishment as a response to a parent implementing a particular decision with respect to such matters.

Plainly, it is possible for childrearing rights to be shared between a number of different agents. We might allow custodial parents and state-mandated educational establishments to share the rights to determine what the child hears and reads, for example, according to some temporal division of rights in which teachers oversee such matters while children are within school and parents have control out of school hours. Or we might confer certain rights on custodial parents such as the right to choose the bedtime story the child receives, while conferring other rights on different agents. For instance, some claim that doctors should have the right to decide whether and when a child should be inoculated, which would place parents under a requirement to take their child to a medical practice for an injection within a particular period of time. But before we decide who, if anyone, are the right-holders with respect to children's upbringing and what the rights and duties of childrearing are, we need a sense of the different interests at stake and the distributive issues that pertain to this issue.

It is clear that children have an interest in who possesses rights over their lives, since they have an interest in having a good upbringing. Any convincing conception of childrearing rights must accommodate these interests in a plausible fashion. But are they the only interests at stake? Two other possible sources of claims for consideration are 'the community' and 'parents'.

The community, let us say, refers to other individuals whose lives might be affected for better or worse by the presence of children, either as children or as the adults they grow up to be. Such individuals have an interest in how children are brought up. If we affirm liberal values, then individuals have an interest in being treated with concern and respect. Hence, an upbringing that encourages children to appreciate and develop a sense of justice and legitimacy is an important part of satisfying the legitimate claims of others to live in a just society. But we must be careful not to weigh in the balance certain desires the community might have with respect to children's upbringing. For example, even if it is in the community's interest to have a productive workforce, it does not follow that it is legitimate for children to be instilled with a work ethic of the kind that inhibits their autonomy with respect to occupational choice. Moreover, it might be better for the community if children are raised in a way that encourages them to have inexpensive tastes, so that others might satisfy their tastes to a greater extent. But again, that kind of social engineering is unjust. Nevertheless, an education in the norms of justice and legitimacy are legitimate interests of the community that might be weighed in the balance when determining childrearing rights.

Notice, however, that there need be no conflict here between the interests of the community and those of the child. While this is controversial, I claim that everyone has an interest in leading a just life. Any legitimate expectation the community has with respect to the child's future conduct is therefore accommodated in an itemization of the child's interest in pursuing a just life, i.e. in leading a life that complies with a legitimate conception of justice. If justice confers rights on others, it also mandates an upbringing that will develop in children a desire to play their part in the achievement of a just society. But it does this in the service of the child's interest in leading a just life and living in a just society, just as much as for others who benefit from justice. If this is right, and there is no conflict between the interests of the child and those of the community, we may proceed by putting the latter to one side.[1] (If I am wrong about the child's interest in leading a just life, a more extended analysis of childrearing rights would be required, but it would not require a substantial revision of the conception I develop.)

Parents are the other agents whose interests might have relevance in childrearing policy. In the context of the revolution in reproductive technology, we must draw distinctions between different kinds of parent. *Genetic* parents, let us say, are those individuals who supply the genes that determine the identity of the resulting child. *Procreative* parents are those responsible for the production of the zygote from which the resulting child develops. The distinction between genetic and procreative parents is clear in the case of a woman (a procreative parent) who conceives a child from a sperm and an egg that are donated (the donors being the genetic parents). Finally, I shall call the *custodial* parents of a child those individuals who have the primary responsibility for the upbringing of the child, as specified by the rights and duties that the conception of justice accords them. Again, one might become a custodial parent through adoption and, therefore, have no genetic or procreative relationship with the child one raises. Some of the key issues that a complete account of childrearing rights must address concern the relationship between these different kinds of parent and the different interests they have. To what extent should we count the desire of genetic, procreative, or present custodial parents to raise their children in the allocation of childrearing rights? I do not offer such a complete account in this chapter. My principal concern is with the rights of custodial parents and the resources to which they are entitled from the point of view of justice. So I do not consider the question of how we ought to resolve conflicting claims to custody or access that might be made by genetic, procreative, and adoptive parents, fascinating though they are.

In addition to a consideration of the relevant interests at stake in childrearing, we must also note certain facts about parenting that are relevant to the issues that concern us. Two facts are salient. First, some individuals are better parents than others. This might be because some are negligently inattentive to their role as parents, or it might be explained by factors for which they cannot be held responsible: some might lack the emotional or intellectual wherewithal to display to the same degree as others do the patience, devotion, creativity, emotional support, and other attributes from which children benefit within a family. Second, some children are more difficult or more costly to bring up than other children. It can be more difficult to cope with children with serious behavioural problems than those who lack them, and plainly it can be more costly to care for a child with certain mental or physical disabilities than her able-bodied peer.

The question is this: What is a just characterization and distribution of childrearing rights? In thinking about this question, we must consider who should bear the costs of poor parenting or of children who are hard to raise. We might, for instance, choose to allocate childrearing rights and resources so that the child's interests are met to the greatest degree possible. This might support placing all the costs on parents who lack parenting ability, by requiring them to transfer their childrearing rights to other individuals when such a transfer is in the interests of the child. Or, the community (or the community of parents) might seek to mollify the effects of bad luck on inadequate parents by offering financial or other support so that they may continue as custodial parents without jeopardizing the child's interests. Or, again, we might place some of the costs associated with poor parenting, or children who are expensive to raise, on the children themselves, by allowing them to endure a less than optimal upbringing. No doubt, various mixed solutions are also possible. To settle these distributive issues, we must assess the relevance and importance of the interests of children and parents respectively, and ask who is responsible for the costs of upbringing.

2.2 CHILD-CENTRED CONCEPTIONS

One influential conception of these matters is child-centred. While different versions of this conception have been proposed, they share the belief that the interests of the child have priority in the determination of childrearing rights. On this view, in decisions concerning the allocation of childrearing rights, if there is a conflict of interest between child and parent, the child's interests should prevail: the interests of parents must always yield to those of the child.

Notice that this conception does not defend a right to the best possible upbringing, since that would imply that those who would be the most able parents are under a duty to take custody of a child. Individuals are under no such duty if we affirm the liberal freedom of occupational choice. We must therefore interpret the conception as requiring the allocation of childrearing rights to *interested* parties whose possession of these rights can reasonably be expected to be in the child's best interests, compared with the possession of these rights by other interested parties. Following Vallentyne, call this the *best custodian condition.*[2]

It is tempting to view the best custodian condition with the image of an auction soon after birth at which interested parties bid for custody rights by promising to devote personal and impersonal resources to the child's upbringing. Perhaps it might be said that the condition demands the continual possibility of interested parties entering the bidding process at a later date if they feel they can outperform a child's present custodial parents. But this would be a caricature. Stable family relationships are an important ingredient in the child's well-being, and security in the possession of childrearing rights might be a condition of able individuals applying for such rights. Recognizing these facts, the best custodian condition may demand a childrearing policy that confers childrearing rights which specify few conditions for their continued enjoyment.

Child-centred views attach no *direct* relevance to the interests parents have in raising their child. Nonetheless, they do not routinely deny the claims of procreative parents to have custody of their children. Even if procreative parents' interests in raising their children do not matter directly, the fact that they have such interests figures in an assessment of who can reasonably be expected to be the best custodian. Various arguments have been offered for the indirect benefits of procreative, or perhaps genetic, parents having childrearing rights over their children. While counter-examples can easily be cited, it is often believed that as a general rule procreative parents are the most motivated to give their child a good start in life; the similarities a genetic relationship between parent and child often produces are sometimes thought beneficial to the child's development of a feeling of belonging or her emerging self-conception. Even if these beliefs are mistaken, and there are very many able and willing would-be parents between whom we cannot choose, we still require some method of allocating childrearing rights. A possible tiebreaker is to allocate these rights to those within the set satisfying the best custodian condition who claim the rights first: typically the procreative parents.[3]

In practice, then, the best custodian condition might support the allocation of childrearing rights to genetic or procreative parents, and does not necessarily make those rights insecure for custodial parents who hold them. Nevertheless, in attaching no direct importance to the interests of individuals in founding or maintaining a family it departs from the widely held dual interest view that attaches direct relevance to the interests of both child and parent.

2.3 THE DUAL INTEREST VIEW[4]

One way of defending the dual interest view is to appeal to the interest we have in pursuing our conceptions of the good life, which in many cases support, and sometimes require, the founding of a family. This general interest we all have generates a *pro tanto* reason to allocate childrearing rights to procreative parents who have conceived their child with the intention of founding a family. And this is the case, irrespective of whether we take up such rights by founding a family. For many, the project of family life with children will not figure in their conception of the good. Nevertheless, even this constituency has an interest in having the opportunity to raise their children if they decide to have children. Of course, this reason is not always decisive: it might be defeated by the independent reason we have to ensure that the child's interests are accommodated, which may, in certain cases, tell against the procreative parents having custody. Nevertheless, the direct accommodation of adults' interests in being parents gives the dual interest view a very different character to that of child-centred conceptions.[5]

It will immediately be objected that we cannot derive a right to found and maintain a family from the general interest we all have in pursuing our conceptions of the good. For the latter must be described as an interest in pursuing *reasonable* or *permissible* conceptions of the good and we have not yet established that a conception of the good that involves holding rights over others is permissible in the relevant sense. The objector insists that the permissibility of a conception of the good turns on whether the interests of others are taken into account in an appropriate manner. For example, we do not have even a *pro tanto* reason to accommodate racist conceptions of the good, because they violate the norms of freedom and equality that are fundamental to liberal society. Similarly, it might be claimed that an individual has the right to raise a child, irrespective of the importance he attaches to that project, only if his enjoyment of that right is in the best interests of the child. Vallentyne makes the point succinctly:

Given that the child has independent moral standing, and the rights at issue are rights to control access to the child, it is quite plausible, I claim, that the child's interests have priority over the potential custodial parents' interests. A man's profound interest in having a relationship with a given woman does not give him any rights to control access to her. The situation with children is no different.[6]

But there is a difference between controlling access to women and children respectively. In the case of the child, someone must have rights to control access to her out of a concern for her interests, whereas this is not true of adult women. The issue before us is this: given that someone must have rights over the child, who should have them? No doubt, some will fall back to the idea that the child's independent moral standing gives her interests priority. But notice that a child is also a potential parent. The individual who is now a child will, in the course of a normal life, come to affirm a particular conception of the good, which may well involve founding a family. As individuals over the course of a life, we have interests as children and interests as adults. Granting the independent moral status of individuals does not allow us to conclude that we must prioritize the interests of individuals as children. Perhaps they are more weighty. Nevertheless, it is not obvious that they always take priority over the interests we have as adults. That requires a further argument.

It turns out, then, that the dual interest view does not describe merely an *interpersonal* conflict between parents and their children, but an *intra-personal* conflict between the interests we have as children and those we have as adults. A policy that serves one's interests as a child may well be one that is detrimental to one's interests as an adult and, indeed, detrimental to one's interests taking one's life as a whole. To take a simple example, suppose in deciding how to distribute scarce medical resources we attach absolute priority to the health of children: if a child's health can be improved, medical resources should be allocated to her care in preference to the health improvement of adults. Prioritizing child health in this extreme way is implausible because the opportunity costs that must be borne by adults are too great. And these adults are the same individuals who the children we are now benefiting will grow up to be. In terms of lifetime health, all things considered, it is surely better to accept some redistribution of resources from paediatric care to other kinds of care, the principal beneficiaries of which are adults. In that way, everyone enjoys access to a reasonable level of health care across her life.[7]

To be sure, the medical rationing case differs from the childrearing case in a number of ways. In particular, both children and adults have an interest in being healthy. With respect to childrearing, the character of the respective interests of children and parents differ. A child has an interest in having a good upbringing where that is defined by reference to a number of variables: emotional security, an education that will develop her physical, mental, and moral powers, and so on. In contrast, the adult's interest is to have the opportunity to found a family: to beget and raise children according to some appropriate standard. However, notwithstanding the differences between these two cases, similar claims about opportunity costs can be made. If we affirm the best custodian condition, this will be best for us as children, for the policy is motivated solely by a concern for our interests as children. But the opportunity cost of this is necessarily that as adults we will have a more restricted access to custodial parenthood: those of us who fail the best custodian test will be refused the right to raise the children we beget.

Some might object that the acceptability of balancing the enjoyment of goods between different parts of one's life, as in the choice between different kinds of medical provision, cannot be applied to the childrearing case. For in this case the proposed balancing is between *exercising control over another* and *having control exercised over one*. The objection is that all rights *of control* must be justified by reference to either the consent or best interests of those who are controlled.[8]

We should reject this view. As we have established, the existence of such control rights is necessary for the well-being of children, and it is not obviously mistaken to claim that individuals might have interests that count with respect to the possession of such rights. Consider the analogous case of democratic rights. Many democrats claim that political institutions have legitimate authority only if they are suitably democratic in the sense that they provide each citizen with equal rights to influence the law. Many democrats accept, in addition, that individuals have an interest in shaping laws that constrain the lives of others (as well as their own). To be sure, we might maintain that the possession of political rights depends upon satisfying certain qualifying conditions, which serve to protect the interests of others. Nevertheless, this does not require political rights to be offered to the set of individuals who would use them to the *greatest* advantage of those constrained by the law. Rather, democracy requires equal rights for all those who satisfy the competence threshold, irrespective of whether some meeting it might exercise them better than others.[9]

It appears, then, that there is nothing counter-intuitive in asserting that individuals can have interests with respect to exercising control over others in cases where control must be exercised. If this is accepted, an adequate account of justice in the distribution of childrearing rights must accommodate our interests as children and as potential parents in a fair way. Responding to this task is not simple, because it is not obvious how much weight should be attached to the respective interests at stake. In the face of such uncertainty about the relative importance of the two primary interests at stake in childrearing, a liberal solution to the problem of accommodation should, I have argued (Section 1.4), be sensitive to our interests as free and equal persons and, in cases where those interests do not supply a sufficiently determinate conception, provide a solution that responds to people's own judgements about how their lives ought to go as children and adults respectively. And that account must deal in a fair manner with the various distributive issues we noted above, namely, that through no fault of theirs some individuals are more effective custodial parents than others are, and some children are more costly or difficult to raise compared to others.

2.4 THE RIGHT TO REAR

My account of justice in the distribution of childrearing rights has two parts. First, I offer an interest-based defence of certain rights with respect to the raising of children. Thereafter, I outline an approach to the distribution of childrearing resources with respect to which the interest-based view gives insufficient guidance. This supplementary account employs Dworkin's ambition-sensitive hypothetical insurance scheme as a way of identifying, among other things, a suitable distribution of financial support for disadvantaged children and parents.

I shall say a little more about the content of the right to rear that can be defended on the basis of an appeal to our interests presently. However, let us begin the interest-based defence of this right by reiterating the objection to the best custodian condition. The condition is objectionable, I claim, because it carries with it unacceptable opportunity costs. While it distributes rights in a way that best serves our interests as children, we pay a heavy price as adults, because it requires childrearing rights to be taken away from custodial parents when other interested parties holding such rights would serve the child's interests better. Consequently, some parents will lose the right to raise the children they beget or with whom they have established a relationship to which they attach profound significance.

The objection to the best custodian condition is not that the parents should never have custodial rights taken from them. Rather, it is that the condition sets the bar for the retention of custody too high. The common-sense view, which, I argue, is based on sound reasons, is that one retains the right to rear if one is a *sufficiently* good parent, rather than the best available parent. So the rejection of the best custodian condition does not supply an argument for childrearing rights that are retained irrespective of parental conduct. It merely argues for a lower threshold of parental adequacy above which individuals may retain custody of their children. How such a threshold is to be determined is a difficult issue, which must be sensitive to the importance we attach to the interests we have as parents and children respectively. I do not propose to resolve that issue here but, instead, to offer some remarks about the relevant considerations that should be weighed when addressing it.

Prior to that, however, we must clarify in a little more detail what is meant by the right to rear. I shall take the right to be a set of claim rights that protect from interference by others certain decisions parents take with respect to their child. It is possible to define the right as a subset of various more particular rights, which may include the right to live with one's child, to determine who she associates with and how she spends her time, to choose the school she attends, to give or withhold consent to various kinds of medical treatment on her behalf, and many more besides. Here, I merely pick out certain rights that fall within the central range of rights defended on the basis of parental interests.[10] On this restricted understanding, the right to rear protects parents in sharing a residence with their custodial child and in excluding others from it. The right justifies holding others under a duty not to relocate their child, take her into foster care, or put her up for adoption by other interested parties. In addition, the parents' right to rear includes the right to determine several of the child's activities such as what she eats how she spends her leisure time, what she reads, and who she plays with.

Other rights that are sometimes claimed to fall within the right to rear are excluded here. For example, the right to give or withhold consent to medical treatment for one's child and the right to choose which school she attends are not included within the right to rear as understood here. Similarly, the right to determine whether one's child engages in paid or unpaid work is not a right that is included. I exclude such rights merely because whether or not they are defensible depends on arguments other than those offered in this section. As I shall argue, the interests that justify the right to rear in the restricted sense offered above are compatible with, but do not provide sufficient justification for, these further rights. Advocates of some or all of those additional parental rights must look elsewhere for supporting grounds.[11]

With this clarification of the right to rear on hand, let us turn to its justification. The analysis in Section 2.3 suggests the particular issue we must address to justify the right to rear. Plainly, some adults neither have the desire to take on parental responsibilities nor attach particular ethical significance to parenthood. In addition, the rejection of the best custodian condition that our defence of the right to rear proposes implies that as children their interests would be served less well than they might be. Thus, our justificatory burden is to explain to such individuals why it is appropriate for them to have had a less than optimal upbringing for the sake of others (their parents) satisfying their desire to parent. We must identify an interest that justifies to them the losses they suffer in childhood without being compensated by the benefits of parenthood, which they reject.

Thus, we are looking for an interest that can be affirmed by free and equal persons holding diverse comprehensive convictions, the acknowledgement of which justifies the right to rear.[12] One that satisfies these desiderata is our interest in maintaining intimate relationships with particular dependent others. In our case, if an individual takes on the role of a parent and forms a relationship with a child, then her well-being is diminished if others terminate that relationship without her consent. A number of reasons can be offered for endorsing this interest. First, if one adopts a parenting role as part of one's conception of the good life, then one's life goes better to the extent that one successfully meets the challenge of parenting. Second, some appeal to the intrinsic value of relationships of this kind that require one to care in an intimate way for a vulnerable child who responds with spontaneous and, perhaps, unconditional love.[13] And, third, some might simply appeal to the natural pleasures one experiences from contact with one's child: from an embrace or from helping her to overcome a seemingly intractable problem.[14]

Thus, the maintenance of an intimate relationship with one's particular child is an interest justified by a number of considerations. Moreover, we can state the interest in terms that abstract from the diverse conceptions of family life that are affirmed, such that even those without the desire to become a parent should recognize its validity within arguments concerning justice. For the interest in parenting is a particular instantiation of the interest each of us has in maintaining an intimate relationship with particular dependent others. That abstractly described interest is recognized by those who care for the dependent elderly, the infirm, or pet animals. One does not have to be a parent, or to value parenthood, to appreciate how devastating it is for others to terminate the caring or nurturing relationship one has with another without one's consent.[15]

The widely held endorsement of the restricted right to rear can therefore be justified in terms of an account of our interests that is acceptable to free and equal persons. Such persons would also agree that the right is conditional upon parents satisfying a threshold of care, such that they may lose the right if their child's care or development falls below a particular standard. However, as I indicated earlier, the appeal to our interests can take us only so far. In particular, we still need to address the claim that parents hold other rights over children apart from the restricted right to rear. For example, should we acknowledge a right to choose which school one's child attends or the kind of medical treatment she receives. Here, the consensus that is achieved on our interest in maintaining a relationship with our children breaks down. And, to introduce another significant set of issues, which I shall consider next, if individuals have a right to rear, what duties, if any, does this place on others with respect to financing the upbringing of children? The restricted right I have defended insists on only a duty of non-interference if parents satisfy a relevant threshold of competence. However, we must also ask whether others have duties to transfer resources they possess to certain parents to defray the costs of parenting. Yet the interest-based argument for the right to rear seems ill-suited to addressing these further questions, because the consensus achieved with respect to the identification of our interests goes only so far, and in the absence of such a consensus any further specification of our interests appears arbitrary or sectarian. Some will insist that the interest that is served by the right to rear is so important that it justifies sizeable transfers of resources from others, while others will think that the parent–child relationship justifies nothing beyond a duty of non-interference. We need to look elsewhere for a conception of justice that can adjudicate between these positions in an attractive way.

2.5 HYPOTHETICAL INSURANCE AND CHILDREARING RESOURCES

In this section, I supplement the interest-based defence of the right to rear by outlining a hypothetical insurance scheme through which we might determine an appropriate distribution of resources for parents and the upbringing of children. In contrast to the best custodian condition, the right to rear, which specifies a threshold of parental acceptability, acknowledges that without compensation some children will be brought up in less propitious family and social environments than others enjoy. In addition, some children are more costly or more difficult to raise compared to others. If we care about justice, we must identify a fair distribution of resources in the light of the unequal distribution of luck that affects parents and children alike. And, in doing so, we must take into account the fact that the benefits of parenting and of a good start in life must be traded off against other goods, such as medical care, employment security, protection against crime, and savings for pensions.

We must therefore consider how individuals who have a sense of the opportunity costs associated with different choices would further specify childrearing rights, granted the restricted right to rear defended above. We require that the choices made must not unfairly discriminate against individuals in virtue of the distribution of brute luck. In particular, neither children nor would-be parents must be unfairly disadvantaged because the former are hard to raise, or because the latter suffer the bad brute luck of possessing inferior parenting resources compared to others. In a just society, the effects of the distribution of brute luck must be fairly shared in a manner that is responsive to the ambitions that individuals have.[16]

An immediate problem that confronts any *ambition-sensitive* account of justice in the distribution of childrearing resources is that very young children lack appropriately formed convictions about how to lead their lives. While we might consult the voice of adults to gauge the nature and strength of their desires to found and maintain families or to pursue other projects, the ambitions of children with respect to their lives as children and their future lives as adults either do not exist or, if they do, are not affirmed authentically and, therefore, do not command the same kind of respect. In the case of children there is no alternative but to act on their behalf.

The most promising approach is to ask what appropriately situated rational adults would choose by way of the distribution of childrearing resources on the assumption that they would relive their lives as children and then adults. In this way we inject ambition-sensitivity into the choice of childrearing policy by allowing ourselves to determine the strength of the two interests at stake—the child's interest in having a good upbringing and the adult's interests in being a parent and pursuing his or her own life—by reference to our own judgements. So let us consider what a suitable hypothetical choice situation might be.

The familiar thought experiment in which we shall engage is to ask what distribution of childrearing resources would be chosen by individuals in a choice situation which guarantees that whatever is chosen is fair. First, we address the issue within an otherwise just society in which resources are fairly distributed and familiar liberal and democratic freedoms are protected. Thus, the first background condition is that, bracketing questions of justice in the allocation of childrearing resources, everyone enjoys a fair share of resources. In a liberal view, the significant inequalities of wealth that are characteristic of modern industrial society would not prevail. Nevertheless, certain inequalities of wealth would remain, justified, perhaps, by incentive considerations or by the ideal that monetary inequalities may justly arise as a product of choice or ambition. On any plausible liberal view of distributive justice, certain inequalities of wealth may legitimately arise in virtue of the different occupational choices people make and the different talents they bring to the market.

Second, our thought experiment stipulates that the parties are rational in the sense they choose in a way that maximally serves their interests as children and adults. Of course, as we have noted, they will have to make judgements about how to balance the different interests they have across a life. Nevertheless, the assumption of rationality ensures that their choices are not inefficient or inconsistent. To realize this requirement we also assume that parties to the choice hold complete general information concerning the relevant inequalities that exist within (the just) society, and an understanding of the costs and effects of the different policy choices they might make. For example, they know that there is a degree of inequality of wealth in society such that some children have parents who have fewer resources at their disposal compared to other parents, and they understand that some children are considerably more costly to bring up than are others in virtue of the physical or mental disabilities they suffer.

Third, to achieve a choice that does not unfairly reflect the unequal distribution of luck which greater wealth-generating or parenting ability might bring, we place the parties under a (partial) veil of ignorance. While they have an understanding of the distribution of such luck, they do not know whether they themselves are advantaged or disadvantaged within this distribution. They do not know, for example, whether as children they have disabilities that make them difficult to raise. Nor do they know what level of wealth or parenting ability their parents enjoy, or they themselves will have as adults. Such a veil of ignorance renders the parties equal in their *ex ante* risk of suffering from bad luck or benefiting from good luck.

Fourth, in deciding the allocation of childrearing resources, parties consult their own convictions about the importance of a good upbringing and the significance of parenthood and other opportunities within their lives. They ask themselves how much value they attach to having the best possible upbringing, the importance they attach to parenthood, and how much they care about maintaining opportunities to pursue goals other than parenting in adult life. In cases where these interests conflict, they must evaluate the extent to which they would be prepared to accept a worse upbringing for the sake of having more resources at their disposal in adult life. They do so in light of the fact that there is an equal risk that they may turn out to have inadequate parents, to be such parents, or to have children who are costly to bring up.

The hypothetical insurance scheme is designed in a way that ensures that whatever is chosen within it is fair and, therefore, just. To be sure, as we shall see, designing childrearing policy on the basis of counterfactual judgements concerning what would be chosen as insurance by suitably situated individuals does not *eliminate* inequalities that are the product of disadvantageous circumstances. At most, it *mollifies* the effects of those inequalities on individuals as children and parents. Nevertheless, the claim to fairness is maintained in virtue of the parties concerned enjoying equal *ex ante* risk of suffering disadvantage. Consequently, any inequalities that are allowed by the chosen policy are not ones that individuals can legitimately cite in a claim against social institutions on grounds of justice. Any such claim can be rebutted with the observation that if they had an equal risk of suffering from the disadvantage in question, individuals would not have bought insurance sufficient to eliminate the relative disadvantage, despite enjoying equal opportunity to do so.

What would be chosen in the hypothetical insurance scheme? This is difficult to answer in detail, because the counterfactual judgements that must be made are difficult to determine with any great precision. There is not simply an epistemic problem of uncertainty about the degree to which an individual would insure against the possibility of being raised by poor parents, for example. In the case of children, we cannot know in advance whether they will grow up to be adults who attach high or low value to founding a family and, therefore, we cannot tailor any childrearing policy to reflect the particular ambitions they will come to hold. I shall return to this problem of indeterminacy below (Section 2.5.5). It is not, though, a devastating objection to the scheme. As Dworkin insists in the course of discussing welfare support for the unemployed, the scheme provides a *structure* that sets the terms of public debate about policy and limits the range of policies that can be treated as just.[17] Moreover, even if we cannot know the future choices of children, we may proceed by addressing the counterfactual question in a *statistical* rather than an *individualized* manner. We can ask what insurance decisions individuals would, *on average*, make, and ask government policy to mirror those choices.[18]

Let us turn, then, to examine the range of insurance decisions that parties would, in all likelihood, take within the hypothetical insurance scheme. A complete account would require a complex set of arguments requiring fine-grained assessments of probability and other relevant information. I shall not attempt to engage in that exercise here. For the purposes of articulating a normative theory through the thought experiment of hypothetical insurance, it is sufficient to outline the principal types of reason that would move parties within the scheme. Consequently, I shall make certain general remarks about the distribution of childrearing resources, and address three main issues: (*a*) inequalities in parenting ability; (*b*) inequalities in parental income; and (*c*) inequalities in the endowments of children. Thereafter, I shall consider how the tax burden for the redistributive policies produced by the hypothetical insurance scheme should be distributed. Finally, I shall reply to some objections that might be levelled against the hypothetical insurance scheme for the distribution of childrearing resources.

2.5.1 Inequalities in Parenting Ability

The right to rear operates as a constraint under which the parties buy insurance that indemnifies them against various harms or losses. The right is conditional in the sense that parents may lose it if the child's upbringing falls below a threshold of acceptability. Above that threshold, the right to rear is secure but, of course, some children will have parents who have better parenting skills compared to the parents of other children. So, insuring parties must decide what kind of insurance they will take out against these eventualities on the assumption that they face an equal risk of suffering them.

First, let us consider matters from the perspective of individuals who want to maintain their role as parents. It would seem rational for such individuals to take out insurance against falling below the threshold of parental adequacy, such that resources are available to ensure that their child's upbringing is brought up to an appropriate level. There are, of course, limits to the extent to which it is rational to purchase such cover. Suppose there exists a sizeable number of parents whose skills are so poor that they can satisfy the threshold of parental adequacy only at very great cost in terms of resources and support. The resources required to maintain parenthood for such individuals necessarily comes at the price of lower provision of other goods, and there is a limit to the extent to which individuals would be willing to sacrifice these other goods for the sake of lowering the risk of losing their relationship with their child. If that is the case, then the childrearing policy must be one that allows some parents to lose their childrearing rights even though resources could be diverted to prevent this. Nevertheless, my conjecture is that since individuals with children generally attach very great weight to their interest in maintaining a relationship with their children, they would buy expensive insurance packages that secure their opportunity to have a relationship with their children. The insurance would pay for parenting classes, educational campaigns, social services provision, which seeks to help families in difficulty in various ways, and much else besides. Here, we have an argument for redistributive policies that trades on the strong desire of parents to maintain their right to rear.

A second, complementary, way of determining a just response to inequalities of parenting skill considers the insurance decisions individuals would on average make when addressing their fortunes as children. Consider, for example, the inequalities in parenting ability that exist *above* the threshold of adequacy. Even if these inequalities are not a concern from the point of view of retaining parenthood,[19] they remain relevant when considering the kind of upbringing one wants as a child. Individuals may want to mitigate the effects that worse parenting might have on their life prospects. Different policies would be available to them, but it is likely that they would opt for those that do not require intrusive surveillance of the performance of particular parents. Apart from concerns related to loss of privacy, such surveillance would be prohibitively costly. It is likely, then, that rational individuals would take out insurance that would pay for such things as educational campaigns, which aim to change parental conduct, free and nutritious school meals to mitigate the problems of a poor diet, and other initiatives that reduce the extent to which children are harmed by having less effective parents.

2.5.2 Inequalities in Parental Income

Parties will also consider buying insurance against being or having children in relatively poor circumstances. Although the hypothetical insurance scheme operates on the assumption of a just background distribution of resources, parties recognize that certain inequalities exist. The productive enjoy a larger share of income compared to the less productive or those who are underemployed. No doubt, these inequalities would be considerably less pronounced than are those that exist in our society. Nevertheless, a certain level of inequality of income would prevail and parties must make decisions about childrearing rights taking this into account. Given that inequality, but not knowing one's position within the distribution as a child or as an adult, parties must gauge whether they should take out insurance against living in a family in a relatively poor environment.

It might be thought that individuals would not purchase insurance against such a possibility on the grounds that money is only one, and perhaps a relatively insignificant, factor in raising a child effectively. But even if that is true, and an effective upbringing requires much more than money, the money required to raise a child might remain significant. It has been estimated by the United States Department of Agriculture, for example, that a middle-income family ($38,000–64,000 in 2000) can expect to spend about $165,630 to buy food, shelter, and other necessities for a child born in 2000 over the next seventeen years; and low-income families (less that $38,000) can be expected to pay $121,230.[20] Now such figures are not definitive of the costs of upbringing if resources were distributed fairly, but we may take the average as something close to the figure that would be the norm in a just society.[21] It seems rational for individuals to take out insurance against the possibility of being parents, or the children of parents, who have insufficient resources to pay for a good upbringing.

Various regimes of child benefit are possible. The choice between them must be sensitive to the alleged problem of abuse. It is sometimes argued that if child benefit in the form of an entitlement to *income* is generous, then adults who have more restricted employment opportunity would have an incentive to found a family as a means of accessing the income offered. Parties to the insurance scheme would, therefore, adopt policies that diminish these incentives in the knowledge that the premiums may otherwise be too costly. Nevertheless, they would not opt for policies that offer only minimal assistance to poor families, for they would reason that as children they have an interest in having a good upbringing, and this remains the case irrespective of the motives of their parents in founding a family. Taking the problem of abuse seriously, but understanding their needs as children, parties may well insure to pay for various *in-kind* transfers from the rich to the poor, which ensure a child's upbringing does not fall below a certain standard despite the relatively low incomes of the parents. The package of initiatives they would buy would enable all children to be well fed, decently educated and housed, and to enjoy opportunities to develop. Such initiatives would also defray many of the costs that children might otherwise place on families with relatively low incomes.

2.5.3 Inequalities in the Endowments of Children

Parties to the hypothetical insurance scheme understand that inequalities also exist with respect to the fortune enjoyed by children and, consequently, the burdens that children place on their parents. For example, some children are more difficult or costly to raise, because they suffer the bad fortune of being born with certain physical or mental disabilities that make educating or caring for them more problematic. It seems rational, therefore, for the parties to insure against being or having a child who is hard to raise, insurance that would pay for additional support for the child and would compensate parents for the burdens placed upon them. Insurance companies in this scheme would write policies that offer compensation in the case of children who are beset by various conditions. The policies would be geared to compensate children directly, through the purchase of items such as wheelchairs, special audio or visual equipment, resources to modify the homes of children with disabilities and to facilitate access to public buildings, special educational assistance, and the like.[22] Since this is the case, governments are required, on grounds of justice, to offer those kinds of provision to children who are difficult or costly to raise.

Children who are difficult or costly to bring up are disadvantaged themselves, but they also disadvantage their custodial parents compared to the parents of children who are easier to raise. Hence, the insurance scheme also supports compensating parents for having children who are hard to raise. The parties would take out policies that would ensure that they can honour their responsibilities as parents without excessively hindering their opportunity to lead a life apart from their parenting duties.

2.5.4 Taxation

One large remaining question asks who is to pay for the policies chosen in the hypothetical insurance scheme to compensate individuals in cases concerning poor parenting skills, children who are hard to raise, or relatively poor families. The scheme itself suggests that the initiatives would be financed through progressive taxation, because in the absence of information about one's earning capacity, it would be rational to choose a premium structure in which premiums are progressively higher, the more one earns.[23]

Nevertheless, in principle, the account does not necessarily require taxing the childless to pay for the childrearing of others. To see why this is the case we must return to the justification of theorizing childrearing policy through the hypothetical insurance scheme in the first place. The background of the scheme is that there exist various inequalities that produce grounds for legitimate complaint from the point of view of justice. That one has parents with inadequate parenting skills while others are free of such burdens, for example, is a ground for complaint, as is being such a parent if the inequality is one for which no one is responsible. The appeal to hypothetical insurance is made as a means of addressing how we should think about responding in a fair, ambition-sensitive manner to the valid complaints that exist.

On this account, however, it is difficult to see how individuals who choose to found a family have a justified case for resource transfers from those who prefer to remain childless. Any inequality of opportunity or income that is the product of having children compared to remaining childless is not the product of unequal brute luck, but rather the result of a difference of ambition. On the liberal account offered here, such inequalities do not necessarily call for redress or compensation. Indeed, they are justified on grounds of treating individuals as free and equal.

To be sure, I do not argue that the childless have no reason to pay for childrearing. There may be self-interested reasons to pay if, for example, a larger population is mutually advantageous and child benefit payments are necessary to encourage the appropriate level of procreation. In addition, it might be that if the childless are not required to pay, then children may suffer a disadvantage, because of their parents' inability to finance an appropriate upbringing. From the point of view of justice, *all things considered*, it may be better to have some tax contribution from the childless. However, even if we accept a universal duty to provide for childrearing, we may continue to believe that parents should shoulder a considerably greater share of the burden compared to the childless.[24]

It might be objected that founding a family is not always a voluntary choice. Individuals often regard themselves as responsible for the raising of the children they beget even when they beget them involuntarily—as a product of rape or unwarranted social pressure—or through ignorance. The objection is, no doubt, sound, and supports compensation for unwanted pregnancy in such cases financed out of general taxation of parents and non-parents alike. But here we are addressing the different issue of whether adults who willingly choose to found a family are entitled as a matter of justice to compensation to defray the costs of childrearing, financed by those who choose to pursue lifestyles without children. On the resourcist view affirmed here, there is no such entitlement as a matter of basic justice.

2.5.5 Reply to Objections

Theorizing justice in the distribution of childrearing rights through the hypothetical insurance scheme is attractive, I have argued, because it enables us to respond to inequalities of brute luck in a way that is sensitive to the ambitions people hold. In particular, the scheme provides a structure for balancing the interests we have as children and as adults. In addition, it enables us to consider the level of provision that childrearing policy should receive, taking into account the opportunity costs of different policies for the supply of other goods, such as health, defence, and consumption.

We must now consider three kinds of objection that might be raised against this account. The first claims that the scheme is too conservative, because it uncritically accepts adults' judgements about childrearing. The second is that it is insufficiently liberal, because its reliance on the choices made on average means that one's entitlements are illegitimately determined by the ambitions of others. The third is that the scheme is insufficiently egalitarian, because it only reduces, and fails to eliminate, the unequal effects of bad luck on the fortune of individuals.

2.5.5.1 Too Conservative?

The first objection does not find fault with the use of hypothetical insurance as such. Rather, it claims that the distinctive position of children places an ambition-sensitive account of childrearing rights on the horns of a dilemma: determining a distribution of childrearing resources on the basis of a hypothetical insurance scheme is either impossible or objectionably conservative. Recall that it was accepted that young children lack authentic ambitions. Their judgements are often ill-considered, inconsistent, unstable, and formed on the basis of mental powers that are often insufficient to justify placing others under a duty to respect them. Consequently, any appeal directly to children's ambitions is impossible.

Avoiding this problem, I argued that we must act on behalf of children by considering what insurance policies would be purchased by suitably situated adults on the assumption that they would relive their lives as children and then as adults. This avoids the impossibility problem because the preferences of adults are authentic and can be used to generate a set of determinate policies. But the objection under discussion insists that while they might be authentic, the particular ambitions held by adults are shaped by the way in which they were brought up. In effect, we are determining the allocation of childrearing resources in a manner that allows the childrearing practices of the past indirectly to influence those of the future, irrespective of the justice or legitimacy of past practices. For example, the scheme determines future childrearing policy on the basis of adult expectations of the extent to which children's interests should be accommodated, expectations that may well be shaped by their own upbringings. A child brought up in a society in which satisfying children's interests is treated as much less significant compared to satisfying adults' interests may come to hold a similar view. The hypothetical insurance scheme would thereby produce a policy that would simply replicate the practices of the past.

The objection is not convincing, because it overlooks the other relevant parts of the conception of justice and legitimacy in upbringing within which the hypothetical insurance scheme is embedded. As I shall argue in subsequent sections, a liberal upbringing is one in which a child is educated to have a sense of justice and the capacity critically to deliberate about ethical and prudential issues such as the relative importance of childhood and opportunities in adult life. Given these requirements, we have little reason to believe that individuals would inevitably come to accept the prevailing expectations about the relative significance of the interests of children and adults respectively. Even if an individual's interests as a child were given little significance in his own childhood, it does not follow that he would choose an allocation of childrearing resources that maintains this arrangement, on the assumption that he is to relive his life as a child.

2.5.5.2 Insufficiently Liberal?

The second objection asserts that the hypothetical insurance scheme is insufficiently liberal to the extent that it fails to accommodate individuals' own distinctive ambitions and allows their entitlements to be determined by the ambitions of others. In fact, there are two objections of this kind. The first is that the scheme allocates childrearing rights that determine the fortune of children according to the choices of others, adults, and we have no reason to assume that their choices match the decisions children would make if they were rational. Call this *the objection to adult choice.* Even if this can be rebutted, the second objection questions the statistical, rather than individualized, nature of the hypothetical insurance scheme. The distribution of childrearing resources is determined by the insurance decisions people would, on average, make. Consequently, an individual might object that the resources she enjoys as a child afforded by average hypothetical insurance are less generous than those *she* would have insured to provide had the scheme been individualized. Call this *the objection to averaging.* In the case of both objections, the criticism is not that entitlements are determined in an ambition-sensitive manner, but that they are determined, in part, by the ambitions of others.

Neither objection is decisive. In response to the objection to adult choice, recall that the scheme does not appeal to adults' ambitions merely as adults, but to their ambitions on the understanding that they will live their lives again as children and adults. So, they must consult their values with respect to childhood as well as adulthood. True, such ambitions are not the ambitions of rational children. But it is questionable whether any determinate content can be ascribed to that notion. It would be inappropriate to hold a child's desires constant and somehow choose on the basis of those desires refined by some rational process, because the process by which we become rational also changes the content of our beliefs and desires. In addition, we cannot decide on the basis of the desires of the adult who the child will grow up to be, because, in a liberal society, the burdens of judgement indicate that a plurality of ambition will exist, and we have no reason to believe that the child in question will grow up to have any particular set of ambitions within that plurality.[25]

We must accept, then, that it is not possible to accommodate the ambitions of children within the scheme. We must accommodate their interests by acting on their behalf. One way of proceeding in this endeavour would be to try to gauge through some sort of philosophical reflection how to balance the interests of individuals as children and as adults. But it is not clear how that balancing can be effected without appealing to some set of ethical convictions. Moreover, we have established that reasonable people differ in the ethical convictions they bring to the balancing problem. Given that we have no reason to believe that a particular child will come to affirm any particular set of convictions within the plurality, he or she cannot legitimately complain if childrearing rights are determined in accordance with the decisions parties would make on average if they assume they will be in the same position as children now are.

Here, some might appeal to the objection to averaging. They may accept that there is nothing inherently mistaken about adult choice on behalf of children. Still, they claim it is illiberal for an individual's opportunities to be reduced below those she would have insured to make available, just because others are more willing to take risks, to gamble with their resources or entitlements. For example, suppose I am risk-averse and would therefore buy expensive insurance against being a child with disabilities. My aversion to risk taking is not shared by others, who take more risks with their childhood, permitting any disabilities they might suffer to have a greater negative impact on their life prospects for the sake of retaining a greater stock of resources to use in pursuit of other goods. Given the mechanism of the hypothetical insurance scheme as proposed, the child benefit to which I am entitled is less generous than that which I would have insured to provide just in virtue of the risk taking of individuals whose attitude to life I reject as reckless or immoral.

The objection to averaging is not an objection to having one's entitlements determined by insurance decisions. It is an objection to entitlements being influenced by the insurance choices of others. Moreover, there is some merit in the objection, for surely if entitlements could be fixed in a way that accommodates each individual's distinctive ambitions, through an individualized insurance scheme, then this would be preferable from a liberal point of view. Nevertheless, the issue at hand is how we ought to determine entitlements when an individualized scheme is not possible due to the complex counterfactual nature of the choice situation. As we have established, there is no way of knowing whether a particular child will be risk-averse or a gambler. The statistical insurance scheme, in which entitlements are determined by choices made on average, seems a suitable second-best approach, for it seeks to resolve the problem of balancing child and adult interests in a way that is sensitive to the range of ambitions held by reasonable people, rather than through some perfectionist standard that might well lie at one extreme of this range.[26]

2.5.5.3 Insufficiently Egalitarian?

The final set of objections offers a more thoroughgoing rejection of the proposed approach to childrearing rights, for it asserts that fixing entitlements to resources on the basis of hypothetical insurance choices, whether individualized or averaged, fails to treat people as equals. A number of different lines of argument have been offered in support of this claim, but I shall focus on one that I shall call *the failure to eliminate inequality objection.*

Some have argued that hypothetical insurance is mistaken as an egalitarian theory, because it permits that which egalitarians seek to eliminate, namely, inequality that is the product of brute luck. A simple childrearing example illustrates the alleged problem. In the scheme I have defended certain children will have a better start in life than others, because their parents satisfy the best custodian condition, while other children's parents do not. Even if the insurance decisions people would make in the face of equal risks would pay for initiatives that *reduce* the detrimental effect of less good parenting on children, it is unlikely that they would buy packages that *eliminate* the differences. On the proposed scheme, such an arrangement is just. But certain egalitarian critics might question this result, arguing that the fact that one child's upbringing is worse than another's through no fault of the child's is a cause for egalitarian concern and, where possible, the disadvantaged child is entitled to a policy that either rectifies the inequality or fully compensates for it.

The central reply to this kind of objection is to emphasize once again the attractiveness of seeking to deal with inequalities of brute luck in a way that is ambition-sensitive. Notice that within the hypothetical insurance scheme insuring parties *could* buy insurance that *eliminates* any inequality of brute luck. Yet they choose not to purchase that policy, because they appreciate the costs it would impose on other parts of their lives. Appreciating the costs that such policies and premiums would impose on their ability to pursue their projects and relationships as adults, parties within the scheme would decline the offer of insurance that would eliminate all inequalities in the quality of their respective upbringings. They would prefer instead policies that mitigate but do not remove such inequalities.

While it allocates childrearing rights in a way that is sensitive to the ambitions of people with respect to how their lives ought to go, the hypothetical insurance scheme remains egalitarian because it insists that the distribution of childrearing resources must be determined in a way that is consistent with individuals making choices in the face of equal risks. To be sure, this is not the only available conception of equality, but it is surely a more attractive account of equality compared to one that prohibits individuals from taking risks with the quality of their lives.[27]

However, I end my discussion of the hypothetical insurance scheme for the distribution of childrearing resources on a promissory note. I have not discussed various other prominent positions with respect to this issue. The dominant liberal conception of justice in the distribution of childrearing resources appeals to the ideal of fair equality of opportunity, under which individuals who are similarly ambitious and naturally able enjoy similar life chances.[28] Others have suggested rather different conceptions of equality of educational opportunity.[29] For all I have said, the hypothetical insurance scheme may be only part of the solution to the problem of justice in the distribution of childrearing resources. However, because I want to discuss other aspects of justice in upbringing I must leave that question standing and return to it on another occasion.

2.6 THE POSSESSION AND EXERCISE OF CHILDREARING RIGHTS

The hybrid liberal conception of justice affords children and parents a set of rights determined by the right to rear and the resources that suitably situated individuals would insure to provide. In this section, I make some further observations about how this conception understands the goods that the claim rights protect and about the relationship between the claim rights and liberty rights of parents.

The distinction between *claim rights* and *liberties* is as follows. The former protect individuals' decisions or interests vis-à-vis other agents. The right to speak, for example, is standardly viewed as a *claim right*, the content of which turns on how it is interpreted. If it is a negative right, it requires others not to prevent the right-holder from speaking, and forbids them from punishing the right-holder for speaking. If it is a positive right, it may, in addition, place others under a requirement to provide a platform on which the individual may speak. The right to speak is also usually conceptualized as a *liberty*. The right grants the right-holder permission to speak or not to speak as she chooses. Whether or not she speaks, the individual is acting within her rights, we might say, and does nothing wrong from the point of view of justice.[30]

On the account offered here, there are several of different right-holders, where rights are interpreted in terms of claim rights. In the first place, children have rights to an upbringing of the kind that would be insured for in the scheme. I have spelt out certain kinds of requirements such rights justify. To be sure they do not enjoy a right to the best possible upbringing, or even a right to parents who are the best available custodians, for those claim rights would violate the parental right to rear. Nevertheless, children have certain fundamental interests—in developing a sense of justice and a capacity for a conception of the good—the satisfaction of which free and equal persons would attach high priority to. This is not to say that children have a right to the development of these capacities, in the sense that others are required, before they pursue other goods, to deliver these goods irrespective of the costs of doing so. Suppose there are a number of children who suffer particular cognitive disabilities, such that their interests in having a sense of justice and being autonomous cannot be realized or can be realized only at very great expense. Parties within the hypothetical insurance scheme may decide that the appropriate response to the problem of cognitive misfortune is to place a limit on the extent to which resources that have only imperceptible benefit for such children should be devoted to improving their lives.

Nevertheless, the scheme does produce an argument for certain rights. Others are under a requirement to fund the provision of certain goods to which children are entitled: child benefit and in-kind benefits that ensure that the negative effects of a disadvantaged environment, disability, and inadequate parenting ability are reduced. The scheme justifies education as a right of children, placing others under duties to provide educational facilities that promote every child's interests in becoming just and autonomous.

I shall offer a more detailed account of some of the content of such an education in subsequent sections. Here our focus is on the kinds of rights that children and parents enjoy. It is clear that children enjoy claim rights placing others under duties to protect their interests in being educated in a certain way. Such duties are positive injunctions that require others not merely to refrain from hindering the child's enjoyment of such an education but also to provide it. But how should those under such duties be characterized, and who has the right to determine the kind of education the child receives? Here it is important to distinguish between issues of *cost* and *authority*. Recall that, according to resource egalitarianism, the rights that are generated from the hypothetical insurance scheme are financed through a progressive tax on parents with, perhaps, some contribution from non-parents. Still, just because non-parents pay nothing or pay less for children's upbringing, it does not follow that they have no *authority* to decide the organization and content of the education to which children are entitled. By this I mean that it does not follow that parents enjoy a claim right that protects their choice of education for their child from interference by others. While the hybrid liberal conception accepts a parental right to rear, that claim right does not include the right to determine the content of their child's education. Whether they enjoy that additional right depends upon further arguments, which we have not yet explored.

Some might suggest that one further argument is that individuals would choose such a right in the hypothetical choice situation described above. However, this is unlikely. While parties would acknowledge that as parents they may have a desire to determine the content of their children's education, they would also reason that as children they have certain interests that need not be satisfied by any particular agent. And to the extent that their interests as children weigh with the parties, they would choose educational arrangements that are most efficient in satisfying these interests. On the basis of this reasoning, then, if their involvement is efficient, non-parents might come to have rights over children's education. Consequently, the child's right to education justifies the allocation of further rights: rights to determine educational arrangements enjoyed by those who are efficient providers of education, which in turn place others—parents and children—under a duty to comply with their demands.

It might be responded that within the hypothetical insurance scheme, individuals would opt for a parental veto over educational choices in order to protect their desire to determine their children's schooling. Now in order to address this claim we need to introduce a different question: What rights as *liberties* do parents enjoy? The holding of claim rights is compatible with either the affirmation or the denial of rights as liberties, i.e. the presence or absence of moral options with respect to the decisions protected by the claim rights. For example, many accept that each person has a claim right that protects from interference by others her decision to buy an expensive car rather than to use her income to prevent people from starving to death. But some, nevertheless, argue that the person does not enjoy the liberty to buy the car, since she is morally required to use her resources to reduce people's suffering.[31] Others believe that an individual's rights include both the liberty to spend money as she pleases, and a claim right protecting her choice from interference.

When discussing claim rights with respect to children's education, we are often discussing claim rights *without* liberties, for the status and interests of the child place parents under certain requirements from the point of view of justice and legitimacy. Developing an account of such requirements is something I shall do in later sections. Here it is sufficient simply to draw a distinction between *general* requirements that everyone is under with respect to children and the *special* requirements parents are under in virtue of their relationship with their children. With respect to the former, general, requirements, the child's status as free and equal and her associated interests in having a sense of justice and in leading an autonomous life place others, parents and non-parents alike, under certain duties not to hinder her fulfilment of these interests. With respect to special requirements, it might be claimed, for example, that even if parents are permitted to some degree to favour their own children over those of other individuals, with respect to their own children, they are required not to favour one child over their other children.

Parents must, therefore, respect certain constraints on their conduct. Given that they would lack liberties in the case of many claim rights, such as in the case of determining the content of the child's education, to what extent would parties insure to protect parental claim rights over their children's education? For some might reason that if they lack an option to X or not, then there is little point in their having the claim right that protects their decision to X or not against interference by others. To illustrate the point with a familiar example, suppose I must assess the value of a claim right protecting my right to shout 'fire' in a crowded theatre when there is no fire, which places others under a duty not to interfere with me doing so, and not to punish me if I so do. Recognizing that I am under a moral requirement not to cause a stampede and, therefore, that I am not at liberty to shout 'fire', it may be rational for me to attach no importance whatsoever to having this claim right, because it is a right that I cannot permissibly benefit from.

However, it is *sometimes* rational to preserve claim rights protecting one's conduct from interference by others even when one is morally required to act in a particular way. This is true in cases in which it matters that an individual performs a required action *herself*, as opposed to the required action being performed by someone else. For example, it might matter to me that *I* care for my sick partner or child. In this case, having claim rights protects me in honouring my moral requirements. Similarly, individuals might value the opportunity to choose the education their children receive, even when the moral options available to them in exercising that right are rather restricted.

Parties within the hypothetical insurance scheme would take such desires with respect to parenthood into account alongside their interests as children. It is doubtful, however, that they would choose a parental veto with respect to their children's education. They would understand that their right to rear protects their relationship with their children. Moreover, given the significant constraints, which, I argue, everyone's interests as free and equal persons place on the liberty of others in educating children, and a concern to ensure good educational provision for their own childhood, it is likely that parties would choose to allow suitably qualified non-parents to exercise some, perhaps considerable, authority in matters of educational provision.

Thus, the dual interest view offers an account of childrearing rights in which both parents and non-parents might have rights to determine different aspects of the child's upbringing. This is because the interests of both parents and children count in the allocation of childrearing rights. The particular regime that will be adopted will depend on a number of contingent factors, such as who is best placed to take decisions that are in the child's interests, and the extent to which individuals care about being protected from interference by others with respect to honouring the requirements that children's status and interests place them under. The conception offered allows circumstantial differences with respect to such variables to influence the shape of a just childrearing policy.

Let us finish this outline of the dual interest view as theorized through the right to rear and hypothetical insurance by briefly examining two alternative conceptions of childrearing rights. The first conceives parental rights as merely liberties or privileges. On this conception, parents are permitted to determine their child's upbringing, but they do not enjoy claim rights protecting their choices from interference by others. If the effect of their decisions is that the child's interests or rights are not best served, then others—e.g. teachers, doctors, or social workers—are permitted to cancel the parental privilege, or to interfere with their decisions out of a concern for the child.[32]

An extreme version of this view denies the justice of *any* parental rights when these are interpreted as claim rights. But we should reject this extreme view. Even if we believe that parents hold no claim rights protecting all their decisions from teachers, doctors, and the like, we may retain our belief that they hold claim rights rights against certain other adults who express a desire to shape their child's education. If a stranger approaches a parent with the intention of directing her child's upbringing, the parent can legitimately decline the offer with an appeal to a claim right that protects her childrearing conduct from interference by strangers.[33]

We should also reject a second alternative conception that occupies the opposite extreme of the range of positions. This conception asserts that if a parent holds claim rights protecting certain choices she might make with respect to her child against interference by others, then also holds a liberty within the protected range, such that she is permitted by morality or justice to choose to exercise the protected choice in any way she wishes. However, the flip side of the point made above, that even where parents lack liberties (moral options) they may still value having claim rights protecting their decisions, is that enjoying such claim rights against others does not imply that one enjoys liberties with respect to how to exercise those rights. Children themselves have claim rights and interests, so even though we may protect parental choice by placing injunctions on others, parents remain duty-bound, as others do, to act in the interests of the child.

The dual interest view is rightly compatible with the justice of claim rights. It allocates these rights according to the right to rear and the decisions that fairly situated free and equal persons would make on the assumption that they would live their lives again as children and then adults. But, as I have indicated, justice and legitimacy in upbringing has a wider focus than merely the distribution of childrearing claim rights. True, injustice or illegitimacy can obtain through a misallocation of such rights. But it can also be the product of right-holders *exercising* their rights in an unjust or illegitimate way.

NOTES

1. See Dworkin, *Sovereign Virtue: The Theory and Practice of Equality*, pp. 260–7.
2. Vallentyne, 'The Rights and Duties of Childrearing', *William and Mary Bill of Rights Journal*, 11 (2003), 991–1010. For other statements of such a view, see Arneson, 'Democracy is Not Intrinsically Just', in Keith Dowding, Robert E. Goodin, and Carole Pateman (eds.), *Justice and Democracy: Essays for Brian Barry* (Cambridge: Cambridge University Press, 2004), p. 46; Brighouse, 'Civic Education and Liberal Legitimacy', *Ethics*, 108 (1998), 737 (Brighouse now

rejects the view: see Brighouse and Swift, 'Parents' Rights and the Value of the Family').

3. For critical discussion of such arguments, see Archard, 'What's Blood Got to Do with It? The Significance of Natural Parenthood', *Res Publica*, 1 (1995), 91–106, and his *Children, Family and the State* (Aldershot: Ashgate, 2003), pp. 82–6. For a Lockean 'first-come, first-served' argument for genetic and procreative parents holding childrearing rights, granted a fundamentally child-centred argument, see Simmons, *The Lockean Theory of Rights* (Princeton, NJ: Princeton University Press, 1992), pp. 177–84.
4. I take the label 'dual interest' from Hubin's unpublished paper, 'From Children's Rights to Parents' Rights' (2000). The view is also defended on different grounds by Brighouse and Swift, 'Parents' Rights and the Value of the Family'.
5. See Section 2.4 for a fuller defence of the interest in maintaining a family.
6. Vallentyne, 'The Rights and Duties of Childrearing', 1001.
7. The strategy of theorizing certain interpersonal issues, such as apparent conflicts between the interests of the young and old, in intrapersonal terms is advanced by Norman Daniels, though I do not follow his particular way of pursuing the strategy. See Daniels, *Just Health Care* (Cambridge: Cambridge University Press, 1985); *Am I My Parents' Keeper? An Essay on Justice between the Young and Old* (New York: Oxford University Press, 1988).
8. See Arneson, 'Democracy is Not Intrinsically Just', pp. 46–8.
9. The view that rights of control or authority are fiduciary in the sense that they must be justified on the basis of the consent or best interests of the governed is associated with Locke. Locke sought to reject Filmer's argument for the non-fiduciary rights of kings, which appealed, in part, to an analogy between sovereigns and parents. One natural Lockean response is to insist that parents do not have substantial non-fiduciary rights and, therefore, it is illegitimate to use the analogy between parents and kings to support the political position Filmer defended. But an alternative response is available, to wit, that absolute monarchs are in one respect unlike parents. If we assume that every child will have the opportunity to become a parent, the existence of some non-fiduciary parental rights does not exclusively benefit one group of individuals over another, as is the case in granting non-fiduciary rights to monarchs. A similar claim might be made on behalf of democracy in which everyone rules and is, at the same time, ruled.
10. Brighouse and Swift call such rights *fundamental* rights of parents to highlight the fact that they are justified by a direct appeal to our interests as adults or parents, rather than rights that are justified by an appeal to the interests of the child. To be sure, children's interests do justify parental rights, as the best

custodian condition accepts. Since our present concern is to rebut that condition, we put such child-centred arguments to one side to establish which rights, if any, are justified by a direct appeal to the interests of adults or parents.

11. Similarly, I do not consider the important issues of the right to procreate or to found a family, or issues concerning the allocation of childrearing rights where there is a conflict of interest between different parents. My aim is to set out the considerations that apply to the central case. Once this is done, it may be possible to apply the conception to deal with other cases concerning the rights of parents or would-be parents.
12. The general strategy of elucidating an account of interests beyond those immediately derived from our interests as free and equal persons, while conforming with liberal constraints of the kind Rawls defends, is elaborated by Scanlon, 'The Moral Basis of Interpersonal Comparisons', in Jon Elster and John Roemer (eds.), *Interpersonal Comparisons of Well-Being* (Cambridge: Cambridge University Press, 1991), esp. pp. 39–44.
13. For this kind of argument, see Brighouse and Swift, 'Parents' Rights and the Value of the Family'; Schrag, 'Justice and the Family', *Inquiry*, 19 (1976), 193–208, esp. 200–08.
14. See Hubin, 'From Children's Rights to Parents' Rights'.
15. In fact, an even more abstractly defined interest might be sufficient. Persons who invest their personality in, and devote their life to, a particular work of art may well be devastated by the removal or destruction of that work. Such persons might see the nurturing of a child in a similar light, even if they think that having a child themselves would destroy their artistic life.
16. See Dworkin, *Sovereign Virtue*, especially chs. 2–3 and 7–9; Williams, 'Equality, Ambition, and Insurance', *Aristotelian Society Supplementary Volume*, 78 (2004), 131–50.
17. Dworkin, *Sovereign Virtue*, pp. 322, 333.
18. Here, again, I follow Dworkin's similar remarks in the context of welfare reform. See ibid. pp. 340–6.
19. They may be relevant from this point of view as well. Parents might want to be *good* parents, not merely *adequate* ones.
20. Pierce and Webster, 'USDA Estimates Child Rearing Costs', (Washington, DC: United States Department of Agriculture Press Release No. 0097, 2001).
21. Even if justice demands a significant reduction of the mean income of citizens of the USA, this would not diminish the point that expenditure on children is significant as a proportion of household expenditure. This is sufficient for the argument for child benefit.
22. To be sure, this is not the only kind of compensation to which children with disabilities are entitled from the point of view of justice. They are also entitled

to resource transfers from others just in virtue of their disabilities and their diminished prospects of finding gainful employment. Those kinds of consideration are theorized through a parallel hypothetical insurance scheme of the kind outlined by Dworkin: see *Sovereign Virtue*, chs. 2 and 9. Here we are dealing solely with issues directly related to childrearing.

23. Ibid. pp. 99–104.
24. The resourcist position asserted here is also consistent with varying the tax burden in accordance with the number of children one has. For a nuanced discussion, see Casal and Williams, 'Equality of Resources and Procreative Justice', in Justine Burley (ed.), *Dworkin and His Critics*. For related discussion, see Vallentyne, 'Equality and the Duty of Procreators' in David Archard and Colin Mcleod (eds.), *The Moral and Political Status of Children* (Oxford: Oxford University Press, 2002). One possible objection to the argument for taxing only parents is that if a child is less advantaged than a childless adult, then surely the former should be compensated in the name of equality. While this is accepted, it does not follow that it is the childless adult who incurs the duty to compensate. Notice, in addition, that the brief argument offered in the text does not address cases in which the child's contribution to society makes everyone, including the childless, better off. See Casal and Williams, 'Equality of Resources and Procreative Justice', pp. 154–9 for an argument for a similar conclusion in such cases.
25. For discussion of different interpretations of, and problems with, hypothetical choice applied to children, see Archard, *Children, Family and the State*, pp. 50–3.
26. Notice, in addition, that the insurance scheme addresses the distribution of childrearing resources, but not the conditions for the enjoyment of the right to rear. Parents' right to rear, generating a duty on the part of others not to interfere with certain decisions they make for their children, is defended on the basis of our interest in maintaining a relationship with our children and, therefore, is secured irrespective of the extent to which people on average desire such a relationship. In principle, the insurance scheme could be applied to the allocation of custodial rights as well as childrearing resources. My conjecture is that such a scheme would produce very similar results to those produced by the hybrid conception of childrearing rights advanced here. Nevertheless, suppose there is a society in which the majority exhibited only a weak desire for maintaining a relationship with their children. Running the hypothetical insurance scheme for the allocation of childrearing rights in such a society may well produce a result in which the threshold for the retention of the right to rear is set very high and approaches the best custodian condition. The majority might reason that the costs of producing a decent

upbringing by a transfer of rights to more skilful parents would be considerably less than those that must be borne to improve the skills of less able parents so that they might retain their right. In that imaginary society, then, an individual may well lose the right to rear just because others do not attach much significance to the raising of their genetic offspring. To avoid this possibility, the right to rear is not defended by an appeal to the hypothetical insurance scheme. Moreover, this strengthens the case for averaging, since the constrained insurance scheme does not, by hypothesis, determine the presence or absence of goods that we have a fundamental interest in obtaining.

27. For a defence of the inadequacy of hypothetical insurance from an egalitarian point of view, see Otsuka, 'Luck, Insurance, and Equality', *Ethics*, 113 (2002), 40–54; Fleurbaey, 'Equality of Resources Revisited', *Ethics*, 113 (2002), 82–105; Macleod, *Liberalism, Justice, and Markets: A Critique of Liberal Equality* (Oxford: Oxford University Press, 1998), esp. pp. 98–105. Dworkin's discussion of this kind of objection can be found in *Sovereign Virtue*, pp. 340–6; '*Sovereign Virtue* Revisited', *Ethics*, 113 (2002), 106–25, 129–36. For further replies to the failure to eradicate inequality objection, see Williams, 'Equality, Ambition and Insurance'.
28. See Rawls, *A Theory of Justice*, pp. 57–78. For a critique of Rawls's position, see Clayton, 'Rawls and Natural Aristocracy', *Croatian Journal of Philosophy*, 1 (2001), 239–59; Arneson, 'Against Rawlsian Equality of Opportunity', *Philosophical Studies*, 93 (1999), 77–112.
29. See, for example, Pogge, *Realizing Rawls* (Ithaca, NY: Cornell University Press, 1989), pp. 173–81; Nagel, 'Justice and Nature', in *Concealment and Exposure: And Other Essays* (New York: Oxford University Press, 2002); Brighouse, *School Choice and Social Justice* (Oxford: Oxford University Press, 2000), chs. 6–7; Swift, *How Not to Be a Hypocrite: School Choice for the Morally Perplexed Parent* (London: Routledge, 2003), pt I.
30. It is also common to distinguish between two kinds of item that claim rights might protect—*choices* and *interests*. When rights protect choices, they place other agents under (negative or positive) injunctions depending upon a relevant *decision* the right-holder takes. Some argue that choices are the only items that claim rights can plausibly protect. But we should reject this view. Rights can sensibly serve a role in placing others under requirements to protect individuals' *interests*, irrespective of whether the individuals in question are capable of choice. On this view, all children qualify for rights; on the choice-protecting conception, many young children do not. For discussion of these matters see Raz, *The Morality of Freedom*, ch. 7, and the essays by Griffin, Brighouse, and Brennan in Archard and Macleod (eds.), *The Moral and Political Status of Children*.

31. See Kagan's discussion of rights in *The Limits of Morality* (Oxford: Clarendon Press, 1989), ch. 6.
32. For a critique of parental claim rights and a defence of parental privileges, see Dwyer, *Religious Schools v. Children's Rights* (Ithaca, NY: Cornell University Press, 1998).
33. Notice that the parent may refuse even if he or she *knows* that the stranger's intervention would be beneficial for the child.

3

Parents and Public Reason

3.1 COMPREHENSIVE ENROLMENT

In exercising their custodial rights parents face difficult choices with respect to their child's upbringing. Some of these choices are distributive in nature: To what extent does justice require or permit them to prioritize their child's interests compared to those of others—other children they have, other family members, their own interests, or the interests of individuals in other families? In this chapter, I consider a rather different issue, which concerns the ethical content of the ideals or norms that might inform parental conduct. In raising their children, parents usually appeal to what they take to be the right view of the good life and seek to enrol and educate their children into the institutions, beliefs, and virtues of that view. There are countless instances of parental enrolment of children into particular comprehensive practices. Consider, for example, many religiously motivated parents who seek to ensure that their children grow up in, and learn the teachings, practices, and virtues of, their particular religious community. The enrolment of children into such communities is often undertaken in formal ceremonies, such as a baptism, which is regarded as the beginning of a journey with God. For example, in the Anglican baptism of infants, promises are made by parents and godparents to 'draw them by example into the community of faith and walk with them in the way of Christ', to 'help them take their place within the life and worship of Christ's Church'. In the Commission, the minister addresses the congregation, parents, and godparents saying:

> As they grow up, they will need the help and encouragement of the Christian community, so that they may learn to know God in public worship and private prayer, follow Jesus Christ in the life of faith, serve their neighbour after the example of Christ, and in due course come to confirmation.[1]

A salient feature of paedobaptism is that it is *non-voluntary*. Infants are enrolled into a Christian community when they are incapable of giving or withholding morally binding consent, because they lack the capacities necessary to make autonomous judgements about the matter. Baptism might take two other forms: it is *voluntary* when performed on a competent adult who consents to the baptism; it is *involuntary* when performed on a competent adult who is capable of giving or withholding morally binding consent but who withholds his consent or is not consulted. Liberals have written extensively about the role of personal autonomy in dealing with relationships between adults. The liberal view is that voluntary baptism should be legally permitted, while involuntary baptism should be legally forbidden. The issue before us, however, concerns the legitimacy of a particular kind of non-voluntary baptism: whether it is permissible for others to enrol us into a Christian community before we have the capacity to give or withhold morally binding consent.[2] To summarize: the question is whether an account of liberal legitimacy, in which the child's right to autonomy figures prominently, supports or condemns practices, such as paedobaptism, in which children are enrolled into a particular comprehensive doctrine.

If we conclude, as I believe we should, that paedobaptism is illegitimate, this will not justify a secular upbringing in which children are enrolled into some kind of humanist conception. For humanist conceptions are similarly comprehensive on our construal of that term (Section 1.1). If autonomy condemns comprehensive enrolment, we must seek an upbringing that rests on neither religious nor irreligious foundations.[3] My aim in this chapter, then, is not to challenge a religious upbringing alone, but any kind of enrolment of children into comprehensive doctrines.

3.2 INDIVIDUAL AUTONOMY: END-STATE OR PRECONDITION?

According to some, questions of autonomy do not arise in the case of children, because we can override an individual's autonomy only when she possesses appropriately formed desires, which a young child lacks. For example, Glover writes:

> Perhaps my three-year-old son will one day have the ambition to produce a unified field theory. If I do not take steps to see he has an adequate scientific education, this may prevent him even having a chance to satisfy the ambition. But this would... be a matter of restricting his future opportunities. I cannot, if I take a decision about his education now, be overriding his autonomy. This is because... he is not at the stage of development where he even *could* have the desire whose satisfaction I may be ruling out.[4]

Glover's view may seem to imply that a concern for autonomy has no implication for the way in which we raise our children. This is mistaken. To the extent that we are moved by the ideal of individual autonomy we want our children to develop their capacities for a conception of the good so that they enjoy, at least, the opportunity to lead autonomous lives. Thus, we can violate a person's interest in leading an autonomous life by hindering or failing to develop his or her mental and physical capacities. Perhaps all Glover means in his discussion, which is centred on the issue of paternalism, is that we cannot show disrespect for an individual's autonomously held views until he or she has developed a capacity for a conception of the good. That might be true. Nonetheless, the ideal of autonomy prescribes a wider set of duties than merely the duty not to interfere with an individual's pursuit of her relevant goals. The ideal asserts, in addition, that individuals have an interest in developing certain personal capacities, and in facing an environment that offers them an adequate range of options.

3.2.1 Autonomy as an End-state

Acknowledging this wider set of duties, what has become the dominant liberal view asserts the child's right to an open future. Recognition of a child's interest in autonomy justifies others being duty-bound to develop her capacity for a conception of the good and to ensure that, on achieving that capacity, she faces an adequate range of options from which to choose, and enjoys protection from coercion and manipulation. Because they lack the capacities necessary to control their own lives, children are rightfully under the authority of parents and others. The authority of parents or other agents to determine the content of a child's education is, though, restricted or conditional upon the development of her capacities for autonomy so that in due course she will have the mental resources critically to reflect on, and to repudiate, the beliefs she has acquired, should she deem that appropriate on the basis of that reflection.

On this view, autonomy is an *end-state* to be achieved. Whatever else parents do to or with their children by way of a religious upbringing, they must not prevent them from eventually leading an autonomous life. In their choice of education, for example, parents must not restrict below adequacy their child's mental or physical development or prevent her from being exposed to a range of lifestyles from which she may eventually choose goals and projects. Nevertheless, on the end-state view, provided these opportunities are preserved, from the point of view of autonomy it is legitimate for parents to enrol their child into particular comprehensive practices, or to steer her towards particular conceptions of the good. One can legitimately engage in the religious instruction of a child, for example, on condition that this instruction is consistent with the child's development of the mental resources necessary for autonomy.[5]

The end-state view is a demanding conception, which has been deployed effectively in arguments against the demands of certain parents or communities to shape their children's education in certain ways. For example, the view forbids parents from removing their child from classes that expose her to comprehensive doctrines that challenge their own.[6] In addition, the view places various constraints on the way in which children can legitimately be enrolled into comprehensive practices. It condemns parents who seek to instill in their child an *unshakable* commitment to a particular religious community, for example. While it permits comprehensive enrolment, that process must not be effected in a way that leaves children unable to jettison these commitments in later life.

Note, in addition, that the end-state view is not the only constraint that those who affirm it would place upon parents. To be sure, enrolment of one's children into particular comprehensive practices is acceptable *from the point of view of autonomy*, when it is consistent with facilitating their acquisition of the powers of autonomy and their enjoyment of an autonomy-supporting environment. Nevertheless, such enrolment might be condemned on grounds other than autonomy, for individual autonomy may not be one's only concern. For example, certain physical procedures that are performed on children, such as the scarring of cheeks or other mild forms of bodily mutilation, may not be particularly detrimental to their future enjoyment of autonomy.[7] Some would, nevertheless, condemn such activities by appeal to the child's interest in being free from pain (unless undergoing pain is required in the service of some other recognized interest). In the case of adults, their consent might waive the duty of others to protect them from physical pain. For children, however, their lack of the power to give morally binding consent implies that the duty to protect them from physical or mental pain cannot be waived.

The end-state view might be elaborated in a number of ways. First, it is consistent with the view for parents to be either *permitted* or *required* to enrol their children into particular comprehensive practices. On the first, permissive, interpretation, parents enjoy the option of enrolment or not as they choose, provided enrolment is consistent with the maintenance of an open future for their child. On the second, mandatory, interpretation, parents do not enjoy such an option, but are required to enrol their children into a comprehensive practice or, perhaps, some particular comprehensive practice. Which of these interpretations of the end-state view is adopted will depend on the wider political and ethical perspective in which autonomy is located. For example, some claim that a successful life is one that is autonomous but that is also rooted in a sense of belonging, which is delivered by a shared history of comprehensive ends between parent and child. This view might be thought to produce a parental requirement to impart their own comprehensive convictions to their children. Parents under such a requirement would not be permitted to enrol their children into comprehensive practices that compete with their own, or to refrain from enrolment of any kind.

3.2.2 Autonomy as a Precondition

On a different view, the intrapersonal and environmental conditions of autonomy constitute an end-state to be achieved, but this end-state is also a *precondition* of being treated in certain ways. Let us distinguish between two kinds of precondition that such conditions might constitute. The first precondition concerns belief formation and might be stated as follows: others can legitimately seek to impart to an individual particular comprehensive convictions only when she possesses the capacity for a conception of the good and faces an appropriate environment. The second precondition might relate to the inclusion of individuals within particular comprehensive practices. It asserts that others can legitimately enrol an individual into a particular set of comprehensive practices, such as a church, only when she autonomously consents to that enrolment.

If individual autonomy operates as a precondition in either of these senses, paedobaptism is illegitimate, because infants lack the capacity for a conception of the good without which baptism is unacceptable. It would be a violation of the child's autonomy if parents aimed to inculcate in her an allegiance to particular religious ideals or to make her participate in religious ceremonies. This view also offers a somewhat different account of the objection to inflicting physical pain on children, where these practices, such as the scarring of cheeks, are not required to protect other primary goods. To be sure, the precondition view is consistent with the view that we may have reasons to protect children from such pain quite apart from our concern to protect autonomy. Nevertheless, treating autonomy as a precondition allows one to mount an autonomy-based objection to such practices; it is a violation of the child's autonomy, as well as her physical integrity, to be made to participate in a particular comprehensive ritual without her informed consent.

The end-state and precondition views of autonomy offer very different visions of legitimate parenting. Which view is more plausible, and how must we go about justifying our adoption of one rather than the other? The two views offer different accounts of what it is legitimate for parents to do with respect to their children. To get clear on that issue, however, we must clarify the *justificatory burden* that parents are under: to which reasons can parents legitimately appeal in justification of their conduct with respect to their children. As I argued above, in deciding how to raise their children, parents usually appeal to what they take to be the right conception of the good life. Is such an appeal legitimate? In what follows, I defend the claim that the fundamental motivation of parents should be to conform with public reason, i.e. to treat their children in accordance with norms that are capable of acceptance by any free and equal person. I defend that public reason restriction in Section 3.3 and, thereafter, assess whether it permits parents to enrol their children into the beliefs, practices, and virtues of a particular comprehensive doctrine.

3.3 THE PUBLIC REASON RESTRICTION

The claim I shall defend is that the ideal of public reason should be extended so that it constrains *parental* conduct, as well as the conduct of politicians, judges, public officials, and citizens. First, let us recall the ideal of liberal legitimacy, which motivates the idea of public reason:

> Our exercise of political power is fully proper only when it is exercised in accordance with a constitution the essentials of which all citizens as free and equal may reasonably be expected to endorse in the light of principles and ideals acceptable to their common human reason.[8]

The basic argument for the extension of liberal legitimacy to parents is a parallel case argument. Such an argument has the following structure. First, it accepts a normative claim as appropriate in a given domain. Second, it notes certain features of that domain, on the basis of which the stated normative claim is justified. Third, it argues that those justifying features are, *mutatis mutandis*, present in some other domain. The conclusion is then drawn that the normative claim applies in this other domain as well as the first.[9]

Since I have discussed and offered a qualified defence of liberal legitimacy as a political ideal (Sections 1.1–1.3), I proceed on the basis that the first part of the parallel case argument is sound. Turning to the second claim, recall the features of the political domain in virtue of which Rawls believes the ideal of liberal legitimacy is justified. The political domain has three salient features. First, the political relationship is non-voluntary, in the sense that we do not enter or leave it voluntarily. Second, it is coercive in virtue of its power being imposed on citizens backed up by the use of various sanctions. Third, the basic structure of society has a profound effect on the lives of individuals. Their life chances and aspirations are shaped in significant ways by the principles that govern the political, economic, and social arrangements under which they live. I shall return to these features after sketching the remainder of the parallel case argument.

As an initial statement of the argument, note that the relationship between parent and child shares the three salient features of the political domain. It is a non-voluntary coercive relationship that has profound effects on the child's life prospects and her self-conception. It is non-voluntary in the sense that the child does not choose to enter it but, instead, is born into it, or is placed under the custody of her parents by an appropriate public body, and is not permitted to leave it for a considerable period of time. Second, it is coercive because parents have the authority to impose various constraints on their child and to use various kinds of force in their imposition. Third, it is uncontroversial that the family in which one is brought up is a significant causal factor explaining one's life chances, and that it can significantly shape one's beliefs and desires, including one's self-respect.

If the parallels between the political and parental case are sound, the conclusion can be drawn that parental conduct, as well as political conduct, should be in accordance with the ideal of liberal legitimacy. That is, parents should exercise their authority in accordance with public reason, in a way that is capable of acceptance by free and equal persons. Now, public reason is a multifaceted ideal that comprises a set of norms relating to concern and respect for the freedom and equality of citizens, the norm of reciprocity, and a set of substantive political parameters within which public debate must operate. Many of these requirements of public reason are considered in Chapter 4. Here, I focus on just one aspect of public reason, which concerns the ideal that public conduct and its justification must proceed in a manner that is acceptable to free and equal persons.

What would it mean for parents to exercise their authority in a way that is capable of acceptance by free and equal persons? As an initial approximation, let us recall the idea of reasonable comprehensive pluralism. In a free society in which the liberal freedoms of conscience, expression, and association are protected, the burdens of judgement reveal that individuals who are capable of appreciating and acting from a sense of justice, and who have the capacity to form, revise, and rationally pursue an ethical ideal, will inevitably disagree about comprehensive matters. They will divide on the issue of whether religion is the true path or an insidious illusion, over the worth of homosexuality, and on the merits of different goals, projects, and relationships that might be pursued. The ideal of liberal legitimacy insists that political conduct must be guided by ideals and principles that are capable of affirmation by every free and equal citizen, irrespective of the particular reasonable comprehensive doctrine she affirms. In that way, as we established, citizens can realize their *political* autonomy.

In our parallel case, then, liberal legitimacy insists that parental conduct should be guided by ideals and principles that do not rest on the validity of any particular reasonable comprehensive doctrine. The ideals that guide parents must not, for example, be secular or religious ideals, which are disputed by reasonable persons. Clearly, this is a significant restraint that prohibits what many parents believe to be routinely acceptable forms of appeal to ideals and values which animate their lives. Nevertheless, if the parallel case is established, and the claims of political liberalism are sound, this routine conduct of parents must be questioned.

As I have presented it, the ideal of liberal legitimacy insists that parents must embrace one important aspect of public reason, which is that their conduct should be capable of justification by reference to anti-perfectionist ideals, i.e. ideals that do not appeal to the whole truth about ethics or religion. Nevertheless, this does not imply that parents may not legitimately appeal to their particular comprehensive doctrines in justification of their conduct as parents. As Rawls insists in discussion of the proviso on the appeal to such doctrines, it is legitimate to invoke one's comprehensive doctrine in support of one's conduct provided one also supports that conduct by reference to ideals that are capable of acceptance by individuals who hold different and, perhaps, incompatible comprehensive doctrines.[10] The proviso cites a necessary condition with respect to the legitimacy of invoking one's comprehensive doctrine. As such, it rules out an appeal to one's comprehensive doctrine in defence of one's claim or conduct when one cannot, in due course, sincerely offer a matching justification in terms of public reason alone.

While the proviso cites a necessary condition of the legitimacy of a comprehensive appeal, there is, to be sure, room for more or less restrictive versions of the proviso. At one extreme, the proviso insists that public reasons must also be offered, at the time or in due course, for the same conclusion that the comprehensive appeal supports. However, a more modest requirement is that a public reason defence of the conclusion must be *possible*, even if it is not a defence that is actually presented. These are interesting matters, but I shall not pursue them here. The weaker proviso is sufficient for our purposes, for it provides grounds for objecting to parents who do not regard themselves as under an obligation to justify their conduct in a manner that is consistent with publicly justifiable ideals and principles. Even if we decide that child enrolment into particular comprehensive doctrines is legitimate, it remains hugely significant if parents may not defend that enrolment on the basis of their comprehensive convictions without regard to publicly justifiable reasons.

I now elaborate the parallel case argument through considering certain objections that might be levelled against it. The objections question the analogy between the political and the parental on which the argument trades. Discussing such matters will enable us to clarify, qualify, and defend further the parallel case argument.

First, some might question the analogy as stated, namely, that the position of children with respect to their parents is non-voluntary and coercive. There clearly is a disanalogy, because, in the normal course of events, children grow up and escape from the authority of their parents, whereas this is not the case for all citizens. But this difference does not entitle us to claim that children's position is voluntary in the way, for example, that adult membership of a church is voluntary. Children are born into or allocated to a family, just as citizens can be regarded as being born into a particular state. In addition, children are not entitled to exit the relationship for a considerable period of time. These facts are sufficient to make the relationship a non-voluntary one. The fact that, unlike citizens, children leave the familial relationship before death is, therefore, irrelevant to the question of the voluntariness of the relationship.[11]

With respect to coercion, there are also certain dissimilarities between the political and the parental, but the similarities are sufficient for the analogy to work. To be sure, parents are constrained in the force they are permitted to use in execution of their decisions for their child. There is a continuing lively debate, for example, over whether corporal punishment is a permissible sanction to employ in parenting. Nevertheless, it is widely accepted, and rightly so, that children are coerced by social institutions including their parents. Parents do not always coerce their children. Sometimes they make offers that expand the options available to their children. But the child's membership within a family is attended by a range of constraints which mean that she is coerced into certain kinds of conduct. On one conception, coercion involves the sincere communication by the coercer (P), and an understanding on the part of the coerced (V), that if V fails to perform the required action, then P will bring about a consequence that V believes will leave her worse off and supplies her with a reason for performing the action. Parents routinely engage in that kind of practice (and various other kinds of manipulation that are best interpreted in terms that do not invoke coercion).[12]

Second, some might accept that the children's relationship to their parents is non-voluntary and coercive, but insist that there are further features of the relationship that render it inappropriate for the ideal of liberal legitimacy to apply. Or they might cite certain further features of the political domain, that are not shared by the familial, which lead to the same conclusion.

Rawls writes that 'the personal and the familial . . . are affectional . . . in ways the political is not'.[13] Unfortunately, he does not elaborate the distinction or its relevance. One suggestion is that parents have a duty of love or care, which the political community lacks with respect to its citizens. The political community, represented by the government, owes its citizens justice: the range of goods they can legitimately expect given the operation of appropriate principles of justice. In contrast, parents love, or should love, their children, displaying a degree of affection that would be quite inappropriate in politics, which must be governed by dispassionate norms of impartiality and an appeal to principle in judging conflicting claims. There is much that is sound about this observation. It establishes that parental reason must have a different character compared to public reason considered more generally. Parents do not typically regard themselves as adjudicating conflicting claims as public officials do. In a family, it is often said, the presumption is that members regard the well-being of other members as enhancing, rather than as potentially competing with, their own.

Now the claim that the interests of different family members are congruent is overstated. Many familial arguments do centre on issues of fair treatment between siblings: from trivial cases of the equal division of dandelion and burdock, to highly significant ones concerning whether to spend the family's resources in a way that prioritizes the interests of one's cognitively disabled child or one's intellectually gifted child. Nevertheless, putting these objections aside, the presence of affection is insufficient to exempt the non-voluntary and coercive familial domain from the requirements of liberal legitimacy. Imagine a society in which affection obtained universally between citizens, such that each is as concerned about the well-being of others as her own. In such a society, the adoption by the majority, or a plurality, of a particular comprehensive doctrine as the basis for law and public policy cannot be rejected as unfairly serving the well-being of only a particular section of the citizenry, for it can be observed that everyone benefits equally in accordance with that doctrine. However, the choice of a particular comprehensive doctrine as the basis for public policy remains illegitimate, because it might be rejected by reasonable persons. Liberal legitimacy, then, cites a constraint on the *content* of the affection and concern one may impose on others, and not merely on the sacrifices one is permitted to impose on others.[14]

Thus, it is clear that parental power is not itself political power. Parents have special responsibilities to their particular children, and should govern their relationship by norms of love and attachment, and through an intimate and particular understanding of their children. Political virtue, by contrast, requires the opposite norms of general, impartial concern and respect. However, the distinction should not be overstated and it should not be used to overlook the normatively significant features that they share in common, which support liberal legitimacy in each case.

Another disanalogy between the political and the familial concerns the status of the beliefs of citizens and children respectively. An objection on the basis of this disanalogy might proceed as follows. The wrongness of the coercive and involuntary imposition of a comprehensive doctrine is that it violates the freedom and equality of the person on whom it is imposed. Specifying this further, it might be said that citizens are free and equal only when they possess to a mimimum degree the capacity to form, revise, and pursue a conception of the good and are capable of taking responsibility for their ends. But young children lack such capacities. Given these premises, it would follow that it is unobjectionable to impose comprehensive doctrines on children, since children lack the freedom and equality, the violation of which renders such imposition wrong.

We should reject this argument's key normative premise, that one's freedom and equality can be violated by having a comprehensive doctrine imposed upon one only if one already possesses the capacity for a conception of the good and the capacity to take responsibility for one's ends. True, lacking a conception of the good held on the basis of a well-formed capacity to form, revise, and pursue such a conception, a young child cannot herself object to the constraints she faces in a manner that would generate a valid complaint. But this merely establishes that her status and interests must be registered in some other way—through a hypothetical choice situation, or via some representative person or guardian—and that we must act paternalistically on her behalf.

If we appoint a guardian to act on her behalf, we must ask how a guardian should approach the issue of the legitimate treatment of a child in a liberal society. First, the guardian should acknowledge the independent moral standing of the child. He or she will also note the existence of reasonable pluralism, and the fact that free and equal persons disagree about the soundness of different comprehensive doctrines. The guardian should assess which principles the future free and equal adult, who the child will grow up to be, may reject as the normative basis of her upbringing. Given these considerations, the guardian must believe that it is highly likely that the adult who the child will become would object to having been subjected to an upbringing that depends for its justification on a comprehensive conception, which she (as an adult) rejects as mistaken or evil. On the basis of *the possibility of future reasonable rejection*, then, the guardian must object to the appeal to comprehensive doctrines on behalf of the child. The objection is necessary if the individual in question is to maintain her political autonomy, which requires her to affirm the constraints that she faces, and their justification, taking her life as a whole.[15]

Note that here I am not ruling out the imposition of a comprehensive doctrine on the child. I am rejecting its imposition in the absence of an argument from public reason. It is, no doubt, possible for someone to mount an argument from public reason, appealing only to anti-perfectionist considerations, for the enrolment of children into particular comprehensive doctrines. I shall consider arguments of that kind below (Section 3.5). But the position under examination here insists that such arguments are unnecessary. It claims that in virtue of the child's lack of capacities that are related to freedom and equality, the ideal of liberal legitimacy fails to hold in the relationship between child and parent. It is that narrow claim that I reject.

Note, in addition, that the objection to an appeal to comprehensive conceptions, which rests on the possibility of future reasonable rejection, does not speak against an adult's adoption of a comprehensive doctrine on the same grounds, to wit, that she may come to reject that doctrine on further reflection. For the relevant difference in this case is that the constraints that a comprehensive doctrine places on her life are deliberately chosen according to her own considered judgement, and that remains the case even if she comes later to regret that choice. In the case of children, the presence of autonomous choice is absent and, therefore, paternalistic decisions made for them must be attentive not to their own convictions, since they do not have the status of self-authenticating sources of valid claims, but to the comprehensive convictions it is reasonable to suppose they might come to hold. In a liberal society, given the burdens of judgement, there are countless such convictions, and it is impossible to say which will be adopted.

I now turn briefly to Rawls's remarks on the family. In his most extensive discussion, Rawls explicitly treats the family as part of the basic structure of society; it is among the set of social and political institutions, which, together, are regarded as coercive, involuntary, and which profoundly affect people's lives. However, he claims that the principles that apply to any particular institution of the basic structure must be sensitive to the kind of institution that it is. For example, he maintains that the difference principle is not a suitable principle for inclusion within a political constitution, because its implementation requires detailed consideration of complex counterfactual judgements and other technical expertise, qualities it would be unreasonable to expect of judges.

With respect to the family, Rawls writes:

> Political principles do not apply directly to its internal life, but they do impose essential constraints on the family as an institution and so guarantee the basic rights and liberties, and the freedoms and opportunities, of all its members.[16]

The basis of Rawls's distinction between the essential constraints on the family and its internal life rests on the different points of view we have as citizens and as family members. As citizens we have interests in developing and exercising our moral powers and, therefore, we have a reason to constrain family life in the service of these interests. As family members, however, the good of 'a free and flourishing internal life'[17] produces reasons for us to limit the constraints that are imposed on the family. Here, Rawls observes parallels between families and other associations, such as churches, and defends the view that in both cases public reason does not regulate their internal lives beyond the essential constraints that are necessary given our interests and status as free and equal citizens.[18]

Rawls devotes most attention to the problem of gender, and he argues that among the essential constraints on families are those required for the minimization of a gendered division of labour where such a division is involuntary. As in other associations, the relationship between mature family members can legitimately be considerably unequal—as is required by certain comprehensive doctrines—provided social policies are in place which ensure that such inequality is compatible with the individuals' equality as citizens, i.e. equality in terms of the rights and economic resources at their disposal.

The issue of justice with respect to adult members of families, whilst interesting, is not our concern. Notice, however, that when we turn to the problem of upbringing, the analogy between families and other associations breaks down. Unlike the position of mature family members, or mature members of associations, the position of young children is not potentially voluntary, i.e. voluntary given the right background conditions. So the issue of how to devise constraints that aim to minimize involuntary participation is absent. Adequately to theorize the family from the point of view of the relationship between parent and child, we must address its arrangement given its unavoidably non-voluntary and coercive nature with respect to the child.

Rawls strikingly fails to engage with this issue, because he overlooks the salient features that make the child's position within the family normatively akin to the position of citizens within the state. His inclusion of the family as part of the basic structure is motivated by his observation that 'reproductive labour is socially necessary labour':[19] the family is a required institution for the reproduction of society indefinitely over time. He misses the more straightforward case for the family as a basic structural institution, on which the parallel case argument trades.

Rawls does offer certain remarks about the relationship between parent and child. He does not believe that parents are required to act in accordance with political principles. He sees the protection of children from abuse and neglect as among the constraints that should regulate families. Moreover, he says, 'at some point society has to rely on the natural affection and goodwill of the mature family members'.[20] If the constraints

Rawls has in mind are legally enforced constraints, then these remarks have considerable force. But, as we have established, we need not treat normative constraints as always enforceable (Section 1.5). Since that is the case, it is not obvious that there is an inconsistency between relying on the goodwill of parents and holding that they are morally constrained by certain principles or modes of reasoning.

3.4 THE CASE FOR THE PRECONDITION VIEW OF AUTONOMY

If the argument advanced above is sound, then it has revolutionary implications for parents and public authorities. No longer may the enrolment of children into particular comprehensive doctrines be justified by citing the merits of those doctrines as comprehensive doctrines. To pass the test of legitimacy, it must be shown that enrolment is justified in a manner that is acceptable to any reasonable person, even those who reject the validity of the particular comprehensive doctrine in question.

As I noted, however, the public reason restriction is in principle compatible with either the end-state view of autonomy, which permits comprehensive enrolment, or the precondition view, which does not. It is consistent with the former if there is a public reason defence of enrolling children into particular comprehensive doctrines. Some, for example, argue that such enrolment is necessary if children are to develop and exercise the intrapersonal conditions of autonomy, i.e. the power rationally to revise and pursue a conception of the good life. I discuss arguments of that kind in the following section. Here, I present a case for the precondition view, which rests on three ideas. First, I claim that the ideal of political autonomy that motivates the public reason restriction also provides a basis for affirming the intrinsic merits of the precondition view of autonomy. Second, I conjecture that the precondition view is instrumentally valuable in enabling individuals to revise their conceptions of the good. Finally, I respond to certain objections that might be raised against the view.

3.4.1 The Intrinsic Merits of the Precondition View of Autonomy

The precondition view asserts two constraints on the treatment of individuals. First, others are not permitted to enrol individuals into comprehensive practices without their autonomous consent. Second, others are not permitted to seek to impart comprehensive convictions to individuals prior to their possession of the capacity for a conception of the good. The intrinsic merit of these constraints is that they are constitutive of legitimate relations between free and equal individuals. A subtle account of this social ideal is offered by Raz in his discussion of independence, which emphasizes that certain modes of treatment can wrong a person independently of whether they have bad consequences for her. Consider Raz's remarks on the importance of independence to personal autonomy:

> Coercion diminishes a person's options. It is sometimes supposed that that provides a full explanation of why it invades autonomy. It reduces the coerced person's options below adequacy. But it need not. One may be coerced not to pursue one option while being left with plenty of others to choose from. Furthermore, loss of options through coercion is deemed to be a greater loss of autonomy than a similar loss brought about by other means. That is why slaves are thought to lack autonomy even if they enjoy a range of options which, were they free, would have been deemed sufficient. Manipulation, unlike coercion, does not interfere with a person's options. Instead it perverts the way that a person reaches decisions, forms preferences or adopts goals. It too is an invasion of autonomy whose severity exceeds the importance of the distortion it causes.[21]

Raz's remarks alert us to the fact that autonomy can be thwarted not just in virtue of lacking the mental capacities to make autonomous decisions, or by facing an inadequate range of options from which to choose one's goals or lifestyle. Autonomy requires, in addition to these goods, a particular set of social (or interpersonal) relations. People's treatment by others must not be marked by manipulation or coercion, because these forms of treatment involve one being subjected to someone else's will. As Raz observes, they treat one 'as an object rather than as an autonomous person'.[22]

This account relates autonomy to the ideal of respect for persons as self-governing agents. Recognition of a person as a self-governing creature involves treating her in ways that elicit her consent. To do otherwise would be to treat the person as a mere means, as an individual whose goals and activities are chosen by others who are more powerful. She would, thereby, become like a tool, which is used by others in fulfilling their chosen projects (even if their project is her perfection according to their conception of the good).

This view of the right to autonomy involves not merely the absence of involuntary treatment, or being forced to act in ways one rejects. In addition, it involves the positive requirement that one should lead one's life according to convictions that are the product of one's critical and rational reflection. Being used or led by others is problematic whether the person used has autonomous convictions that are ignored, or does not have any autonomous convictions. In short, the view that respect for autonomy has value in itself, because it ensures that each individual is self-determining and the central features of her life are the product of her autonomously held convictions, supports the precondition view of autonomy. This renders it impermissible to steer a person into a particular lifestyle without her consent, and prohibits religious formation that does not prevent a child's development of critical capacities as well as that which does.

This appeal of independence is implicit in many people's objection to the use of techniques of eugenic or genetic selection to shape individuals' characteristics beyond those required to screen out certain disabling conditions, such as cystic fibrosis, Tay–Sachs disease, or Huntington's disease. We do not know the extent to which our phenotypical traits might be shaped by genetic interference. Nevertheless, many are adamant that even if we learn how to manipulate those traits through genetic choice, we ought not to allow parents to select the characteristics of their children in this way. To do so would, they claim, wrongly allow parents to 'play God'. The thrust of this objection, on its more plausible interpretation, is not that it is never appropriate to interfere in nature.[23] Rather, it is that humankind should not treat other people in the way that God is thought entitled to treat humanity, namely, as beings whose abilities and interests can legitimately be moulded to his values. Playing God is wrong because it subjects people in their creation to the will of others. An individual's autonomy is violated if the genes that constitute her and shape her motivations and abilities are manipulated or chosen on the basis of the individual's parents' conception of the good. Even if she possesses the other conditions of autonomy, her life will always have a particular history marked by her interests and abilities having been to some extent chosen by her parents.[24] Viewed from the perspective of the parents, they can be seen to violate their duty to respect autonomy in their procreative choices. Their choice of, say, a girl rather than a boy, or a gene that gives their child a bias in favour of heterosexuality (if such a gene exists) would involve manipulation of a future child's characteristics such that they conform to their own particular conception of the good, a conception that can reasonably be rejected. The precondition account insists that one has a permission to encourage an individual to adopt a particular conception of the good when, but only when, the individual has realized the mental capacities to deliberate rationally about that encouragement. This insistence respects the independence of the individual by ensuring that no one is coerced or manipulated by others. This dimension of autonomy explains the view that while no injustice has been done if a straight child is born through natural reproductive methods, it would be wrong to use genetic screening to create such a child. Whereas in the first case the child's sexuality is not chosen by others, in the second her characteristics are the manipulated product of her parents pursuing their own particular conception of the good.[25]

The precondition conception of autonomy, then, trades on the grounding idea of autonomy as self-rule, which is also the motivation for the public reason restriction. An autonomous life is one in which the individual is the author of her own life rather than that life being chosen by another. Before she has the capacities necessary to take rational control of her own life, it is necessarily the case that she cannot be the author of their own ethical life. She needs the help of others to acquire the capacities necessary to be an author: to form, revise, and rationally pursue a conception of the good. Nevertheless, if others, such as her parents, are concerned that *she* is the author of her life, they will regard themselves as under an obligation not to choose for her, not to try to get her to hold particular beliefs that they find attractive or compelling, or to make her engage in particular ethical practices, such as worship, which they regard as essential to a worthwhile life. These thoughts resonate with the notion at the heart of autonomy, that my life is *my* life and no one else's.

3.4.2 An Instrumental Argument for the Precondition Conception

Our interest in having the capacity for a conception of the good, which involves being able to form, revise, and rationally to pursue such a conception, is justified, in part, by considerations of our fallibility. As Rawls observes in his defence of certain basic liberties:

> There is no guarantee that all aspects of our present way of life are the most rational for us and not in need of at least minor if not major revision. For these reasons the adequate and full exercise of the capacity for a conception of the good is a means to a person's good.[26]

The argument can be presented from the original position. Placed behind the veil of ignorance, individuals lack knowledge of which conceptions of the good are worthy of pursuit. Given the existence of a plurality of conceptions, some which are doubtless more worthy than others, they cannot be sure that the conceptions they individually affirm are best for them. Possession of the capacity to reflect on, and to revise, one's conception is, therefore, a means to their good.

An argument for the precondition view builds on this insight. Let us begin with the observation that there are two different ways in which it can be hard for someone to revise her conception of the good, which employs G. A. Cohen's nice distinction between the *difficulty* and *cost* of performing an action. To fix ideas, consider Daniels' case of Jane:

> Jane's mother raised her to believe that a mother's duty is to stay home with her children and that no woman should pursue a career during her childrearing years. Jane no longer believes that, has had a good career, and now faces the choice about what to do about childrearing. But she feels so guilty at the thought of pursuing her career that she ends up staying home with her children. Not only does this mean she is deeply disappointed about her sacrifice of career, but she resents the burden placed on her by her children (and her mother).[27]

Jane finds it hard to revise her lifestyle, but this is not because she is unable to consider its merits rationally and amend it on the basis of that reflection. In other words, she possesses the capacity to revise her ends. Nevertheless, because of the guilt she experiences when revising her priorities, from staying at home with her children to pursuing a career, it remains hard for Jane to revise her goals. The guilt that she experiences makes the pursuit of a career too costly in psychological terms: she finds the guilt she is beset by, and with which she disidentifies, unbearable and therefore does not pursue the conception of the good she reflectively endorses.[28] Employing Cohen's distinction, it is costly, but not difficult, for Jane to change her goals.[29]

A person's enjoyment of the capacity for a conception of the good is described in terms of the difficulty she has in reflecting on and changing her conception of the good life. In other words, one's enjoyment of the capacity is indicated by one's possession of powers such as *imagination*—the ability to conceive actual and possible alternative lifestyles one might pursue—and *rationality*, which enables one appropriately to evaluate how one's immediate goals relate to the comprehensive ideals one affirms; it also involves the ability to act in a way that satisfies one's goals, to perform the actions warranted by one's beliefs and desires.[30]

Returning to the instrumental defence of the precondition view of autonomy, we can now defend more satisfactorily the claim that individuals are more likely to prefer it to the end-state view, which permits comprehensive enrolment. Even if a child's religious schooling is constrained by the development of her capacity for a conception of the good, she will predictably find it more costly to exercise her capacity in ways that go against the religion in which she is brought up. To do so is often wrenching because of the guilt one cannot help feeling when one goes against the ideals that have guided one's early life. To be sure, such feelings of guilt or disorientation are sometimes the product of the revision of goals one has acquired autonomously. However, the emotional grip of ideals and practices into which one has been schooled during childhood is likely to be greater. Because children lack the capacity for a conception of the good, their early commitment to the ideals into which they are schooled is not the product of independent, rational thought. Like one's allegiance to one's family, commitments developed in the absence of rational reflection are more likely to retain an emotional pull later on, even when one decides that they lack plausibility. Moreover, the mix of family allegiance and comprehensive enrolment adds to the likelihood of costs in revising one's conception of the good. If parents enrol their child into a particular religion, she may find that abandoning it in later life is hard, not merely because the ideals have an emotional grip that she finds costly to shake off, but because she would be rejecting the ideals of her *parents.* If her parents have sought to prepare her for life as a devout Christian, abandoning that life might be wrenching because she feels that she is rejecting the upbringing that they provided and for which she feels a debt of gratitude: she might be beset by guilt, which is the product of regarding herself as ungrateful for her upbringing or as failing to live up to her parents' expectations.[31]

To be sure, these claims about the costs of enrolment in terms of later rational revision are conjectures, which might be refuted on the basis of empirical evidence. They are hardly novel. Wollstonecraft makes a similar point:

> I never knew a parent who had paid more than common attention to his children, disregarded; on the contrary, the early habit of relying almost implicitly on the opinion of a respected parent is not easily shook, even when matured reason convinces the child that his father is not the wisest man in the world.[32]

If these social and psychological conjectures are sound, the precondition view of the right to autonomy has some plausibility. For the conjectures support an extension of Rawls's argument for the instrumental value of having the capacity for a conception of the good. Placed behind the veil of ignorance, in which individuals lack knowledge of which conceptions of the good are worthy of pursuit, parties would adopt the capacity for a conception of the good as a means to their good. They would also consider the issue of the *costs* of revising their conceptions of the good given different kinds of parental conduct. Suppose that we lack knowledge of whether our parents' conception of the good is worthy of pursuit. Other things equal, it would be rational to ensure that our upbringing equipped us with the intellectual and emotional means to revise and, perhaps, abandon any particular conception of the good if we find that it is not the most valuable one for us to pursue. But we might also consider the claim that the costs of such revision are higher if we have been schooled in a conception of the good than if our parents had not attempted to recruit us to that conception before we possessed the intellectual and emotional strength that secures for us an independent perspective from which to evaluate the merits of different conceptions. Parties in the original position who acknowledge these possibilities would, other things equal, rationally adopt the precondition account of autonomy as a means to their good. They would regard the possession of the capacity for a conception of the good *prior* to others attempting to recruit them to particular conceptions as a bulwark against being swayed by emotional ties or intellectual deficiencies, over which they have little control and which may lead them into errors that are costly to rectify.

3.4.3 Does the Precondition View Condemn Too Much?

In response to an earlier presentation and defence of the precondition view, Andrew Mason asks:

> Why should we suppose that religious instruction violates the child's right to autonomy? If the point is just that it involves imparting a particular 'comprehensive' conception of the good, then respect for autonomy, so understood, would be highly restrictive. It would seem to rule out cultivating in children virtues such as kindness and generosity, or a particular aesthetic sensitivity, and prohibit feeding a child fish, meat or even dairy products (to the extent that this presupposes the permissibility of exploiting fish and animals for this purpose).[33]

The principal charge is that my view condemns too much or is too restrictive. Now, it is true that the precondition view condemns many aspects of parental conduct that are widely regarded as permissible or even mandatory. Nevertheless, it is not as restrictive as Mason thinks. First, the view does not rule out the cultivation of generosity or kindness, since these virtues are instrumental to, or constitutive of, children developing a sense of justice, which parents are required to develop, or to allow others to develop (Section. 4.3).

Second, the precondition conception rules out certain kinds of *intentional conduct*, not particular kinds of behaviour or outcomes. For example, on the issue of feeding children meat, let us assume that meat eating is not unjust; if it were, parents would not be permitted to feed their children meat, just as they are not permitted to ask their children to steal from others. If parents provide their children with a balanced diet, expose them to a variety of different conceptions of eating, and display a sensitivity to the emerging gastronomic conceptions of their children, then on the precondition view they do not violate their autonomy. They would violate their autonomy if they fed meat to their children with the aim of cultivating another meat eater. Similarly, parents who take their children to church to enable them to experience the traditions and practices of the church, who also allow their children genuinely to become familiarized with other religious and irreligious traditions, may not violate their children's autonomy. To make their children worship, incorporate them in the ceremonies of the church, and seek to cultivate Christian virtues, which is what parents promise to do in the baptism ceremony, does violate their autonomy according to the precondition view. Similar claims can be made about education with respect to other comprehensive matters. Two children can have the same thing happen to them—they are fed meat, for example—but, nevertheless, the motivation of the parents can be markedly different in a way that is relevant to the children's autonomy. One parent might be motivated solely by the aim of providing a balanced diet while another might aim to create carnivores.[34]

In this respect, the precondition view operates as a constraint on *aims* in a way that is familiar to the tradition of liberal thought. For example, although it is contrary to public reason to prohibit Sunday trading on the grounds that it is contrary to particular Sabbatarian faiths, this is consistent with restricted Sunday trading if a sound public reason argument for a common rest day can be offered.[35] The notions of 'enrolment' and 'seeking to impart comprehensive convictions' make reference to particular aims in this respect, namely, the aim of having one's children be part of a comprehensive practice, or having them adopt the comprehensive convictions in question. Conduct motivated by such aims is prohibited by the precondition view of autonomy. But this is consistent with introducing children to comprehensive doctrines when the ambition is not to make them participants or believers.

The precondition view might be thought to be too restrictive in another sense, because it fails to provide sufficient space for parents to pursue their reasonable comprehensive doctrines. Many comprehensive doctrines are evangelical in the sense that they require their adherents to convert non-believers into believers. The precondition view significantly reduces individuals' freedom to pursue such doctrines, since its elaboration of the status and interests of children implies that any attempt to convert them prior to their enjoyment of the capacity for autonomy is illegitimate. Few parents, it might be suggested, would accept such a position.

The problem with this objection is that if it is sound, it is unclear why it does not generalize in a way that would permit adults to use the coercive power of the state to convert others to the comprehensive views they affirm. As we have established, considerations of autonomy, particularly political autonomy, generate a set of reasons that support the claim that citizens should constrain their use of political power by norms of public reason that are acceptable to reasonable persons. That constraint limits the means by which individuals may evangelize or seek the comprehensive conversion of others. If the critic accepts that argument, he or she must explain why the extension of it to the case of children is not valid. In the absence of such an argument, we should affirm the illegitimacy of parents enrolling their children in comprehensive doctrines, even if few parents agree with us.

A similar response is available to those who criticize the precondition view on a child-centred basis. Some, who adhere to a conception of salvation by baptism, would complain that if parents are not permitted to baptize their child, the child suffers incalculable harm, because her sins are not washed away. They might argue that the good of autonomy is insignificant compared to the good of salvation. If we have to choose between them, the transcendent value of baptism must defeat the good of treating others as autonomous agents.

This is perhaps the most threatening argument against the precondition view. But notice again that its implications extend far beyond the case of children. The appeal to transcendent values to defeat the requirements of autonomy, if sound, defeats the appeal to public reason in the case of *adult* relations as well as the relation between adult and child. Liberal philosophers must therefore offer reasons that support the claim that the reasons we have to be concerned about, and respectful of, the autonomy of others override, or in some other way defeat, the claims made by individuals who align themselves to comprehensive doctrines that embody transcendent values of this kind.[36] I shall not discuss this general problem for liberalism here. It suffices to point out that the appeal to transcendent values to defeat the precondition view cannot be invoked by those who affirm autonomy as a regulative ideal. Those who accept the end-state view of autonomy cannot employ this argument in criticism of the precondition view.

3.5 ARGUMENTS FOR COMPREHENSIVE ENROLMENT CONSIDERED

The arguments above support two claims. First, in justifying their treatment of children individuals must abide by the public reason restriction, which requires them to defend their conduct in a manner that cannot reasonably be rejected by free and equal persons. Second, the precondition view of autonomy, which prohibits adults from enrolling children into particular comprehensive doctrines prior to their enjoyment of the capacity for a conception of the good and in the absence of their consent, is an attractive conception of the legitimate treatment of children, given the ideals that motivate the public reason restriction, and given the plausibility of certain claims about the rational revision of conceptions of the good.

Yet the dominant liberal account of upbringing affirms the end-state view, which permits parents to enrol their children into particular comprehensive practices and traditions, and to shape their comprehensive convictions prior to their development of the capacity for a conception of the good. Various arguments might be deployed in defence of that view. First, I discuss a set of arguments that offers a parent-centred defence of a parental liberty to enrol children into comprehensive doctrines. Consider the rather compressed argument offered by Galston for this commonly held view:

> [T]he ability of parents to raise their children in a manner consistent with their deepest commitments is an essential element of expressive liberty.... {1} [P]arenting is typically undertaken as one of the central meaning-giving tasks of our lives. {2} We cannot detach our aspirations for our children from our understanding of what is good or virtuous.... {3} [L]oving and nurturing a child cannot in practice be divorced from shaping that child's values. {4} In doing so as parents, we cannot but draw on the comprehensive understanding that gives our values whatever coherence and grounding they may possess. Moreover, {5} we hope for relations of intimacy with our children, as they develop and when they are grown. But estrangement is the enemy of intimacy. It is understandable for parents to fear their children may become embroiled in ways of life they regard as alien and distasteful and, within limits, to act to reduce the risk that this fear will be realized.[37]

It is unclear whether Galston can be categorized as affirming the end-state view of autonomy. In some places, he asserts that autonomy is only one value among many different ideals of living, and that a non-autonomous life can be a very good one. At other times, however, he argues that an upbringing or association must accommodate a meaningful right of exit from relationships and associations, which he elaborates in a manner that is similar to Rawls's specification of the capacity for a conception of the good.[38] But whether or not he affirms it, the quoted remarks might be invoked in defence of the end-state view of autonomy or some ideal close to it.

In evaluating Galston's argument we must distinguish between different claims—which I have numbered in added parentheses—that are distinct. The first claim in defence of a parental liberty to enrol children into comprehensive doctrines {1} asserts an interest that many adults have in parenting, and rightly justifies that interest by reference to the intrinsic value of parenting. If one of our central projects in life is to found a family, we have an interest in having the opportunity to meet the challenges that parenthood poses. If we successfully respond to these challenges, our lives to that extent go better. For many, it is hard to see what would contribute more to their well-being than succeeding as a parent.

Galston's second comment {2}, that our aspirations for our children are informed by our comprehensive judgements, is also sound. Some pray for their child's soul, while others hope luck will be kind to theirs, or that their child will pursue a lifestyle that is fulfilling rather than unrewarding. Aspirations of these kinds are an unobjectionable, some would say an inevitable, part of parenthood. However, it is too strong to claim that parents cannot detach their aspirations for their children from their own specific conception of what is good or virtuous. If parents hold comprehensive pluralist views, as Galston does, and think there is a plurality of good lives, then they need not believe that the virtues they practise must also be the ones that their children should pursue. Many parents hope their children will lead successful lives, even if they are ones that they (the parents) barely understand, still less pursue. Moreover, appreciating their own fallibility with respect to ethical matters, parents might hope that their child will *reject* their comprehensive commitments if they are mistaken. Nevertheless, we can accept that it is not illegitimate for parents' aspirations for their children to be informed by their comprehensive convictions.

The third claim is that shaping one's child's values is an unavoidable part of parenting. No one disputes this. The dispute between the rival accounts of autonomy and parenting turns on the nature of the constraints of legitimacy with respect to this unavoidable activity. Adherents of the precondition view believe that seeking to shape children's comprehensive convictions is illegitimate, while imparting the virtues that are constitutive of public reason may not be. Those who hold a version of the end-state view operate with less demanding constraints of legitimacy so far as comprehensive ideals are concerned.

The first pivotal statement in the argument is {4}: the inevitability of parents drawing on their comprehensive understanding when shaping their children's values. From the point of view of the dispute that presently concerns us, the nature, implications, and plausibility of this claim are far from evident. Consider three different interpretations of the claim. First, Galston might mean that parents inevitably understand their role as parents, including the unavoidable shaping of their children's values, by reference to their own comprehensive convictions. This may be true, but it is not sufficient to generate the conclusion that they are permitted to shape their children's beliefs so that they affirm those comprehensive values. For example, one may understand one's parenting as expressing one's religious duty to found a family and yet abide by the public reason restriction when deciding how to parent. On this interpretation, then, the inevitability of appealing to one's comprehensive doctrine is compatible with the requirements of the precondition view.

A second interpretation asserts that it is inevitable that parents will steer their children towards their own comprehensive convictions. But if this is the claim, no evidence is offered in defence of it. Moreover, even if we accept the inevitability of parents affecting some of their children's comprehensive beliefs, the extent to which this happens surely remains dependent upon the choices parents make with respect to their children's upbringing. For instance, those persuaded by the instrumental benefits of the precondition view will seek to minimize the degree to which the upbringing they provide influences their children's comprehensive convictions. In addition, the inevitability claim does not threaten the distinction outlined above, in the context of the reply to Mason, that there is a relevant difference between intending to influence a child's comprehensive values and foreseeing such influence as a by-product of one's conduct that is differently motivated. Two parents may offer their child a balanced diet, but do so by offering different kinds of food. The inevitable effect of the different diets will be a difference in eating preferences when the child becomes an adult. But, if the aim of the parents is simply to offer a balanced diet, this inevitable shaping of the children's preferences, does not constitute a violation of their autonomy. Thus, the claim of the inevitability of shaping one's children's comprehensive values cannot be stated in a way that is both plausible and threatens the precondition view.[39]

Third, perhaps {4} should be read normatively. Given the comprehensive aspirations that parents have for their child, and the unavoidability of their shaping her values, they *ought* to impart their comprehensive beliefs to her. But this short argument trades on an invalid inference. We must distinguish between an individual's *hope* that someone else comes to affirm her atheism, say, and her *seeking to make it true* (*or more likely*) that he does. As we have established, a possible position asserts that even if the shaping of certain values is unavoidable, the principles that guide that process may not permit avoidable comprehensive shaping. Since the precondition view is a possibility, we cannot infer a liberty to impart one's comprehensive convictions to one's child from the hope that she will come to share them.

3.5.1 The Argument from Intimacy

If {4} cannot do the work required to justify the liberty of parents to impart their comprehensive convictions to their children, then perhaps the seemingly independent argument from intimacy {5} can. Indeed, Galston is not alone in appealing to intimacy to ground such a liberty. For such an argument to succeed, we require a conception of intimacy that is in tension with the constraints the precondition view imposes on parental conduct. However, it is difficult to judge this argument, because few offer an account of intimacy that is sufficiently rich to judge its relevance for the issue at hand. Galston's argument, for example, is too quick because it simply asserts the claim that parents tend to become estranged from their children if the latter take up lives that their parents find 'alien and distasteful'. It is incontrovertible that parent–child intimacy is sometimes lost when children develop views that challenge their parents'. But this is not a universal phenomenon, and we may question the motivations of parents who allow a disagreement over such matters to reduce their willingness to enter into the kinds of activity that characterize an intimate relationship with their children.

A richer account of intimacy between parent and child is provided by Brighouse and Swift, who notes its uniqueness as follows:

> The love one receives from one's children, [. . .] especially in the early years, is spontaneous and unconditional, and, in particular, outside the rational control of the child. She shares herself unselfconsciously with the parent, revealing her enthusiasms and aversions, fears and anxieties, in an uncontrolled manner. She trusts the parent until the parent betrays the trust, and her trust must be betrayed consistently and frequently before it will be completely undermined. Adults do not share themselves with each other in this way: intimacy requires a considerable act of will on the part of adults interacting together. But with children, while parents are prone to spontaneity and intimacy, their fiduciary obligations often require them to be less than wholly intimate (despite the child's unconditional intimacy with the parent). The good parent sometimes masks her disappointment with, sometimes her pride in, her child, and often her frustration with other aspects of her life.[40]

Many adults treat the successful maintenance of such an intimate relationship with a child as necessary for a flourishing life. Brighouse and Swift maintain that the need for such a relationship grounds an interest that adults have in having the opportunity to pursue relationships of this kind. They then proceed to cash out this interest in being a parent with an intimate relationship with one's child in terms of a number of rights. In doing so, they distinguish between associational and control rights. The associational rights, which the interest in intimate relationships justifies, include rights to be with one's child: to live and spend time with her, and to reveal one's enthusiasms and convictions to her.[41] Such rights depend upon parents enjoying certain control rights, because, as Brighouse and Swift argue, an entitlement to determine how the child spends some of her time, which books they share together, what kinds of recreational activity she pursues, and the kind of religious or non-religious organizations she attends is a means of facilitating an intimate relationship between parent and child. But they insist that control rights above and beyond those necessary for the appropriate kind of associational rights are not justified by reference to the good of intimacy. In particular, rights to control one's child's future development is conditional upon that control being in the interest of the child, and cannot be defended by an appeal to intimacy.

This account of parent–child intimacy has considerable plausibility.[42] It is worth adding a few comments with reference to the dispute between end-state and precondition accounts of autonomy. The precondition view is primarily an account of how parents ought to exercise their associational rights, which may be defended on the basis of considerations of intimacy. The appeal to intimacy, if sound, generates a set of claim rights, which entitle parents to determine the joint activities of the family—whether the family sees a particular play, or attends a particular church—such that others may not interfere with these choices. As Brighouse and Swift note, granting such rights is often practically indistinguishable from protecting parents who seek to enrol their children into particular comprehensive doctrines or to impart their faith to them. But holding such claim rights does not imply that parents enjoy a liberty right to engage in such enrolment. Even if we protect the opportunity to enrol one's child, we may continue to hold that enrolment wrongs the child from the point of view of liberal legitimacy (Section 2.6).

Brighouse and Swift's conception of intimacy enables us to appreciate that the precondition view of autonomy leaves room for intimate relations between parent and child to flourish. For the liberties and entitlements required for intimacy are compatible with parents not enrolling their children into the beliefs, traditions, and ceremonies of their comprehensive conceptions. Just as a parent can take pride in the accomplishments of her children as dancers, scouts, footballers, or musicians, without becoming any of these herself, so children may witness and take pleasure in their parents' comprehensive accomplishments without being schooled in the virtues and practices of the comprehensive conception or affirming its value. To be sure, if the instrumental argument for the precondition view is sound, a parent must be attentive to the possibility that her children may develop an allegiance to their comprehensive views, which they will find costly to shake off even if they come to reject their merits. Thus, in pursuing shared projects and goals there should be a presumption that the shared activities of the family should be determined by reference to the child's developmental needs and enthusiasms rather than the parents'. And, in revealing her beliefs and desires a parent should be clear that reasonable people disagree about their merits. Nevertheless, these kinds of restraint leave room for intimacy between parent and child.

We can go further and observe that the value for a parent of maintaining intimacy with her children is conditional on her recognizing their moral standing in the appropriate way. Consider Scanlon's remarks on a related issue:

> [O]ne cannot take the same pleasure in one's cooperative relations with others as members of the same firm or university, say, if one comes to believe that they are being asked to participate on terms they could reasonably reject, and the meaning of one's own successes and accomplishments is undermined by the thought that they were attained on terms that were basically unfair.[43]

In Scanlon's view, the requirement of justifying one's conduct to others is not merely a constraint, the violation of which is a source of guilt or shame. Rather, it is part of a positive account of the way in which we ought to live in unity with others. For example, friendship, he claims, 'involves recognizing the friend as a separate person with moral standing—as someone to whom justification is owed in his or her own right, not merely in virtue of being a friend'.[44] The good of friendship is jeopardized if one fails to recognize the independent moral standing of the friend.

These remarks can be extended to qualify the ideal of intimacy between parent and child. The value of that relationship is dependent upon it being justifiable to the child (or a representative) as an individual who is born with the status of a free and equal person *on terms that she could not reasonably reject*. As I have argued, that standard of justification supports the public reason restriction and, for parallel reasons, the precondition view of autonomy. If those arguments are sound, then not only is honouring the precondition view compatible with the good of intimacy between parent and child but its violation even jeopardizes that good.

3.5.2 Is Enrolment by Parents Necessary for the Pursuit of an Autonomous Life?

Finally, I turn to a child-centred argument for the end-state view. This argument claims that enrolment within a specific comprehensive doctrine enables the child to become autonomous: enrolment is autonomy's friend, not its enemy. This is the case, the argument goes, because beneficial effects flow from comprehensive enrolment in terms of the child's development, and later exercise, of a capacity for autonomy.

Before we assess arguments of this kind, notice that the advocate of enrolment must establish more than the compatibility between enrolment and the child's development and exercise of her capacity for autonomy. For if both end-state and precondition views are capable of delivering an upbringing that will equip the child with the capacity for autonomy, we must select the precondition view. As was highlighted in the discussion of its intrinsic merits, the precondition view is sensitive in the right way to the interpersonal dimension of autonomy—the ideal of independence or political autonomy. If the end-state view is to cancel or defeat the reasons parents have not to enrol their children, which are motivated by this interpersonal dimension, then it must clearly be established that it facilitates the other dimensions of autonomy—the intrapersonal or environmental conditions—more successfully than the precondition view does. The empirical difficulties of establishing such a claim are considerable. A child's development of the capacity for autonomy is enhanced or hindered by a variety of background conditions quite apart from her parents' choice of whether or not to enrol her into a particular comprehensive practice. And it is not clear that any empirical investigation could control for these other determinants in a satisfactory way. Nevertheless, one simple reply that might be made on behalf of the precondition view trades on the observation that there are countless individuals who as children were not enrolled by their parents into particular comprehensive practices, but who, nevertheless, developed and now exercise their capacity for autonomy. The common-sense observation is sufficient to require this particular argument for enrolment to pass a reasonably strict scrutiny test if it is to defeat the constraints recognized by the precondition view.

With this in mind, let us now consider some arguments for comprehensive enrolment that appeal to its beneficial effects in terms of the child's development of autonomy. Advocates of comprehensive enrolment often appeal to cultural coherence as a precondition of leading an autonomous life. Individuals cannot engage in rational reflection, it is claimed, if they do not hold normative commitments on the basis of which they can evaluate the validity and strength of other putative reasons, or rationally reflect on the worth of other commitments they hold. It is mistaken to think that autonomous self-creation involves individuals somehow determining their character for themselves out of nothing. Rather, the pursuit of an autonomous life presupposes a set of reasonably stable convictions on the basis of which one evaluates other convictions.[45] On this view, there can be no objection in principle to parents imparting their convictions to their child, because her holding such convictions is a precondition of her development of the power rationally to deliberate about, and choose between, alternative comprehensive conceptions. Call this *the argument from autonomous deliberation.*

Various problems beset this argument. First, children are not blank slates, which must be filled with convictions if they are to develop the powers necessary for autonomy. As is well known, children are born with particular proclivities and will in due course acquire particular interests and beliefs as they experience alternatives that are offered to them. So even if the possession of convictions is necessary for the development of autonomy, it is not obvious that children will lack them in the absence of being enrolled into a particular comprehensive conception; instead, they might simply pick up convictions with respect to various matters, and develop projects, goals, and a desire to engage in different kinds of relationship, as they grow up. And it is not the case that convictions acquired in this way need be any less stable than ones into which one has been enrolled by one's parents.

Even if the child needs to be enrolled into certain convictions, it does not follow that those convictions must be comprehensive in character. For example, parents might give their child a sense of identity, a sense of belonging to a particular societal culture, by imparting its language, a sense of its history, and the values and virtues that animate its public culture. A sense of embeddedness within a liberal culture, then, can supply a raft of commitments and convictions, relating to the freedom and equality of individuals, a related conception of social cooperation, and of the norms that constrain individual conduct which flow from these ideals. Even if the possession of normative convictions is a precondition of meaningful rational reflection, we might ask why this set of liberal convictions is not sufficient.[46]

One response to this possibility claims that the public or political convictions one receives through an appropriate upbringing in liberal values fail to equip one with the intellectual wherewithal to raise questions and deliberate about comprehensive matters, such as the nature of the universe, religion, the value of different personal projects and relationships, or aesthetic value. Holding firm convictions that others are free and equal and affirming the norms of respect and reciprocity which that status imply, it might be said, do not enable one to assess the merits of Mozart and Dylan as composers, or Vermeer and Rothko as artists, or the debate between atheists and theists on the question of God and our place in the world. But this seems doubtful. When we educate children to be respectful and just towards others we confer on them a commitment to certain norms and values and, more generally, a sense of the seriousness and responsibility of normative commitment (Section 4.3). In addition, if we are successful, they will have the ability to reflect on different accounts of these values and the ability to see that alternative political values are unattractive. But they will not be exposed to the full range of alternative conceptions of how we ought to live together in society. Instead, their upbringing will, we hope, be sufficient for them to reflect in a rational and reasonable manner on different political proposals that are put to them, on the basis of the convictions they already hold and the intellectual tools they possess. If they possess such critical capacities, they will be able to assess whether alternative beliefs are irrational, rest on beliefs that hang together in the right way, depend on arbitrary or dangling distinctions, and so on. It is difficult to see why this kind of liberal upbringing would be insufficient to enable children to engage in autonomous deliberation about comprehensive matters as well. For autonomous deliberation about comprehensive matters seems to rest on the same intellectual capacities and orientation as deliberation about public matters. Children must have a sense of the potential seriousness of the comprehensive issues at hand, and an understanding of the comprehensive practices and the beliefs that ground them. If they have developed, in addition, the intellectual capacity to subject different beliefs to critical scrutiny, as described above, we have no reason to suppose that they cannot employ their capacity for deliberation to address comprehensive issues.[47]

The argument for comprehensive enrolment from autonomous deliberation may be extended in a way that denies these claims. According to McLaughlin, enrolment within a set of particular religious practices enables a child to gain an understanding of religion *from the inside*. It facilitates a rich and detailed acquaintance with the beliefs, reasoning, and traditions of a particular comprehensive practice on the basis of which the child can come to reflect on its merits.[48] On the basis of this kind of view, it might be thought that engagement with political values and public reason is insufficient to reflect adequately on religion or on other comprehensive practices; or it might be argued that religious understanding is impossible without religious practise.

Interestingly, McLaughlin himself does not defend these claims, but the more modest one that practising a religion may be beneficial, if not necessary, for religious understanding. Yet it is not obvious that the modest claim is sufficient to justify parental comprehensive enrolment. For example, consider an adult who, we would judge, satisfies the conditions of autonomy. She possesses the powers of rational reflection necessary for autonomy, faces a range of religious and non-religious views, and is free of coercion and manipulation. It seems possible for her to reject as erroneous any number of religious beliefs if atheism is the product of her rational reflection on questions concerning the origin of the universe, or the nature and place of humankind in the world. Her atheism may be autonomously held, and she may autonomously reject a particular religious view—Islam or Christianity—without attending to the practices of the particular religion in question. Her convictions are quite generally irreligious, but nonetheless, autonomously held. It is entirely possible, then, for individuals to adjudicate autonomously between different comprehensive conceptions in the absence of an inside understanding of the different conceptions.[49]

No doubt there are other versions of the argument that comprehensive enrolment is significantly beneficial for the development of the child's capacity for autonomy. It is doubtful that there is a general refutation that can be deployed against every version of the argument. Nevertheless, the two central ideas invoked above suggest that most challenges of this kind will prove to be unsuccessful. First, the development of the child's sense of justice is a significant benefit in terms of the child's development of the capacity for autonomy. Second, given an appropriate education for a sense of justice, it is not necessary to enrol individuals into particular comprehensive conceptions for them to be able autonomously to consider their merits. To be sure, the appeal to cultural coherence is the right kind of argument, given the public reason restriction defended above. However, given that the precondition view respects the political autonomy of children, and in the absence of a compelling argument for the necessity of enrolment for the development of autonomy, we may conclude that the precondition view of autonomy is the best response to the issue of whether it is permissible for parents to enrol their children into particular comprehensive doctrines.

NOTES

1. The Archbishops' Council of the Church of England, *Common Worship* (Church House Publishing, 2000), pp. 352, 358. Compare the instructions to godparents in *The Book of Common Prayer*:

   '[Y]e must remember, that it is your parts and duties to see that *this Infant* be taught, so soon as *he* shall be able to learn, what a solemn vow, promise, and profession, *he hath* here made by you. And that *he* may know these things better, ye shall call upon *him* to hear Sermons; and chiefly ye shall provide, that *he* may learn the Creed, the Lord's Prayer, and the Ten Commandments, in the vulgar tongue, and all other things which a Christian ought to know and believe to his soul's health; and that *this Child* may be virtuously brought up to lead a godly and a Christian life.'

   Church of England, *The Book of Common Prayer* (Oxford: Oxford University Press, 1969), pp. 330–1.
2. There are other cases of non-voluntary enrolment that differ from the non-voluntary enrolment of children. In the case of children, their enrolment is effected *before* they are competent to give or withhold consent. In this respect, they are unlike many demented individuals who were, but no longer are, competent. In the latter case, one possible justification of non-voluntary baptism is that the individual would have consented to the ceremony, but that dispositional consent cannot be inferred in the case of children. For

further discussion, see Feinberg, *Harm to Self* (New York: Oxford University Press, 1986), p. 181ff.

3. Rawls is insistent that the ideal of public reason is not a secular ideal. See 'The Idea of Public Reason Revisited', pp. 583–4, 587–8.
4. Glover, *Causing Death and Saving Lives* (Harmondsworth: Penguin Books, 1977), p. 77.
5. Advocates of the end-state view include Feinberg, 'The Child's Right to an Open Future', in his *Freedom and Fulfillment: Philosophical Essays* (Princeton, NJ: Princeton University Press, 1992); Gutmann, 'Children, Paternalism, and Education: A Liberal Argument', *Philosophy and Public Affairs*, 9 (1980), 338–58; McLaughlin, 'Parental Rights and the Religious Upbringing of Children', *Journal of Philosophy of Education*, 18 (1984), 75–82; Rawls, *Political Liberalism*, pp. 313–14; Macleod, 'Conceptions of Parental Autonomy', *Politics and Society*, 25 (1997), 117–40; and Levinson, *The Demands of Liberal Education* (Oxford: Oxford University Press, 1999).
6. A number of legal cases in the USA have provided the occasion for asserting the demands of the end-state view. The two most prominent cases are *Wisconsin v. Yoder* and *Mozert v. Hawkins County Public Schools*. For discussion of the former, see Feinberg, 'The Child's Right to an Open Future'; for discussion of the latter see Levinson, *The Demands of Liberal Education*, pp. 53–4, 60; Callan, *Creating Citizens*, pp. 141–2, 157–61.
7. It is worth stressing that some forms of bodily mutilation must be condemned on grounds of autonomy as well as bodily integrity. It is well documented, for example, that the genital mutilation of young girls involves extreme pain, and can cause significant gynaecological and other medical problems, and, sometimes, death. Even if there is no autonomy-based objection to extreme pain, the other risks to which such young girls are subjected do fall foul of the duty to promote their autonomy. For an account and critique of the different practices of female genital mutilation, see Dorkenoo, *Cutting the Rose—Female Genital Mutilation: The Practice and Its Prevention* (London: Minority Rights Publications, 1995), pp. 1–58.
8. Rawls, *Political Liberalism*, p. 137.
9. See Joshua Cohen, 'The Economic Basis of Deliberative Democracy', *Social Philosophy and Policy*, 6 (1989), 27, for a discussion of the structure of the parallel case argument and an application of it in a democratic defence of socialism.
10. Rawls, 'The Idea of Public Reason Revisited', pp. 584, 591–4.
11. See Rawls, *Political Liberalism*, pp. 40–1. On p. 136, n. 4, Rawls is explicit that the possibility of emigration does not render political association voluntary. Perhaps there are certain voluntary relationships in which, like

the parent–child relationship, there is no option with respect to entry. The proposal of opt-out schemes for organ donation is a case in point. Everyone is included within the scheme from the outset, but there is an immediate right of exit. But if the right of exit is conferred only after some period of time, the lack of an option with respect to entry implies that the relationship is not a voluntary one.

12. For a discussion of coercion, see Raz, *The Morality of Freedom*, pp. 148–57. Notice that establishing the presence of parental coercion may not be necessary for the parallel case. We are assessing whether the conditions that require liberal legitimacy in the political domain are also present in the parent–child relationship. In Section 1.5, I argued that a non-coercive relationship is evaluable from the point of view of justice and legitimacy if it is involuntary and has profound consequences for individuals' lives.
13. *Political Liberalism*, p. 137.
14. See Nagel, 'Rawls on Justice', in Norman Daniels (ed.), *Reading Rawls: Critical Studies on Rawls' 'A Theory of Justice'* (Stanford, CA: Stanford University Press, 1989), pp. 7–8.
15. This accords with Rawls's account of the principle of paternalism. See *A Theory of Justice*, pp. 218–20.
16. Rawls, 'The Idea of Public Reason Revisited', p. 597.
17. Ibid.
18. In the context of churches, for example, the essential constraints include the right of exit and the impermissibility of punishing apostasy. But this is consistent with a sexist construal of authority within the church.
19. 'The Idea of Public Reason Revisited', pp. 595–6.
20. Ibid. p. 598.
21. Raz, *The Morality of Freedom*, pp. 377–8.
22. Ibid. p. 378.
23. That version of the objection was effectively rebutted by Hume, 'On Suicide', in Stephen Copley and Andrew Edgar *Selected Writings* (eds.), (Oxford: Oxford University Press, 1993).
24. Note that the objection does not lose force if it is pointed out that the genetic choice produces only a tendency to develop certain phenotypical characteristics.
25. For further discussion, see Clayton, 'Individual Autonomy and Genetic Choice', in Justine Burley and John Harris (eds.), *A Companion to Genethics* (Oxford: Blackwell, 2002).
26. Rawls, *Political Liberalism*, p. 313.
27. Daniels, 'Equality of What: Welfare, Resources, or Capabilities?', in his *Justice and Justification: Reflective Equilibrium in Theory and Practice* (Cambridge:

Cambridge University Press, 1996), pp. 220–1. Daniels uses the example to address the different issue, which does not concern us at present, of whether egalitarian justice should compensate people for shortfalls in welfare.

28. It could be that reflectively she does not want to continue her career, because she knows how unbearable would be the guilt she would feel if she did so. We can think of conscious (character planning) and unconscious (adaptive preference formation) ways of this happening. Nevertheless, it remains the case that she would prefer not to experience that guilt and, therefore, be free to revise her conception of the good in a relatively costless manner.
29. See G. A. Cohen, *Karl Marx's Theory of History: A Defence* (Oxford: Oxford University Press, 1978), pp. 238–9; see also 'On the Currency of Egalitarian Justice', 918–19: there Cohen remarks that '[a]t the far end of the difficulty continuum lies the *impossible*, but it is the *unbearable* which occupies that position in the case of costliness'.
30. For instructive remarks on rationality in this sense, see Rawls, *A Theory of Justice*, pp. 358–72; Elster, *Sour Grapes: Studies in the Subversion of Rationality* (Cambridge: Cambridge University Press, 1983), pp. 2–26; and Raz, *The Morality of Freedom*, pp. 292–4.
31. Similar remarks are made by Green, 'Internal Minorities and Their Rights', in Will Kymlicka (ed.), *The Rights of Minority Cultures* (Oxford: Blackwell, 1995), pp. 264–7.
32. Wollstonecraft, *A Vindication of the Rights of Woman*, in Janet Todd (ed.), *Political Writings* (Oxford: Oxford University Press, 1994), p. 235.
33. Mason, *Community, Solidarity and Belonging: Levels of Community and their Normative Significance* (Cambridge: Cambridge University Press, 2000), p. 164.
34. Here it is important to note that the aims in question refer to both *ultimate* and *immediate* aims. T. H. McLaughlin rightly observes that parents might have the ultimate aim of equipping their children with the intellectual wherewithal autonomously to reflect on different religious views, yet consistently with, and partly in the service of, this aim, enrol them in a particular religious community. In this way, their immediate, or short-term aim, is the development of their faith, though the ultimate aim is the development of autonomy. See McLaughlin, 'Parental Rights and the Religious Upbringing of Children', 79. It should be evident that the precondition view operates with a constraint prohibiting action motivated by either kind of aim to enrol one's child into a comprehensive practice.
35. See Mill's discussion in *On Liberty*, ch. IV, par. 20; Jeremy Waldron, 'Legislation and Moral Neutrality', in R. E. Goodin and Andrew Reeve (eds.), *Liberal Neutrality* (London: Routledge, 1989), p. 61.

36. Indeed, this is not a task merely for liberals, but for any political theorist who aspires to offer a justification of political authority that does not rely on theocratic foundations. Hobbes was well aware of this. See *Leviathan*, ch. 31 and pt III. For a discussion of this problem as it presents itself with respect to political liberalism, see Clayton, 'Political Liberalism, Disagreement, and Sectarianism', *Polis: Revistă de Ştiinţe Politice*, 6 (1999), 85–9.
37. Galston, *Liberal Pluralism: The Implications of Value Pluralism for Political Theory and Practice* (Cambridge: Cambridge University Press, 2002), p. 102.
38. Ibid. p. 123.
39. Amy Gutmann argues that since all ways of arranging educational institutions and curricula will inevitably bias children in favour of certain comprehensive conceptions and away from others, parents should have the presumptive freedom to determine the biases of their children. But she offers little in defence of the inference, apart from an appeal to the liberal ideal of respect for the plurality of reasonable comprehensive doctrines and the right of parents to live their own lives freely. See Gutmann, 'Children, Paternalism, and Education: A Liberal Argument', pp. 351–3. But respect for alternative comprehensive practices is compatible with the precondition view of autonomy and, therefore, cannot be used in criticism of it. In addition, it is not obvious how an adult's interest in pursuing his or her comprehensive conception renders him or her free to impose that conception on others, in this case the children. Finally, Gutmann seems to overlook the fact that even if any upbringing biases a child's comprehensive view, the extent of that biasing might be a matter of degree, and the origin of the biasing might remain significant. She argues that if parents allow their children to understand that eating pork is considered reasonable by others in society, they have a right to prevent their children from eating it. In response, we should note that this instance of biasing is avoidable and, if my argument is sound, there are sound intrinsic and instrumental reasons for avoiding it. Consider the analogous argument with respect to a possible future world of genetic screening: 'Since this child will inevitably have genes which biases her towards a gay, straight or bisexual lifestyle, it is parents who should determine which of these biases constitutes her.' The inference is invalid, because it is preferable from the point of view of autonomy for no one else to determine this kind of bias, and to leave the biasing process to nature.
40. Brighouse and Swift, 'Parents' Rights and the Value of the Family', pp. 16–17.
41. Ibid. sec. 7.
42. For another account of familial intimacy, see Schrag, 'Justice and the Family', *Inquiry*, 200–08. The good of intimacy constitutes one ground for the parental right to rear I defended earlier (Section 2.4), though that right was

defended on a number of grounds and need not depend on the good of parent–child intimacy.

43. Scanlon, *What We Owe to Each Other* (Cambridge, MA: The Belknap Press of Harvard University Press, 1998), pp. 163–4. This view is similar to Dworkin's claim that justice is a parameter with respect to the good life. See Dworkin, *Sovereign Virtue*, pp. 260–7.
44. Scanlon, *What We Owe to Each Other*, p. 164. For related discussion, see Callan, *Creating Citizens*, pp. 82–7.
45. See, for example, Feinberg, *Harm to Self*, p. 33; Levinson, *The Demands of Liberal Education*, pp. 30–2.
46. Levinson, who emphasizes the need for cultural coherence, concedes this possibility. See *The Demands of Liberal Education*, pp. 133–5.
47. For more on the first personal dimension of ethical integrity, see Dworkin, *Sovereign Virtue*, pp. 270–1.
48. McLaughlin, 'Parental rights and the Religious Upbringing of Children', pp. 81–2; Galston, *Liberal Pluralism*, p. 105.
49. To be sure, in many cases it is preferable to gain an understanding of a comprehensive practice from the inside. We can criticize a person for not investing sufficient time or resources to gain an adequate appreciation of a particular comprehensive practice before rejecting it. But we need not insist on such an understanding for her rejection to count as autonomous.

4

Education for Justice

4.1 POLITICAL EDUCATION AND CONSENT

In this chapter I turn from issues concerning the child's acquisition of a comprehensive doctrine to the problem of political education. I address the problem in the following way. First, I discuss the issue of the permissibility of shaping children's political convictions from the perspective of ideal theory, i.e. under the assumption that existing arrangements are just or legitimate, or nearly so. In such a society, a number of questions concerning political education arise. Is it legitimate for the state to stabilize these ideal arrangements through cultivating a desire in children to comply with and support them? If it is legitimate to cultivate such motivations, how should we describe the content of the political education we offer to children—are the norms they ought to acquire purely procedural, or might they include certain substantive commitments as well? Second, having clarified the proper place of political education from the point of view of ideal theory, I address the problem of citizenship education as it presents itself in non-ideal circumstances. Citizenship education is a part of the educational provision of many countries that falls short of justice to varying degrees. Even if no single conception of citizenship education is appropriate for all such non-ideal circumstances, we might, on the basis of our ideal theory, sketch a conception of how we ought to respond to different educational practices or initiatives in this domain.

We must begin by drawing a distinction between two models of citizenship education. On the model of *political literacy*, as I shall call it, the aim of political education is to cultivate in individuals knowledge of the nature and history of the political instititutions and laws that govern their lives, an understanding of the principles that purportedly justify those institutions and laws, and of the rival political conceptions that have been articulated and defended. But the model of political literacy requires more than a comprehension of the different conceptions of politics that might be affirmed. It also offers an understanding of the ways in which political change might be effected, both violent and non-violent, and aims to impart to individuals the skills that enable them to reflect rationally and critically on political matters, and to participate politically, should they so desire. Yet, fundamentally, the model of political literacy eschews any attempt to shape the political motivations of individuals. It does not aim to encourage individuals to participate in political life. Whether or not individuals participate, indeed, whether or not they affirm an obligation to obey the law, is a matter left entirely to them. On this model, the shaping of children's political convictions is beyond the remit of citizenship education.[1]

Political literacy is contrasted with the model of political education as the *shaping of political motivations.* This model facilitates political literacy, but goes beyond it by shaping educational curricula and the organization of educational institutions so as to cultivate in individuals certain political beliefs and the desire to participate in political life in permissible ways. To be sure, there are many different versions of the political motivation model of political education, depending on which conception of political morality is in operation. Whereas liberals who affirm the model will favour an education for justice or legitimacy, socialists might seek the inculcation of an egalitarian or fraternal ethos among individuals, and communitarians and nationalists will cultivate an allegiance to the particular ethical and political understandings of the group. There is a range of possible positions. Plainly, affirming this model of political education does not commit one to the view that individuals' beliefs and desires can legitimately be shaped *irrespective* of the content of the beliefs and desires in question. For instance, it is consistent for liberals to tailor their choice between the two models to the political circumstances in which they find themselves. They might advocate the political literacy model if they recognized that permitting the shaping of political convictions would license a dominant illiberal majority to inculcate what liberals take to be a sense of *injustice* in children. I shall return to strategic issues of this kind in due course (Section 4.5). Nevertheless, it suffices for present purposes to note that on the political motivation model the cultivation of beliefs and desires is, *in principle*, permissible.

Notice, in addition, that the political motivation model need not rest on a particular account of human motivation in general. There has been considerable debate, for example, on the question of whether to explain human action we must cite an appropriate kind of desire on the part of the agent. The Humean view is that beliefs are motivationally inert and, therefore, in explaining an action we must necessarily cite the presence of a desire that is connected in the right way to the conduct of an agent. An alternative view holds that people can be motivated directly by reasons, or the belief that a course of action is appropriate. On this view, it makes sense to explain an action by appeal to the agent's recognition that she had a reason so to act, even though she had no desire to do it.[2] These are interesting matters, but I do not pursue them here because the political motivation model is compatible with either view. The shaping of motivations can be viewed in terms of influencing people's desires or placing them in a position that will enable them to recognize the reasons that apply to them. The legitimacy or otherwise of shaping political motivations is independent of this philosophical dispute.

Which model of political education should be adopted? In the first instance, we address this question from within ideal theory. Thus, we suppose that prevailing political and legal arrangements are legitimate according to liberal principles. We ask whether it is permissible for these arrangements to be stabilized by deliberately shaping individuals' beliefs and desires such that they generally comply with the law and are prepared to defend liberal institutions against various kinds of threat.

A prominent critique of the political motivation model, offered by Harry Brighouse, appeals to the need for free, informed, and rational consent for political legitimacy. In his view, political literacy is required for the continuing legitimacy of liberal political institutions, but shaping political motivations is forbidden on grounds of legitimacy.

Before considering this argument, it is worth briefly mentioning the nature of problem of legitimacy. It is useful to distinguish between two rights that might be associated with political legitimacy. First, if a set of political and legal institutions (call it the state) is legitimate, then it has the right to use the powers at its disposal to force individuals to conform with the laws it issues. So, it may forcibly prevent people from breaking the law and punish transgressions of the law. Second, if it is legitimate, the state has the right to rule, which justifies the claim that citizens have political duties or obligations towards it and, at the very least, they have a standing reason to comply with the commands of the state.[3] For the purposes of our present inquiry, we must establish what are the necessary and sufficient conditions for the attribution of political legitimacy. In addition, we must ask whether those conditions place educational constraints upon the conduct of governments or other political actors as a means of facilitating the conditions for legitimacy.

Brighouse claims that the conditions of legitimacy place significant constraints on the kind of political education that might be offered to children. He cites two necessary conditions of legitimacy. First, political arrangements must conform to principles that would be chosen by suitably motivated (reasonable and informed) individuals. What this amounts to is a matter of some dispute, but we might interpret the hypothetical choice condition, without detriment to the argument, in terms of a choice from something like Rawls's original position, which seeks to eliminate bases of choice that would render the resulting choice unfair.[4] Nevertheless, Brighouse insists that hypothetical consent is insufficient for legitimacy:

> A state to which no one consents even though all *could* consent should not congratulate itself on its legitimacy. So some concern that the state aspire for the actual consent of at least a majority, and preferably a vast majority, is usually added to the hypothetical conditions.[5]

Thus, the second necessary condition is that political legitimacy requires the *actual* consent of the governed. But this must be free, informed, and rational consent. If the consent is coerced or manipulated, or poorly informed, or premised on inadequate formal powers of reason, then it is not morally binding consent. It is not, that is, the kind of consent that establishes an obligation to obey the law.

The second necessary condition of legitimacy in Brighouse's view evidently favours the model of political literacy over the political motivation model. First, if actual consent is necessary, it must be informed and rational consent. Consent that is offered on the basis of ignorance of what it is one is consenting to, or of the feasible alternatives, carries no morally binding force. Neither does consent that rests on inadequate powers of reasoning: no one seriously thinks that a young child's consent to her parents places her under a duty to obey them, because the child lacks the capacity to render her beliefs and desires consistent and mutually supportive and, consequently, we have no reason to believe that her consent is given on the basis of a settled judgement informed by her critical reflection. Such desiderata justify a programme of political education that fosters political literacy, which enables the child to become politically informed and to bring general analytical and critical capacities to bear on issues of political relevance.

Second, if a person's consent is to be given *freely*, it must not be generated coercively or manipulatively. And this explains why the political motivation model of political education fails the test of legitimacy. As Brighouse notes: 'If we carefully foster the virtues among those who are not yet able rationally to assess the legitimacy of the state itself, what basis do we have to think they would have freely supported it on the basis of their reason alone?'[6] Notice the qualification 'not yet able rationally to assess the legitimacy of the state'. In this view, we might have a *qualified* rejection of the political motivation model. Seeking to shape the political motivations of autonomous individuals who are informed, rational, and enjoy options sufficient for free choice, if it is done openly and not behind people's backs, might be unobjectionable from the point of view of the consent requirements of legitimacy. Such motivation shaping, through persuasion or mild financial inducements that encourage participation, appears unobjectionable because individuals enjoy the wherewithal to give or withhold unmanipulated and uncoerced consent. But in the case of children, these conditions are absent, because children lack the rational and critical capacities, and the information required, to judge the state on the basis of their autonomous reason alone. So, even if the appeal to consent does not condemn every instance of political motivation shaping, it is sufficient to forbid it in the case of children. From the point of view of the education of children, then, the appeal to actual consent establishes a preference for political literacy over political motivation.

We should reject the consent-based argument for the political literacy, because we should reject the second proposed condition of political legitimacy, which requires the actual consent of the governed. Brighouse claims that the introduction of the second condition is *usually* added to the requirement of hypothetical consent, because hypothetical consent is too easy to satisfy. Yet this is mistaken in two respects. First, it is not the case that actual consent is usually added as a necessary condition of legitimacy, at least if 'usually' refers to the most prominent liberal accounts of political legitimacy. It is significant that the three leading liberal thinkers of recent times—Rawls, Dworkin, and Raz—argue that actual consent is not a requirement of legitimacy. Rawls, as we shall see, develops an account of political legitimacy on the basis of our natural duty of justice; Dworkin defends a conception of associative obligations, in which political obligations are justified in a similar manner to involuntary obligations to family; and Raz develops, what he calls, the normal justification of political authority, in which a person can have an obligation to obey the law, without having consented to it, when complying with the law enables her better to act on her reasons for action.[7] And, second, it is not the case that satisfying political legitimacy would be too easy if it could be obtained without the actual consent of the governed. As I shall argue, a plausible account of legitimacy that rests upon the ideals of justice and democracy places significant demands on political principles and institutions. That few societies, if any, have managed to fulfil these conditions is indicative of how hard they are to satisfy.

4.2 LEGITIMACY VIA JUSTICE

Justice and legitimacy are distinct political virtues. Nevertheless, a degree of justice is an important element of legitimate political arrangements. Indeed, our concern to act legitimately can be viewed as a product of, and shaped by, our duty to act justly.

Consider a natural challenge that consent theorists face. Any plausible moral conception recognizes the existence of moral duties that apply to individuals irrespective of whether they have consented to them. For example, we are duty-bound not to wrong others by violating their rights even if we do not voluntarily accept such a duty. If obeying the law enables us better to act on those duties, it is unclear why a duty of obedience is not also justified by appeal to the duty not to wrong others, independently of our consent. True, obligations to obey the law can be generated through consent. But there are other justifications of such obligations that do not rest on voluntaristic foundations.

Thus, an obligation to obey the laws of a just society can be justified as an element of the natural duty of justice. Moreover, if we take our duty to act justly seriously, we must recognize a duty to comply with laws that are somewhat unjust. Let me explain this position by setting out the content of the natural duty of justice, and its relationship to legitimate law and democracy.[8]

The natural duty of justice is the duty to support, comply with, and promote a just basic structure. Specifying it further, we can say that if just institutions do not prevail, one must do one's fair share in advancing the prospects of their realization. Where just, or nearly just, institutions exist one must do one's fair share to support them. In addition, if the basic structure that governs one's life is just, one is duty-bound to comply with its requirements. This is an aspect of the normal justification of political authority. Acting under authority involves acting on a content-independent, exclusionary reason for action. It is content-independent, because I have a standing reason to obey the law, without consideration of its content. If the law has legitimate authority, I should obey the law that prohibits theft because it is the law, not because it is wrong to steal. In addition, my reason to obey the law is exclusionary in the following sense. In so far as I have a reason to obey the law, I disregard the independent reason I have not to steal, and act on the basis of the reasons generated by the law alone: the fact that it is legitimate law provides me with sufficient reason so to act. But even though I disregard the wrongness of stealing at the point of deciding how to act when under authority, the basis for ascribing authority to the law prohibiting theft depends upon the reasons and duties that already apply to us independently of our relationship to those who claim authority. A set of principles and institutions have legitimate authority, then, if our compliance with them (i.e. acting from them because they supply content-independent exclusionary reasons for action) enables us better to conform with the reasons and duties that already apply to us.[9]

Thus, the natural duty of justice can generate a duty to obey the law, if such compliance enables us to conform with justice better than if each of us acted according to our own judgements of the demands of justice. If the principles and institutions that govern our lives are just, in all likelihood we are under a duty to obey them. For if political institutions and the law are just, it is highly unlikely that individuals would realize justice as effectively by acting on their own individual judgements concerning the requirements of justice. Just collective action requires the coordination of everyone within society, and assurance that the benefits and burdens of social cooperation are fairly distributed. The possibility of realizing the required kinds of coordination and assurance through individuals acting on their own independent views of justice is remote.

Do individuals have a duty to obey laws that do not fully realize justice? On the basis of what I have said so far, it would appear that they do not, because if a law prescribes unjust conduct, it might very well be the case that an individual would realize justice better by not surrendering her judgement to the putative authority but, instead, by acting on her own conception of justice. But this conclusion is too quick, and it fails to acknowledge the relationship between justice and democratic legitimacy.

Principles of social justice *include* rights of democratic participation. Such rights include 'the equal right to take part in, and to determine the outcome of, the constitutional process that establishes the laws with which [citizens] are to comply';[10] free and fair elections; protections for freedom of conscience, speech, and political association; and provisions to ensure the fair value of these rights. The conclusion that democratic rights are required by justice can be reached in a number of ways. Let us review just three kinds of argument.

First, there are plausible reasons for believing that democratic institutions will produce more just outcomes compared to non-democratic ones. There are many different kinds of argument for this claim. One argument, which derives from Condorcet's jury theorem, states that if individuals are on average more likely than not to judge the requirements of justice correctly, our confidence that the majority decision of a group of independent individuals is right increases exponentially as the size of the group increases. This explains why juries have twelve members rather than three, and why well-functioning democracies are more likely to realize justice than autocracies.[11] Other, less formal instrumental arguments, which are perhaps more attentive to the realities of representative democracies, appeal variously to the beneficial effects of free and fair elections and democratic deliberation and debate. Democracies serve an important protective function, because individuals whose interests are not satisfied, or who are wronged in others ways, may campaign for greater recognition and seek to influence the government through the electoral process, petitioning, or media campaigns, to effect a change of law or policy. In addition, common sense suggests that a majority view informed by democratic deliberation is more likely to produce just outcomes than the deliberation of only a few individuals: the exchange of ideas and arguments mitigates against our natural partiality, and widens our understanding of the issues by adding to the information that is available to us and enabling us better to appreciate the range of arguments that apply to a particular issue. As Rawls suggests, 'the effects of common deliberation seem bound to improve matters'.[12]

Second, democratic procedures are a valuable means of ensuring that certain procedural values of justice are realized. A familiar liberal requirement is that justice must be capable of being seen to be done (Section 1.5). Each individual must have the opportunity to acknowledge that the governing institutions give their interests due consideration. Thus, we need political principles and institutions that realize justice in a manner that provides each individual with the opportunity to regard herself as having been treated as a person with equal moral standing. Now, if a small group imposed a set of laws on society without consulting the views of citizens, then, irrespective of the soundness of their judgements of justice, this would fail to realize justice, because those on whom the law is imposed would reasonably feel that they are treated as having lower moral standing. This is the case for reasons similar to those advanced above. Legislators are fallible and subject to various kinds of cognitive bias in favour of their own interests. Recognizing such natural limitations, individuals will treat other people's views about their interests and entitlements with suspicion. Thus, given our natural limitations, democratic procedures seem necessary institutional conditions to facilitate individuals seeing themselves as having been treated as equals. Even when we aim for just outcomes, we must aim for them via democratic procedures that offer everyone the opportunity to believe that her judgement is taken seriously.[13]

A third argument for democracy observes a more intimate connection between democratic rights and the interests and status of free and equal persons. The two arguments above specify a set of goods that can be described without essential reference to democratic procedures. In the first, justice is described without reference to any kind of decision procedure and the task of institutional design is to fashion a procedure that will best realize justice so construed. In the second, justice is described in a manner that, among other things, makes reference to a certain procedural interest: the interest in being able to see that one's interests are given due consideration. But in this argument there is an instrumental argument for democracy as the best means of satisfying this interest: while other political regimes could, in principle, satisfy that interest, democracy is best suited to the task, given human limitations. The third argument, however, offers an account of our interests and status that makes an essential, and not merely a contingent, reference to the enjoyment of democratic rights.

As I have noted, an anti-perfectionist liberal view does not operate with an account of our interests that appeals to full information about well-being. Instead, it rests on a limited set of claims about the interests we have as free and equal persons. We have fundamental interests in developing and exercising our two moral powers: the capacity for a sense of justice and for a conception of the good. It is the first moral power that is relevant to our present concern. The capacity for a sense of justice is the capacity to understand, to apply, and to act from a conception of fair terms of social cooperation. Rawls's view is that an adequate set of principles of justice must cater for this interest and our status as full and equal citizens in virtue of possessing a sense of justice to a minimally sufficient degree. Exercising a sense of justice requires an individual to form judgements about fair social cooperation and to be included in the decision-making body that applies such judgements in the formation of authoritative laws. If citizens are equal in virtue of possessing a sense of justice so construed, it is not sufficient for each to be included within the law-making body; each must be included *on equal terms*. Thus, a full description of our interests in exercising a sense of justice, and the equal status that is conferred in virtue of having such a power, necessarily leads to the inclusion of a principle of equal participation within the principle of basic liberties that is our just entitlement. In this view, we have an interest in having an equal right to bring our sense of justice to bear on issues concerning fair social cooperation.[14]

There are, then, multiple bases for our commitment to democracy, each of which begins with the fundamental ideal of just social cooperation. The upshot of these arguments is that taking justice seriously implies taking democracy seriously, which means that the democratic decisions of citizens motivated by a sense of justice carry legitimate authority. The natural duty of justice supports compliance with such democratic laws, because justice demands democratically determined law.

Let us now readdress the question of whether individuals have a duty to obey laws that do not fully realize justice. We have not yet fully answered this question, because for all we have established it might be thought that to have legitimate authority the law must be democratically decided *and* fully just. While we should reject this extreme view, it contains a kernel of truth. The justice-based defence of democracy does not regard democratic law as unconditionally legitimate. Instead, law has legitimate authority if it is the *democratic outcome of citizens bringing their sense of justice to bear on issues of social cooperation.* Thus, the ideal of just social cooperation supports not merely the establishment of democratic institutions but it also requires individuals who participate within these institutions to be motivated in the right way—each must act from a sense of justice, rather than from a sense of her rational advantage.

We are edging closer to the educational implications of this account of political legitimacy. We are confronted with the question of what it means for individuals to be motivated to act from a sense of justice. I shall discuss the content of the idea of a sense of justice in Section 4.3. Here I want to make a preliminary remark on the need to invoke a threshold of justice in the context of our discussion of democratic legitimacy. The extreme view of legitimacy cited in the previous paragraph holds that the law is legitimate only if it is both *fully* just and democratically determined. We must reject this view, because it is often better from the point of view of justice to have somewhat unjust laws than to have no authoritative law at all. As we have seen, effective social cooperation requires authoritative laws, which coordinate the conduct of many and provide individuals with the necessary assurance that their cooperative endeavour will be reciprocated by others. Even if a particular law is unjust, we may still have a reason to comply with it in the service of effective cooperation that generally conforms with justice. In short, we have a standing reason of justice to obey the body of laws that applies to us if it is sufficiently just.

We face the problem, therefore, of defining the threshold of justice above which democratic law is legitimate (even when it is not fully just). To resolve the problem, there seems no alternative but to appeal to an ideal of just social cooperation. But we should distinguish two different ways in which this project might proceed. In *the shortfall from full justice view*, as I shall call it, we begin by describing a complete conception of justice that specifies a set of determinate principles of justice. Rawls's two principles of justice and Dworkin's account of liberal equality are two different conceptions, which are candidates for the label 'complete' in the sense I have in mind. On the basis of our affirmation of such a conception of justice, the shortfall from full justice view asks us to determine a threshold by reference to that conception of justice. For example, if we adopted Rawls's two principles, educational policies that violate the principle of fair equality of opportunity would be more worrying from the point of view of justice compared to the failure to realize the difference principle in the distribution of wealth and income. Eventually, we would need to identify which kinds of departures from full justice are so significant that they render democratic institutions illegitimate.

In a second view, call it *the adequate realization of fundamental ideals*, we seek to identify the threshold by reference to the fundamental ideals that are constitutive of just social cooperation. In Dworkin's liberalism, this is defined according to the two grounding commitments of ethical individualism: the principle of equal objective importance of individuals' lives and the principle that individuals have special responsibility for the lives they lead.[15] In Rawls's work, the fundamental political ideal is defined in terms of fair and well-ordered social cooperation between free and equal persons. On the basis of this ideal, he offers an account of the interests of individuals as free and equal persons, as having the moral powers for a sense of justice and a capacity for a conception of the good, and of their equal status in virtue of the possession of these powers. From these he derives an account of certain properties that is constitutive of a reasonable political conception of justice. Such a conception must, first, he argues, include a principle that gives priority to the protection of basic democratic rights, familiar liberties such as freedom of conscience, association, and expression, and opportunities to pursue office. And, second, it must distribute resources so that everyone can make 'intelligent and effective use of their liberties and opportunities'.[16]

In Rawls's view, justice as fairness is the most reasonable conception of justice in the sense that it works up the ideals of fair social cooperation between free and equal persons most adequately. However, as we noted earlier (Section 1.3.1), Rawls is aware that the burdens of judgement apply to conceptions of justice as well as to conceptions of the good and, therefore, he acknowledges that there exists a family of reasonable conceptions of justice. While other conceptions of justice might not be as reasonable as justice as fairness, they are, nonetheless, reasonable in virtue of satisfying the properties described above that are derived from the fundamental ideal of fair social cooperation between free and equal persons. In this way, law that is premised on a reasonable conception of justice is legitimate, even if other more reasonable conceptions of justice are available. This is simply an acknowledgement of the need for political settlement and the deployment of majoritarian decision-making procedures as a means of effecting that settlement between adherents of different conceptions that satisfy the threshold.

There may not be significantly different outcomes between the two approaches to setting the threshold of justice for political legitimacy. Nevertheless, the adequate realization of the fundamental ideals view coheres better with the ideal of political autonomy defended earlier. Recall that the ideal asserts the desirability of offering individuals the opportunity to regard themselves as under laws they set themselves; that they affirm the principles that constrain them. Given the inevitability of reasonable comprehensive pluralism, political autonomy so understood favours anti-perfectionist principles of justice. With respect to pluralism over conceptions of justice, acknowledging the need for a reasonable political conception, but also the need for a political settlement between adherents of different reasonable conceptions of justice, the ideal of political autonomy supports an approach to that settlement which offers individuals the opportunity to regard the principles that constrain them as legitimate. Principles might be regarded as reasonable, if not fully reasonable, when they satisfy the threshold of reasonableness cited above; they can be treated as legitimate in virtue of being a democratic choice between different conceptions that satisfy the reasonableness threshold.[17]

This completes the sketch of an account of liberal legitimacy in which justice and democracy play key roles without the consent of the governed. Because legitimacy is constituted by the democratic will of citizens bringing their reasonable convictions of justice to bear on public issues, it is essential that citizens have a sense of justice that satisfies the relevant threshold of acceptability. Contrary to the consent-based critique of the political motivation model, then, the ideal of liberal legitimacy as outlined here does not simply reject the need for the free and informed consent of the governed but it also provides positive reasons for shaping the political motivations of children as a means of getting them to hold sufficiently reasonable political convictions such that, collectively, their democratic will becomes authoritative law.

I finish this section, however, by qualifying this conclusion in the face of a natural objection that arises from the role played by the ideal of political autonomy in this account of political legitimacy. For some might argue that the ideal of political autonomy supports citizenship education according to the model of political literacy rather than the political motivation model. Even if we reject the consent-based critique of motivation shaping, there is, some would insist, an autonomy-based critique that trades on the same concern about manipulation that the former has. Stated as a worry about autonomy, the argument might run as follows. If we care about individual autonomy, we should enable individuals to develop and exercise their own convictions about justice free from manipulation by others. That seems to be the implication of the appeal to independence in defence of the precondition view of autonomy with respect to matters of religion and other comprehensive doctrines (Section 3.4). If others wrong me by enrolling me into a particular controversial comprehensive practice before I have the mental powers to give or withhold morally binding consent, then surely the same goes for those who seek to enrol me into a controversial family of conceptions of justice. In short, is it not a violation of my autonomy if I am enrolled into reasonableness?

There are two ways in which this challenge might be rebutted. First, we might believe that the ideals of individuals becoming autonomous and them developing a sense of justice are independent. On this view, while shaping children's motivations so that they have a desire to act justly would be, in one way, good for them as free and equal persons; it would be worse for them in another way, because the manipulation involved in the process would reduce their autonomy. But even if this is accepted, it remains plausible, I claim, that the badness of their loss of autonomy may well be outweighed by the benefits of their developing a stable sense of justice. This is the case because even if some autonomy is lost, the principles of justice to which they are educated protect and promote their interests in leading autonomous lives through the range of institutions and policies they justify. Moreover, it is not even clear that the model of political literacy would protect their interest in autonomy to a greater extent, because, by hypothesis, the political asset of having a suitably motivated citizenry may be realized to a lesser degree, which would, in turn, make it more unlikely that liberal principles would prevail. Nevertheless, in this view, some autonomy would be lost by the shaping of children's political convictions, even if this may be the price that must be paid for liberal institutions that protect autonomy, among other things.[18]

A different view, which is more compelling, holds that the good of autonomy is conditional upon the agent acting reasonably: the value of leading an autonomous life is dependent upon that life being a reasonable one, i.e. one that complies with a reasonable set of principles of justice. In this view, a person whose life is autonomous in the sense described in earlier chapters, but who successfully pursues goals that are beyond the pale, does not lead a life that is even in one way successful, or good for him or her.[19] Of course, it is consistent with this view to say that it would be better for us if our sense of justice is developed without manipulation. Yet the view does not necessarily hold that it is better for us to have unmanipulated political convictions *tout court*. Given the *conditional* value of autonomy, it may well be better for us to have a manipulated sense of justice rather than an unmanipulated sense of injustice.[20] According to this interpretation, the political motivation model of education is worse only for those who would have developed a sense of justice without being so manipulated. This generates an interesting response to the choice between two models with which we began this chapter. If we are optimistic about the capacity of human nature to develop a sense of justice without the involvement of educational institutions to form or shape that sense, the liberal ideal may support the model of political literacy. Motivation shaping would, because it may threaten valuable autonomy, be illegitimate as well as unnecessary. If we are less optimistic, however, and see the need for a sense of justice to be imparted to individuals, then, because the value of autonomy is conditional upon the agent's reasonableness, there is no threat to autonomy in developing children's sense of justice. Thus, the shaping of children's political motivations is just if it is necessary.

4.3 THE AIMS OF CITIZENSHIP EDUCATION

In Section 4.2, I rebutted a prominent critique of the political motivation model of citizenship education, which rests on the claim that the actual consent of the governed is necessary for political legitimacy. That critique rightly claims that the conditions for free and informed consent require political literacy and forbid the shaping of children's motivations. However, the critique fails, I argued, because legitimacy is possible without the actual consent of the governed. Indeed, we have a natural duty of justice that consists of a duty to support and promote just institutions and to comply with sufficiently just democratic institutions that apply to us. In this section, I elaborate an account of the aims of citizenship education in a liberal society, i.e. a society that already adheres to one of a family of reasonable political conceptions.

I reiterate at the outset the limited nature of my inquiry. As in other debates about principles of educational provision, many, perhaps most, of the important issues we face are technical and strategic in character. If, as I have claimed, motivation shaping in citizenship education is, in principle, permissible or required from the point of view of legitimacy or justice, there remain large questions to address concerning which techniques of belief formation or desire formation, if any, would successfully develop a sense of justice in children. For example, some might argue that citizenship education in schools is unnecessary, because individuals can develop the required sense of justice through participation within democratic institutions, voluntary associations, or the family. Others claim that while these are important seedbeds of a sense of justice, so too are formal educational institutions.[21] And if we accept that the latter should seek to cultivate a sense of justice in children, we need to ask which educational means are best suited to deliver this aim. Recently, the national curriculum of England was revised to include citizenship as a part of the core educational entitlement. Yet there are other ways, apart from through the formal curriculum, in which the shaping of motivations might be effected. It could, instead, be fostered through the rules and ethos of the school and by enabling children to cooperate with their peers in the right way. In addition, if we decide that the formal curriculum is an appropriate means by which to form a sense of justice, we need to assess whether citizenship should be taught as a separate subject, or whether it is better realized through other subjects, such as the study of literature, history, or geography.

While I touch briefly on some of these matters in Section 4.5, as a way of illustrating certain issues liberals face in developing a sense of justice in citizens in non-ideal circumstances, I do not offer a thorough examination of them, important though they are. Instead, in formulating a theory of justice and legitimacy in upbringing that sees the formation of a sense of justice as a required activity, my remarks are largely restricted to setting out the appropriate *aims* of education for justice. Much of the work in itemizing these aims has been done in previous sections. Nevertheless, it is worth setting out reasonably systematically the different features of a sense of justice and the associated political virtues liberal educators should seek to develop. I do so under two headings: public reason and deliberative virtue; and compliance and participation.

4.3.1 Public Reason and Deliberative Virtue

Recall then that a sense of justice consists in understanding and being motivated to follow a reasonable conception of justice. Thus, a liberal citizen understands the political relation in a certain way. She understands political conceptions, principles, institutions, and policies as items that should be evaluated at the bar of justice. This offers a distinctive account of the relationship between citizen and politician compared to a prevalent understanding within contemporary liberal democracies. For the latter treats citizens as permitted to use the political influence at their disposal to press for law and policies that serve their rational self-interest, irrespective of the justice of the laws in question. Choosing between political parties solely on the basis of the question 'what's in it for me?' is contrary to the ideal of liberal citizenship. Of course, liberal democracies protect an entitlement of citizens to participate in such a self-serving manner, through the guarantee of freedom of speech, equal votes, and a secret ballot. We cannot therefore forcibly prevent citizens from exercising their votes in ways inimical to the liberal standard. Nevertheless, in so far as citizens fail to address political matters from the point of view of justice, the ideal of liberal legitimacy remains unrealized.

A liberal citizenry is, then, a morally motivated citizenry. In addition, acting from a sense of justice is a deliberative enterprise. It exhibits some of the qualities that Burke cited in describing ideal parliamentarians. In explanation of his claim that Members of Parliament owe their constituents their judgement as well as industry, he remarked:

> If government were a matter of will upon any side, yours [the constituents'], without question, ought to be superior. But government and legislation are matters of reason and judgement, and not of inclination; and what sort of reason is that in which the determination precedes the discussion, in which one set of men deliberate and another decide, and where those who form the conclusion are perhaps three hundred miles distant from those who hear the arguments?[22]

Plainly, Burke was no liberal of the kind we have in mind. Nevertheless, the ideal liberal citizen, like Burke's ideal parliamentarian, rejects conceptions of the political relation that view it in terms of the aggregation of personal preferences, or a fair bargaining procedure to determine which coalition of personal concerns should prevail. Instead, ideal liberal citizens regard themselves as under a duty to use their deliberative capacities to form, revise, and apply a conception of justice.

Before we add any further content to the idea of a liberal citizenry that acts in compliance with legitimacy and justice, we can generate a number of educational aims from the ideal of political deliberation alone. Such aims are common to all conceptions of deliberative politics, whether guided by socialist, liberal, libertarian, or conservative political ends.[23] In the conception of politics as deliberation, the ideal of citizen engagement has a particular character. Citizens regard themselves as addressing questions concerning what they owe to each other through the principal political, social, and economic institutions of society. These significant questions, they take it, are ones that admit better and worse answers, and citizens regard themselves as under a duty to engage with such questions with the appropriate level of seriousness. Treating the subject responsibly, citizens aim to form, revise, and operate with political reasons that exhibit a number of desirable properties. Jointly, we might call these the ideal of common human reason.[24] They include the following: one's political conception should be internally consistent; its different ideals and values should hang together, and not rest on dangling distinctions, so far as this is avoidable; and it should be appropriately sensitive to the evidence and principles of valid inference and of other kinds of reasoning.

Just as in confronting questions about the good life, political deliberation is enhanced by vigorous public debate about political matters, in which individuals and groups exchange ideas and argue with each other. Ideally, those debates should be ones in which citizens and politicians recognize the possibility that their present views might be mistaken or only partially right and, therefore, are willing to engage with those who hold contrary beliefs. Thus, the deliberative citizen is one who is committed to modes of discourse in which appropriate forms of reasoning rather than rhetoric are the modus operandi. To be sure, it is not part of the ideal that citizens seek to avoid causing offence to others; offence is an inevitable outcome of the exchange of ideas, and may have positive effects in terms of getting people to reflect on convictions they tend to affirm in an unreflective manner.[25] Nevertheless, personalized insults should be minimized in democratic debate, because they tend to distract us from reasoned deliberation about politics. Thus, deliberative citizens display a set of skills and virtues related to deliberative interaction: skills related to articulating a position and the reasons for its affirmation; listening skills; the ability charitably to understand the views of others; analytical skills that facilitate a critical assessment of different positions; an appreciation of the benefits of exchanging ideas; and a commitment to reason rather than to employ attractive slogans or rhetoric.

In addition to a commitment to deliberation, which is common between a number of different political conceptions, the liberal view places distinctive constraints on the kinds of reason to which citizens may appeal. Among the most significant constraints under which citizens operate are those generated by the duty of reciprocity, which includes the duty of civility. First, I shall discuss civility. Citizens honour the duty of civility if they are:

> able to explain to one another on those fundamental questions [concerning constitutional essentials and matters of basic justice] how the principles and policies they advocate and vote for can be supported by the political values of public reason. This duty also involves a willingness to listen to others and a fair-mindedness in deciding when accommodations to their views should reasonably be made.[26]

Although liberal citizens are guided by moral norms, they are not necessarily guided by the whole truth about morality or ethics. For, as we have established, the ideal of liberal legitimacy requires agreement between reasonable individuals in the service of the political autonomy of each citizen. Consequently, the reasons we offer to each other as citizens must be grounded on reasons that can be acknowledged by other reasonable citizens, given the reasonable comprehensive pluralism, which is the inevitable product of free institutions. The public reason restriction, then, operates as a constraint on the reasons to which we may appeal in political deliberation. Earlier, I defended the extension of that restriction to govern parental conduct (Section 3.3). Here, we see that the public reason restriction generates further important educational aims. Children should be raised to appreciate the merits of deliberation through public reason and taught the associated virtue of political restraint. In particular, the aim must be that they acknowledge the importance of holding comprehensive values they endorse, or come to endorse, in a liberal spirit.[27] This means that as citizens, they refuse to use the institutions of the basic structure of society as instruments for the promotion of the particular comprehensive doctrines they affirm. Furthermore, they see that the ideal of liberal legitimacy requires them to articulate reasons for law and policy that do not depend upon controversial comprehensive claims.

The virtue of political restraint is an interpretation of the virtue of tolerance, but it interprets that idea through the ideal of liberal legitimacy and its requirement of anti-perfectionist political conduct: to tolerate another individual is to refrain from engaging in conduct that is unwelcome to him, conduct that we regard as prima facie justified on the basis of our assessment of his behaviour or character.[28] Tolerance in this general sense is not restricted to the political domain. A believer may display tolerance towards an atheist by not ridiculing the latter's beliefs or lifestyle in her presence when the believer sincerely believes the atheist leads a degraded life. This kind of tolerance can characterize one's non-political relationships and need not make any reference to the political domain. The virtue of political restraint, in contrast, is a political ideal and relates to the basic structure, rather than to one's conduct within that structure. To be sure, as we noted earlier, this does not imply that political restraint is a virtue that is limited to our use of coercion, because conduct can be basic structural without being coercive (Section 1.5). Nevertheless, political restraint is an ideal of citizenship, not a comprehensive ideal that tells us how to deal with others within the various relationships and associations that are permitted by the basic structure. To take a topical case, consider the issue of gay and lesbian rights to hold office. We must distinguish between public office and the offices of an association, such as a church. If we are tolerant in a general and comprehensive way, within a church, say, then we may well support proposals to permit gay clergy, even if we regard homosexuality as a sin. Yet the ideal of political restraint does not insist on that kind of generalized tolerance. It is sufficient for political restraint that citizens put aside their comprehensive convictions when considering candidates for public office and different principles and policies to govern the basic structure.[29]

Let me now turn to reciprocity, which is the norm of sincerely proposing principles, laws, and policies that realize fair terms of cooperation between free and equal persons, i.e. persons who possess a sense of justice, the capacity for a conception of the good, and who follow a particular comprehensive conception. Part of the duty of reciprocity is civility, because we must propose a conception of social cooperation that can be accepted by others without them having to reject their different reasonable comprehensive doctrines. But the duty of reciprocity has a richer content than civility. For example, certain libertarian conceptions respect the requirement of civility, because their political morality is relevantly anti-perfectionist. In Nozick's libertarian conception of political morality, for example, individuals and groups are free to associate with whomever they choose. His argument for the self-ownership rights and the particular regime of private property he defends does not rest on controversial claims about the good life, but on a conception of what we may not do to one another. In this respect, Nozick's libertarianism is a political conception.[30] But it not a liberal conception, because it fails to satisfy the liberal criterion of reciprocity.[31]

Reciprocity, in general, is satisfied by a political conception that attaches priority to the protection of basic liberal and democratic rights, and that offers every citizen a fair share of the social and economic means to develop and exercise her fundamental interests as a free and equal person and to pursue the comprehensive doctrine she affirms. With respect to the latter, Rawls specifies a set of conditions that keeps social and economic inequalities within a range that satisfies reciprocity so understood: the ideal of politics, which is free of manipulation by powerful economic interests, that justifies the public financing of elections; the provision of educational opportunity so that everyone can contribute to public debate; a distribution of wealth and income that provides everyone with the wherewithal effectively to use her freedom; employment provision that offers everyone meaningful work, which facilitates the maintenance of her self-respect; and basic medical provision for every citizen.[32] This list further specifies the idea of a liberal political conception by offering a conception of the adequate realization of the fundamental ideal of fair cooperation between free and equal persons (Section 4.2).

In the liberal view, then, the realization of reciprocity is necessary for political legitimacy. The consequences for education are profound. The aim of citizenship education must be to develop in individuals a commitment to democratic deliberation that is constrained by both civility and a sense of the significant social and economic requirements of reciprocity. Just as children should be educated to abhor law and policy that discriminate on racial or sexual grounds, they should also be brought to appreciate the injustice of political ideologies that do not afford citizens the right kind of concern and respect. The failure of a certain kind of libertarian conception to offer sufficient guarantees to citizens in respect of health, opportunity, wealth and income, and political participation is a case in point.[33]

4.3.2 Compliance and Participation

We have reviewed the important constraints that the ideal of deliberation through public reason places on citizens and, consequently, on education for justice. But we have not yet considered the extent to which individuals should be political active, or the legitimate kinds of activity in which individuals might engage to effect political change. For, first, it is quite coherent to believe that (*a*) *if* individuals engage in politics, they should do so on certain terms shaped by the requirements of public reason, but that (*b*) the liberal state is not permitted to shape people's motivations such that they form a desire to participate politically. We need, therefore, to discuss educational aims with respect to the extent of political engagement. Call this the question of participation. And, second, we must discuss whether an education for justice should encourage compliance with the law or equip individuals with the skills and virtues to challenge the law through legal and illegal means. Call this the question of compliance.

To answer the question of compliance we must return to the natural duty of justice. Part of that duty states that we have a duty to comply with just institutions that apply to us. If a person resides in a territory governed by a just, or nearly just, basic structure, then she has a standing reason to obey the law. The justification of such a duty appeals to the normal justification of political authority. Our fundamental duty is to act justly—to do our just share in a scheme of social cooperation that respects the freedom and equality of everyone. Now, if our compliance with the law enables us better to do our fair share in such a scheme, compared to acting on our own individual judgements about what justice demands, then we have a duty so to comply.

Some have argued that the natural duty of justice cannot generate a duty of compliance. For instance, Simmons argues that a just institution can apply to us territorially without producing a duty to obey its rules. His example is a geographically bounded philosophy institute into which the sons and daughters of philosophers are born. In every respect, we are asked to suppose, the activities of the institute are just. The children are considered philosophers at least up to the point at which they are grown up and choose to exit from the area. Simmons claims that it is clear that the institute and its rules apply to the children in a territorial sense, but it is, nonetheless, counter-intuitive to assert that they have a duty to obey its rules.[34]

But Simmons's example is an inadequate test for the claim that the natural duty of justice can generate duties of obedience, because we may question the justice of the institute. The institute is defined according to a particular comprehensive doctrine that can be rejected by reasonable people. In this respect, it is like an association guided by a particular ethical vision rather than like a just political domain. To be sure, Simmons is right to claim that an association of civil society has no right to rule over children merely in virtue of being a just association and the fact that the children are born to its existing members. But this truth is compatible with the justification of political authority, which the natural duty of justice follows, and, therefore, does not supply an argument against it.

The justification of authority rests on the idea that one is duty-bound to comply if compliance both enables one better to act on one's reasons *and it is better for one to conform with reason than to act according to one's own judgement.*[35] Yet, there are many cases in which it is better to act according to our own judgement even if it means that we fail to conform with the reasons that apply to us. If I dine out with someone who unilaterally takes it upon herself to choose my meal, then I may refuse her choice and choose my own meal, however bad I am at choosing in that particular restaurant. Similarly, however good the reasons are to pursue a life of philosophical reflection, the decision as to the kind of life one leads should be left to oneself.

A better analogy to test the duty to comply with just institutions that apply to us territorially is one in which there is no question about the justice or legitimacy of the rules of the institution in question. One example is the just family home. If a child is born into a home that is governed by just principles and rules, does she have a duty to obey those rules? Here, common intuition supports the answer that the child does have such a duty. Since the familial and political domains are relevantly similar, in being non-voluntary relationships for children and citizens respectively, this intuition supports the claim that there is a duty to comply with a just set of political institutions that applies to us territorially.[36]

The natural duty of justice, then, involves a duty to obey the laws of a just basic structure. As we have discussed, it also supports a standing reason to comply with a nearly just political regime, one which adequately realizes the fundamental liberal ideal of fair social cooperation. In a nearly just society the standing reason to obey the law means that there is a similarly weighty reason to obey each law, irrespective of the justice of the particular law in question. To take a familiar example, many people believe that laws prohibiting euthanasia are unjust, because, among other things, they unfairly deprive individuals of the freedom to avoid a painful or undignified death. But if the basic structure satisfies the relevant threshold for legitimacy, such people have a duty to obey this law that is as strong as their duty to obey laws, the justice of which is unanimously and rightly acknowledged. Yet the presence of the standing reason to obey the law is not always decisive, because the standing reason is only a *pro tanto* reason. In other words, the reason we have to obey the law of a legitimate society is a weighty reason, but there may be competing reasons that, when all the relevant reasons are balanced, tell against obedience. One such reason stems from the good of civil disobedience: non-violent, public law-breaking as a means of bringing to the attention of the majority one's sincerely held conviction that a particular law is unjust. A liberal regime accepts the (by definition moral but non-legal) right of civil disobedience in the sense that it accepts the permissibility of engaging in such law-breaking when certain conditions hold. In addition, it resolves to judge and punish such illegal activity leniently: the penalties it imposes on the civilly disobedient are less burdensome than those imposed on similar law-breaking that is not motivated by the desire to bring a perceived injustice to the public's attention.[37]

The aims of education for justice should be attentive to these considerations. Individuals should understand the nature and justification of political authority and how it is related to the ideals of justice and the need for political settlement on controversial issues. They also need to appreciate the various means by which perceived injustices might be challenged. An understanding of the legal mechanisms of political change is clearly a large part of that appreciation, but they should also be familiarized with the nature, justification, and role of civil disobedience in a liberal society. Moreover, liberal citizens must have a sophisticated set of political dispositions that, on the one hand, leads them to surrender their judgement by acknowledging the authority of law in a legitimate society, and, on the other, to be vigilant in assessing the justice of particular laws and to have the courage to challenge the majority view through legal and, sometimes, illegal channels.

Let us turn now to the question of participation, with respect to which we might distinguish three views. First, political participation might be viewed as a requirement of liberal citizens. Second, it might be treated as optional.[38] Third, we might treat it as a conditional requirement. In the third view, participation in politics is required if certain conditions hold; otherwise it is optional. The conditions might cite times of war, or other circumstances in which the survival or flourishing of the liberal polity is in jeopardy.

To adjudicate between these views, we must first clarify what is meant by participation. There is clearly a broad range of activities that fall under this description. Willing obedience of the law, paying taxes, and contributing to the economy through one's labour are all forms of participation that are preconditions of any stable political regime. The kinds of political participation that are controversial, however, concern voting, acquainting oneself with the issues on the political agenda, holding politicians and officials to account, engaging in campaigns for public office, and, in more threatening conditions, fighting for just political institutions. The natural duty of justice asks us to do our fair share in promoting and supporting just institutions. It is therefore hostile to the idea of these kinds of political participation being optional. If the justice of a society is threatened by external aggression, apathy, or internal corruption, individuals are duty-bound to do their fair share to overcome these threats.

Given our liberal foundations, one argument for required participation lacks legitimacy. This is the civic humanist idea that one's well-being depends upon participating as an equal in political affairs. Since this rests on a comprehensive account of what makes one's life go well, which is rejected by many reasonable persons, it cannot be the basis of an argument for required participation within a liberal conception. But as Rawls notes, the classical republican idea that our freedom is secure only if citizens are willing to participate in political affairs does provide an acceptable argument for such a requirement, since the republican insight is compatible with liberal legitimacy.[39] However, the republican view supports only the conditional participatory requirement: that one is duty-bound actively to participate if a flourishing liberal political regime demands it. Yet in all likelihood, such a flourishing regime is facilitated by merely *widespread* participation; it does not depend on the participation of each and every citizen.

One reply that might be made on behalf of required participation appeals to the duty to do one's fair share to support justice. In this view, even if a just society is possible without my participation, I act unjustly if I free-ride on the cooperative efforts of others who participate to realize this good. Each must shoulder a fair share of the burden of political participation. There is some merit in this reply, but we must be clear that its force relies on a particular account of 'the cooperative efforts of others'. If others treat political participation as a *burden* that must be endured for the sake of maintaining justice, the duty to do one's fair share does indeed support a participatory requirement. But suppose that the overwhelming majority consider it beneficial from the point of view of their well-being to participate politically; suppose, then, there is a widespread commitment to civic humanism. In that case, the majority that maintains just institutions does not experience political participation as a burden. Now consider the few individuals who reject civic humanism and who also think that political participation takes 'too many evenings'. Are they nevertheless required to participate? I do not think they are, because there is no objectionable free-riding in this case.

Thus, the duty to shoulder one's fair share of the burden of realizing and maintaining just institutions supports the conditional requirement to participate. In practice, however, the conditional requirement supports required participation, because the imaginary society overwhelmingly populated by civic humanists is not our world. In our world, political participation is a burden that should be fairly shared between citizens. Hence, we have a further aim of education for justice: individuals should be able and willing to participate politically; to form a desire to register their political convictions; and to hold politicians and officials to account.

4.4 QUESTIONS ABOUT NATIONALITY AND GLOBAL JUSTICE

I turn now to two questions of great significance for political education. First, should we, as some have claimed, foster a sense of nationality in children? And, second, what moral attitudes should we seek to inculcate in children with respect to people living in other political societies, with particular reference to the pervasive and severe poverty and other injustices that beset the world?

In the account I have offered, the fundamental aim of political education is the development of a sense of justice. To the extent that individuals possess such a sense, they are disposed to support and comply with legitimate political institutions that apply to them and to promote justice in other contexts. In addition, the liberal view is committed to a set of political and economic institutions that ensure, among other things, that everyone has the social and economic wherewithal to maintain their self-respect and to revise and pursue their comprehensive goals. This set of institutions depends upon a certain kind of tolerance and restraint on the part of a citizen and also a willingness to abide by the outcome of deliberative democratic procedures, even when her interests are not satisfied as much as they might be. Significantly, this account does not require the cultivation of a sense of belonging or mutual sympathy between individuals, or a sense of national identity.

Some have sought to establish a connection between justice and nationality, which supports the claim that an important part of political education should be the development of a sense of nationality. There are various conceptions of what nationality might consist of. To fix ideas, let us take Miller's conception as our reference. In his view, a nation is 'a community (1) constituted by shared belief and mutual commitment, (2) extended in history, (3) active in character, (4) connected to a particular territory, and (5) marked off from other communities by its distinctive public culture'.[40] As he points out, it is a mistake to conflate 'nation' with 'state'. Whereas the latter is defined by reference to a set of political institutions, the former connotes a particular kind of community in which members regard themselves as belonging together and hope to organize their affairs in common with each other.[41] A person who acknowledges a national identity is someone who believes she belongs together with others in a community marked by the characteristics Miller lists.

Our question concerns the relationship between national identity and political education. It is worth distinguishing between two positions. Let us call the inculcation of a national identity by educational institutions *education for nationality.* Advocates of this kind of education propose that educational and political institutions should develop a sense of belonging and affective ties between individuals, such that they feel duty-bound to come to the aid of others in the national group. These aims often generate a call for children and immigrants to be initiated into the public language of the group, to have an understanding of its history, and to be able to participate in maintaining and developing its public culture. This position can be contrasted with *nationality-shaping education*, which holds that although educational institutions should not inculcate a sense of national identity, they should nevertheless respond appropriately to the fact that many people do align themselves to particular nations. Nationality-shaping education aims to employ educational mechanisms to influence an individual's sense of nationality so that it complies with liberal principles.

Miller's defence of nationality lends support to education for nationality. He rejects the view, implicit in my account of political education, that the broadly liberal, democratic, and egalitarian arrangements characteristic of liberal political philosophy are possible between individuals bound together by merely common citizenship, as opposed to common nationality:

> Let us try to imagine how the rights and obligations of citizenship might look if the citizens were tied to one another by nothing beyond the practice of citizenship itself, and were motivated by the principle of fairness. They would insist on strict reciprocity. In other words, each would expect to benefit from their association in proportion to his or her contribution, taking as a baseline the hypothetical state of affairs in which there was no political co-operation between them. So, for instance, redistributive taxation would be agreed to only in circumstances in which each person thought it was rational to insure him- or herself through the state against the possibility of falling below a certain level of resources.[42]

Miller's view appears to produce three different sources of duty, each of which depends upon the kind of relationship that prevails between us. First, we have duties to humans as such, which correlate to a set of basic rights to which every human is entitled. Second, duties of (pure) citizenship require us to uphold institutions that benefit each in accordance with her contribution. Third, obligations of nationality are determined by the public culture of the particular nation in question. Having a national identity disposes one to attach 'special weight to the interests of fellow members'[43] to come to the aid of fellow nationals in need, where need is defined by reference to the national public culture.

We should reject Miller's conception and, in particular, his claim that our reasons to favour liberal and egalitarian political arrangements depend upon the existence of ties of nationality. Consider a counter-example offered by Williams:

> [I]magine there exists one nationalist faction amongst a group of multinational shipwreck survivors, stranded on a moderately abundant desert island. Appealing to the obligations they owe to each other, they exclude non-members from the island's most productive resources, and permit non-members only sufficient resources to guarantee basic security.[44]

As Williams points out, Miller's conception, which seems to countenance such exclusionary behaviour, goes against our intuitive reaction to the case, which is that the nationalist faction is not entitled as a matter of justice to the higher than average living standards they enjoy in virtue of excluding non-nationals.[45] Reflecting on this example, we can appreciate the merits of an education for justice as outlined in previous sections. Being a shipwreck survivor changes the context in which individuals must operate. In the absence of a well-ordered set of political institutions, the survivors must create a fair scheme of social cooperation afresh. The island on which they land is a natural limit, and a salient point of reference, by which to characterize the scope of their duties. Given the status of each survivor as free and equal, the salient political arrangement is to construct a scheme of social cooperation that aims to treat each justly irrespective of her nationality or previous citizenship. Thus, we should reject Miller's meagre account of the duties of citizenship.

Advocates of education for nationality might retreat from claims about our normative reasons to claims about the importance of nationality in terms of motivating individuals to do what justice—theorized independently of nationality—demands. Without a shared national identity, the argument might go, citizens will fail to realize justice. Or, more modestly, the cultivation of a national sentiment might be a beneficial, if not a necessary, means of motivating individuals to pursue justice.[46]

Notice that the modest claim is insufficient to justify education for nationality over nationality-shaping education. This is the case, because from the point of view of liberal legitimacy there are costs to the cultivation of nationality. Thus, if justice can be realized without the inculcation of a particular nationality, just by seeking to shape people's existing national sentiments without favouring any in particular, then this strategy is preferable from a liberal point of view. Let me explain.

Nationality involves the idea that there exists a group characterized by certain shared understandings and practices, the members of which regard themselves as belonging together. Typically, members take pride in the accomplishments of the group and experience shame for its wrongdoing, even if the achievements and moral mistakes of the nation happened before their birth. Furthermore, some nations are essentially related to a particular religion and, as many note, in many cases nation-building begins with the inculcation of a particular language.

From a liberal point of view, the objection to education for nationality in this sense lies in the fact that the merits of having a national identity, and the attractiveness of different particular nationalities, are disputed among reasonable people. Some cosmopolitans, for example, reject the idea of belonging to a nation, and the alleged special obligations that derive from it, preferring instead to identify with globally defined groups according to other criteria, such as religion, occupation, or gender. Moreover, those who do accept the importance of nationality may not share the same national ties. Some British citizens, for instance, define their national identity differently from their citizenship: they see themselves as Indian, Australian, Chinese, and so on, while holding a British passport. Just as the religiously devout are committed to particular groups, traditions, and customs defined by their respective religions, some individuals express national commitments in the sense that they believe they have affective ties, or special obligations, to their fellow nationals who form a subset of the citizenry. But in Britain, as in many others countries, there is no agreement on one conception of nationality.

Other things equal, the ideal of liberal legitimacy favours a model of political education that does not take a stand on the diverse conceptions of living embraced by free and equal persons. So, given the many different conceptions of nationality and of its moral importance, liberal legitimacy has a presumption against adopting some controversial view of national identity into which children ought to be enrolled. It follows that an adequate defence of education for nationality must establish a stronger claim for nationality with respect to justice. It needs to explain why the cultivation of a particular nationality is necessary for the maintenance of legitimate institutions, or why it is an unrivalled means of realizing liberal legitimacy.[47]

These are empirical claims, the soundness of which ultimately depends upon a detailed examination of human moral psychology. Nevertheless, there are reasons to doubt the liberal nationalist's case. As Mason suggests, we must distinguish between a sense of belonging to a polity and a sense of belonging together. In his account, 'a person has a sense of belonging to a polity if and only if she identifies with most of its major institutions and some of its central practices and feels at home in them'.[48] In addition, he offers two empirical hypotheses—(*a*) that liberal political arrangements are possible without a shared national identity; and (*b*) even where there exists a sense of belonging together as fellow nationals, it is citizens' sense of belonging to the polity, rather than the nation, that best explains the stability of their liberal institutions—and on the basis of an interpretation of the politics of the USA, Switzerland, and Belgium, argues that there is some empirical support for them.

In addition, there are certain general considerations that suggest that we can be motivated to pursue justice without shared nationality. First, in the shipwreck case, we believe not merely that the *reasons* that apply to survivors do not depend upon nationality but also that a reasonably just scheme of social cooperation is *feasible* without shared nationality. Second, few seriously suggest that all duties of justice depend upon shared nationality. It is generally recognized that individuals are duty-bound not to kill, physically harm, or steal from others, irrespective of the nationality of the others in question. Moreover, we treat such negative duties as weighty constraints on what we may permissibly do in the service of those to whom we have special attachments.[49] Even if parents may buy better than average football boots for their child, we believe they are morally forbidden from disabling another child who is competing with theirs for a place in a football team. Similarly, while some believe themselves to be under special duties to come to the aid of members of their church or nation, they accept that they may not steal from those outside these communities in order to do so. Part of the task of education for justice, then, is to get individuals to recognize that the duty of justice requires them, in the first instance, not to impose unjust institutions on others, i.e. to honour their negative duties not to wrong others. Common-sense morality, which affirms the stringency of negative duties to others, supplies us with a foundation upon which liberals can build. The task of a liberal political education is to develop a heightened awareness of justice such that individuals come to appreciate that withholding the taxes they owe, say, is not just failing to aid the less advantaged, but is theft in the sense that they are preventing others from enjoying their just share. In this way, a sense of solidarity or shared membership will come to be thought to be irrelevant from the point of view of justice. Thus, the claim that we cannot be motivated to pursue justice in the absence of shared nationality is demonstrably false in the case of many negative duties of justice.

If the development of a sense of justice without nationality is a feasible and appropriate aim of political education, issues remain concerning the attitudes individuals should be encouraged to have with respect to the fate of people in other societies. I have in mind people who live in different political jurisdictions.[50] There are significant differences with respect to the degree to which different societies are legitimate in the liberal sense. Some societies reject the ideal of individual autonomy, fail to honour human rights and basic associative, expressive, and democratic freedoms, and lack the rule of law that is characteristic of good government. Thus, questions arise about the attitude individuals in liberal societies should adopt with respect to non-liberal societies: what are the appropriate limits of toleration? To what extent, if at all, should individuals act to reduce injustice in other societies? Moreover, is it permissible for liberal societies to intervene in the internal affairs of illiberal societies, or to exclude such societies from international cooperative arrangements?

We must also consider liberal political education in the context of the severe poverty that disfigures our world. If we think of severe (absolute) poverty in terms of a lack of access to basic necessities for minimal well-being—to safe food and water, shelter, medical care, and education—the global poverty statistics are appalling: it is estimated that 831 million are chronically undernourished, 1,197 million lack access to safe water; 1,000 million lack adequate shelter; 2,000 million lack essential drugs; about a third of all human deaths each year have poverty-related causes; 876 million adults are illiterate; and 170 million children (between ages five and fourteen) in developing countries do hazardous work.[51] Consider, in addition, the disparities in wealth between the world's rich and poor, as observed by Pogge: 'For the world as a whole, annual *per capita* income is $5,150. With annual *per capita* income of $85, the collective income of the bottom quintile [1,211 million] is about $103 billion annually, or one-third of 1 percent of aggregate global income.'[52] If education is to foster a sense of justice, what should individuals be taught about their duties with respect to global poverty and inequality?

We cannot answer these questions by simply noting the educational implications of liberal political morality on these questions, as if the nature of liberal international political morality is uncontested. For the increasing interest of liberal thinkers in global questions has brought to the surface a profound disagreement between two positions concerning the scope of justice. Cosmopolitan liberals hold that justice has universal reach: fundamentally, every person has equal status, irrespective of citizenship, nationality, religion, or other group-differentiated association; and our duties to others are general in the sense that we are duty-bound to display concern and respect for each person, not merely to one's compatriots or fellow nationals. In this view, any special duties we have towards our fellow citizens, say, must be defended on the basis of these fundamental ideas. We might have particular duties with respect to the basic structure that applies to us, for example, but cosmopolitans insist that the test for the justice of a country's basic structure turns on whether that structure is consistent with our honouring the general duty we have to treat each person in the world with equal concern and respect. We may have a duty of justice to contribute through taxation to the maintenance of the particular social and political institutions of our society, for example, but the defence of that duty must show how our political regime does not jeopardize the fulfilment of our duties to those who live in other societies.

In contrast, social liberals hold that global justice is a matter of just relations between different societies or peoples.[53] They claim that social justice is primarily a matter of individuals receiving their just share through the societal basic structure that governs their lives. Justice between peoples is conceived as fashioning principles to govern the relationship between separate just, legitimate, or, perhaps, decent, peoples. If a particular society reaches a threshold of moral acceptability, it has equal standing within a so-called 'society of peoples', and is then governed by a law of peoples, which is a law that each people can agree to consistently with it preserving its self-government. In Rawls's version, the principles of the law of peoples include respect for a people's freedom and independence, the right of self-defence, and a number of duties: to observe treaties, of non-intervention in other people's affairs, to respect human rights, of justice in the waging of war, and to assist peoples who are failing to realize justice or decency because of unfavourable circumstances.[54]

Some social liberals hold that justice is the price to be paid for the right to rule. If a basic structure claims political authority over a particular jurisdiction, and thereby asks its citizens to surrender their judgements to its laws, the legitimacy of that claim depends on whether the basic structure treats its citizens justly.[55] In this view, justice has a restricted scope. The British state must ensure a just distribution of benefits and burdens between its various citizens. But the question of a just distribution of benefits between its own citizens and individuals living outside its authority does not arise, because, by hypothesis, the British state is not claiming the right to rule over the latter. To be sure, social liberals who reject global duties of *justice* to individuals do not reject global duties *tout court*. Most acknowledge the existence of duties of humanity, duties not to coerce or enslave others, and to come to the rescue of those in dire need. Moreover, there may remain issues of justice between different peoples. But if every person has access to a minimally decent life, questions of justice between individuals may not arise in virtue of the significant inequalities that prevail between one's own citizens and those in other societies.[56]

Cosmopolitans address issues of global justice by asking questions about the fundamental entitlements of individuals. States and peoples have only secondary importance from the point of view of justice. However, social liberals address global justice in terms of principles to regulate the cooperation between independent societies or peoples. The claims of individuals are considered only in setting a threshold, which determines whether a society has standing in what Rawls calls 'a society of peoples'. Once that is settled, the different peoples themselves have standing as self-determining units for the purposes of selecting principles of international political morality.

Theoretically, the distinction between cosmopolitan and social liberalism is profound. The dispute goes to the heart of our understanding of justice and political morality. Here, I do not attempt to decide between these different liberal conceptions. More modestly, I claim that, in practice, a set of global duties can be generated by any plausible interpretation of either conception. Call the set of such moral norms the minimum content of international political morality. It includes various human rights: the right to life, including rights of access to the necessary conditions of minimal human well being, such as safe food and water, shelter, and medical care, freedom from enslavement and torture, security from genocide, freedom of conscience, the right to personal property, and the rule of law. It also includes the claim that everyone is under duties generated by human rights. Here, it is crucial to register the distinction between negative and positive duties. As noted above, it is commonly believed that it is morally worse for one to impose a harm on a person compared to one failing to prevent a harm being imposed on her by another. Furthermore, it is often thought that it is worse to fail to compensate an individual for a harm one has imposed upon her than to fail to rectify a harm she has suffered at someone else's hands.[57] We have duties, then, of a less stringent kind to come to the aid of individuals who are suffering human rights abuses at the hands of their own governments. Having a less stringent duty, does not, of course, mean that we lack a duty. There has been considerable debate on the question of the extent of our duties to come to the aid of others in dire need.[58] But we need not delve too deeply into this debate to characterize the minimum content of international political morality. Pogge observes that the richest 955 million humans, who share about 81 per cent of the global product would need to give up just 1 per cent of that product to raise the least wealthy 44 per cent of the world's population (2,735 million) above the World Bank's $2 per day poverty line.[59] It is hard to see how anyone acknowledging the existence of positive duties to come to the aid of those in extreme poverty could reasonably object to a tax regime that raised the necessary 1 per cent of global income to eradicate severe poverty worldwide.

But a similar conclusion can be reached if we reflect on our negative duties. As Pogge argues, severe poverty and other human rights abuses in the world are, at least in part, caused by the policies of, and international agreements between, rich nations. Contrary to claims that global poverty can be fully explained by factors specific to particular political regimes, he shows how various global institutional practices in which rich countries participate harm the globally least advantaged. Such practices include protectionism through the use of tariffs, import quotas, export credits, and subsidies to domestic industries; the unwillingness of rich countries to sign up to rules that ensure every country pays for the negative externalities, in terms of pollution and resource depletion, it causes; and the recognition by rich countries of corrupt or oppressive governments in developing countries, which involves extending to such governments privileges with respect to borrowing, resources, and arms purchases that perpetuate the poverty and other human rights violations to which the people are subjected by their oppressive rulers.

In these and other ways, then, the governments of rich and powerful countries are partially responsible for the harm the poor and oppressed suffer in other societies. Moreover, we need not specify any particular conception of harm in this context in order to establish the claim. One of the theoretical and polemical attractions of Pogge's account is its ecumenical notion of 'harm'. The world's poor and oppressed are harmed by rich and powerful nations whether we appeal to a Lockean account of the conditions under which individuals may be excluded from using the world's resources, a Nozickean account of the requirement to rectify historical injustices, such as colonialism, or a liberal account in which harm is construed as being subject to social institutions, which avoidably provide one with less than some specified amount.[60]

Pogge teaches us that rich nations do not simply routinely fail to come to the aid of other people in severe poverty, but they wrong these people by collectively imposing global rules that harm them. Thus, citizens of rich countries cannot legitimately be satisfied by their more or less generous responses to appeals for famine relief funds. Instead, they need to rethink the problems related to global poverty and other human rights abuses as problems that they collectively, through their governments, have partially caused and continue to perpetuate. If we should be taught that it is our duty to challenge the injustices of our society through legal and illegal means, then part of that duty, perhaps the most important part given the gravity of its effects, is to campaign for a more just foreign policy.

4.5. POLITICAL EDUCATION IN NON-IDEAL CIRCUMSTANCES

Having sketched a liberal account of political education for nearly just societies, I turn now to issues that arise in non-ideal circumstances. Plainly, a society might fall short of political legitimacy in more or less serious ways, and the account of political education we affirm must be sensitive to such differences. At the most abstract level, I propose a consequentialist conception of political education that coheres with the natural duty of justice. On this view, we favour educational policy or other educational inititiatives that can reasonably be expected to promote the realization of legitimate political arrangements. Given the claims made above concerning the need for a citizenry motivated to promote, support, and comply with legitimate institutions, it follows that whether liberals should support a particular educational initiative depends upon the kind of political understanding and motivation that it would produce. In non-ideal circumstances this will turn on a number of factors, which must be gauged with due consideration of the empirical facts. However, I shall not discuss these empirical questions. From the point of view of outlining a theory of political education, it suffices to raise the pertinent questions that must be addressed.

A consequentialist approach to education for justice in non-ideal circumstances will necessarily recommend different responses to different kinds of unjust circumstances. It will consider, for example, the nature and gravity of the problem of injustice in a particular society, the political agenda that might be more or less fixed in the society in question, and the political and social context that affects the likely consequences of the different decisions we might take with respect to education.

In the first place, a liberal consequentialist will not always recommend a state-directed policy of political education. In certain environments it may be better for liberals to side with consent theorists and others who deny the legitimacy of any kind of motivation-shaping political education, if adopting such a rule would effectively constrain the activities of seriously unjust states with respect to inculcating an acceptance of injustice through schooling and other techniques. If liberation must be won by the oppressed themselves, as many suggest, the kind of education required for liberation may have to take a particular form. As Friere has pointed out in the context of the role of educators in liberating the oppressed:

> Critical and liberating dialogue, which presupposes action, must be carried on with the oppressed at whatever stage their struggle for liberation has reached. The content of that dialogue can and should vary in accordance with historical conditions and the level at which the oppressed perceive reality. But to substitute monologue, slogans and communiqués for dialogue is to try to liberate the oppressed with the instruments of domestication. Attempting to liberate the oppressed without their reflective participation in the act of liberation is to treat them as objects which must be saved from a burning building; it is to lead them into the populist pitfall and transform them into masses which can be manipulated.[61]

Friere adds that the liberating dialogue should not take place in the open: 'that would only provoke the fury of the oppressor and lead to still greater oppression'.[62] At first glance, Friere's conception of education appears non-consequentialist, because it seems to invoke the thought that individuals are ends in themselves and that there are certain educational practices that fail to respect this constraint and that are, therefore, forbidden for reasons that are independent of their consequences. That may be part of his view. However, the tenor of his remarks strike me as consequentialist. Friere has a particular Marxist account of the requirements of stable liberation from oppression that turns on the oppressed recognizing their situation for what it is and, in the light of that appreciation, taking revolutionary action to abolish the prevailing oppressive social relations. In his view, liberating revolutionary action requires critical recognition and a self-understanding on the part of the oppressed. Without that understanding, the beliefs and desires of the oppressed will continue to be prone to be manipulated and, therefore, any victory over oppression they achieve will be short-lived.

My aim in reporting Friere's view is not to endorse his Marxist account of politics and historical change, but merely to cite it as an example of how a consequentialist account of political education might be elaborated in seriously unjust societies. Whether or not we agree with Friere, his view is instructive as an example of how education for justice in non-ideal circumstances must tailor a conception of education to respond appropriately to the nature of the injustices of a particular society, how people's motivations are shaped by the social conditions under which they live, and how educators might seek to help to overcome these problems in the difficult circumstances in which they operate.

A very different illustration of the issues that arise with respect to political education in non-ideal circumstances is the recent introduction of citizenship education in England. Citizenship education was introduced into the revised National Curriculum in 2000 and, from August 2002, became a statutory subject for secondary level students (11–16).[63] The introduction of citizenship education followed a report of the Advisory Group on Citizenship chaired by Bernard Crick, *Education for Citizenship and the Teaching of Democracy in Schools* (henceforth the 'Crick Report').[64] The Advisory Group reported some analysis of the poor state of citizenship among young people in the UK and recommended citizenship education in schools as a means of rectifying the problem. Among its recommendations were that citizenship education should be a curriculum subject in its own right, and also taught through other subjects such as history, geography, and literature; that schools should be required to establish that they are meeting given learning outcomes at each key stage in secondary education (at ages fourteen and sixteen respectively); and that citizenship education should inform the ethos and organization of the school as well as the curriculum.

The revised National Curriculum largely follows the Crick Report recommendations and its understanding of citizenship as requiring (*a*) an appreciation of key moral and political concepts (such as democracy, autocracy, equality, justice, freedom, community, and so on); (*b*) knowledge and understanding of the political process, institutions, and issues; (*c*) the possession of various skills and aptitudes, such as the ability to cooperate with others, engage in deliberative reasoning, and place oneself in others' shoes; and (*d*) the possession of certain values and dispositions, including a concern for the common good and human dignity, to resolve conflicts, to work with others, to practise tolerance, as well as a commitment to equal opportunities, gender equality, and voluntary service.[65] The National Curriculum programme of study for citizenship does not have as its aim the development of the values and dispositions suggested by the Advisory Group. Instead, its restricted concern is to produce informed citizens who have skills of enquiry and communication who are capable of participation and responsible action, and it includes a detailed set of learning outcomes for those who are fourteen and sixteen years old respectively.[66]

While some objections have been raised, the introduction of citizenship into the National Curriculum has been overwhelmingly welcomed by educationalists and politicians. From the point of view of education for justice, the test for its worth depends upon whether it improves the realization of political legitimacy as described in previous sections. With this in mind, I offer a few observations about citizenship education as it is currently conceived in the public debate in Britain.

The Advisory Group's argument for the good of citizenship education in schools is contentious. Its argument has two parts. First, it argues that an improvement in skills, understanding, and motivations related to citizenship is necessary because of the low level of political literacy and participation exhibited by young people in the UK. Second, it places its faith in citizenship as part of the National Curriculum as a remedy for the problem. Both claims have been challenged. For instance, Tooley has argued that before we accept the *Crick* recommendations we must address the question of whether the ad hoc citizenship education that individuals receive outside the school environment—through various kinds of media and social interaction—is insufficient or any worse than that which might be provided through formal classes.[67]

The Advisory Group reports a limited set of data that reveals the low level of political competence and participation exhibited by young people in the UK. Its conclusion is that even if 'things may not be getting dramatically worse, they are inexcusably and damagingly bad, and could and should be remedied'.[68] However, we need to know more about the nature of the lack of political literacy and participation in the young to gauge whether it is a cause for concern. For example, if levels of political literacy and participation generally improve in the life cycle without government intervention, then low levels in the young may not indicate a permanent problem that generates the need for a solution of the kind proposed by the Crick Report.[69]

With respect to the Advisory Group's second claim, that citizenship education as part of the National Curriculum would improve political competence, it is odd that no pilot study of the effects of such an education was conducted before recommending its introduction. The Group reports the findings of a pilot initiative in drugs education, which indicated that individuals who received the education displayed a lower incidence of experimentation with drugs.[70] It is not clear, however, that the potential value of citizenship education can be read off from this case, since part of the alleged explanation of low political literacy is that politics is disconnected from the daily lives of young people. Since the issue of drugs resonates with young people to a greater degree compared to politics, it is less likely that drugs education would fall on deaf ears. Thus, the proposal for citizenship education as a component of the National Curriculum would carry more weight if it were made in the light of comparative data, which, controlling for other factors, indicate that political literacy and participation is heightened by the kind of citizenship education in question. No doubt studies of this kind will be conducted now that the provision has been included within the National Curriculum.

Another set of concerns that has been raised about the introduction of citizenship in schools relates to the problem of political bias. Tooley criticizes the Advisory Group for failing to realize, or not caring about, their particular political biases 'creeping into the report at every stage'.[71] One response, offered by some who defend the Advisory Group, points out that citizenship education cannot avoid controversial issues, and that the Report includes a sensitive discussion of different teaching strategies for dealing with the problem of bias.[72] From the point of view of education for justice, however, it is important to ask what is meant by 'bias'. In one view, being biased is being disposed to engage in belief formation and desire formation in an irrational manner.[73] In another view, political bias means holding political convictions that are not shared by others. The problem Tooley raises relates to the second interpretation of bias. Citizenship education will, he claims, inevitably involve encouraging children to adopt disputed political beliefs, either because the conception of citizenship that motivates the learning outcomes is disputed or because it is inevitable that teachers' political convictions will be imparted to children through their teaching of citizenship. Tooley cites the following example:

> It is pretty easy to spot a tad of political bias creeping into the report at every stage. After all, '*ethical trading, peace-making and peacekeeping*' and '*poverty, famine, disease, charity, aid, human rights*', all seem to be recognizably the building blocks of a discernible political creed, one focused on the problems of underdevelopment, the evils of capitalism and how the United Nations can put it all right. Meanwhile '*prejudice, xenophobia, discrimination, pluralism*', and '*commitment to equal opportunities and gender equality*' likewise could be (perhaps less exclusively) the building blocks of another left-wing political creed, this time one focused on the institutionally racist and sexist (and no doubt homophobic) society we live in.[74]

Leaving aside the questionable inferences that Tooley draws from the italicized ideals and concepts he quotes from the Crick Report, we must ask what is problematic about educating for an understanding of these phenomena and for a commitment to the stated ideals. Education for justice has no principled objection to this kind of teaching, because it takes political legitimacy to depend on citizens being committed to such ideals when exercising their democratic rights. True, the ideals are disputed. It is easy to cite certain minority political parties, such as the British National Party, which campaign against many of the ideals mentioned above. Fortunately, there is a wide consensus across the major political parties within Britain with respect to the liberal norms of reciprocity, tolerance, and human rights. If citizenship education can be framed in a way that is both congenial to these dominant parties and advances the aims of liberal citizenship, then there are good reasons to support it.

Finally, we might ask questions about the *site* of citizenship education. The Advisory Group claims that formal schooling is an appropriate context for citizenship education. It recommends a portion of the National Curriculum be set aside for the development of political understanding, democratic skills, and the development of responsible political conduct. It also suggests that schools should consider how the development of citizenship should be taken into account in determining the ethos and organization of the school. The adoption of school councils to hear and discuss the views of pupils, and young people's engagement in projects in the local community, are often cited as examples of how various virtues of citizenship might be encouraged in individuals. But these issues may run deeper than these examples suggest. If the ideal of liberal citizenship is to get individuals to approach political questions by asking what is just rather than what is in it for them, we must ask whether the educational system as a whole serves this purpose well. Writing in 1961, Richard Wollheim addresses this problem in the context of a selective education system (which remains in place in certain areas of England):

> Schooling is becoming like a long steeplechase from start to finish. Every stage that is traversed is regarded as a prelude to the one that follows, every examination that is passed is merely a means of manoeuvring for position for the next.... [A]n educational system, which is conceived primarily as a method of social selection, is bound to have the effect of instilling into those who pass through it the morality of competition and a view of life in which streaming and grading are natural elements.[75]

Now Wollheim accepts the need for a meritocratic ideal of education in which there exists competition for places of higher education, say. He claims there are reasons of both efficiency and justice for the ideal of equality of opportunity, in which social selection prefers natural talent over social standing. Nevertheless, given the detrimental cultural effects that attend meritocracy, he asks the question: '[H]ow is it possible to preserve what is good in the theory of educational opportunity without setting an undesirable premium upon intellectual ability or establishing competitiveness and ambition as the central values of our society?'[76]

Education for justice must take Wollheim's claims and questions seriously, especially in contemporary England where, once again, children are routinely required to perform and compete in public tests just as they were under the selective system that worried him. If we want individuals to be creative, deliberative citizens who treat other citizens with concern and respect, and who are willing to meet their obligations of justice to individuals in other parts of the world and future generations, then we need to ask whether a schooling system informed by the steeplechase ideal of education Wollheim describes is best suited to that task. As before, I offer these remarks as indicative of the issues and questions that education for justice must address in non-ideal circumstances, and to illustrate the different kinds of response to proposals for political education that it might adopt, depending on the particular circumstances of the society under consideration. With respect to the site of education for justice, we must ask questions about the school curriculum, the ethos and organization of the school, and the unintended cultural side effects of educational policy. And, in addition, we must also ask whether other social policies and arrangements relating to the family and workplace serve individuals in their acquisition of liberal convictions.[77]

NOTES

1. For an elaboration and defence of this model of education for political literacy, see Brighouse, 'Civic Education and Liberal Legitimacy', *Ethics*, 108 (1998), 719–45, and his *School Choice and Social Justice* (Oxford: Oxford University Press, 2000), ch. 4. In the latter, Brighouse describes his view, which proposes an autonomy-*facilitating* rather than an autonomy-*promoting* education as *character-neutral*, because while it seeks to equip individuals with the capacity to pursue an autonomous life it does not impart to them a desire to pursue such a life, still less a life of political virtue. The coherence of this distinction is questioned by Callan, 'Liberal Legitimacy, Justice, and Civic Education', *Ethics*, 111 (2000), 141–55, esp. 146–7.
2. For the Humean account, see Hume, *A Treatise of Human Nature*, eds. L. A. Selby-Bigge and P. H. Nidditch (Oxford: Clarendon Press, 1978), bk II, pt III, sect. III; *An Enquiry Concerning the Principles of Morals*, eds. L. A. Selby-Bigge and P. H. Nidditch (Oxford: Clarendon Press, 1975), app. I; Smith, *The Moral Problem* (Oxford: Blackwell, 1994), ch. 4. For discussion and defence of the view that reasons can motivate us directly, see Scanlon, *What We Owe to Each Other*, ch. 1.

3. Some hold that while the two rights associated with a legitimate state are analytically distinct, they are normally normatively connected. True, there are certain cases in which the state might legitimately use its coercive powers to force conformity with the law, in the absence of a duty on the part of individuals to obey it. Such cases, however, are the exception. Normally, if the state lacks the right to rule in a way that correlates with a duty on the part of citizens to obey its laws, it will also lack the right to use its coercive power to force conformity with them. See Dworkin, *Law's Empire* (London: Fontana Press, 1986), p. 191.
4. It is not detrimental to Brighouse's argument, because all the work required to defend the political literacy model in preference to the political motivation model is performed by the second condition of legitimacy.
5. Brighouse, 'Civic Education and Liberal Legitimacy', 720.
6. Ibid. 723.
7. See Rawls, *A Theory of Justice*, sects. 19, 51–4; Dworkin, *Law's Empire*, pp. 190–216; Raz, *The Morality of Freedom*, pt. 1. Note also that neither Raz nor Dworkin appeal to hypothetical consent in addressing legitimacy. To be sure, there is a tradition of liberal thought, deriving from Locke, which affirms the necessity of actual consent for legitimacy. See, for example, Locke, *Two Treatises of Government*, ed. Peter Laslett (Cambridge: Cambridge University Press, 1988); Simmons, 'Justification and Legitimacy', *Ethics*, 109 (1999), 739–71; Green, 'Associative Obligations and the State', in Justine Burley (ed.), *Dworkin and His Critics*; Otsuka, *Libertarianism without Inequality*, ch. 5. The point here is merely that the shared rejection of this condition by the leading liberal thinkers of our time suggests an alternative account of legitimacy.
8. What follows is an interpretation of Rawls's remarks in *A Theory of Justice*, sects. 19, 51–4, and *Political Liberalism*.
9. Here I follow Raz's conception of the normal justification of political authority. See Raz, *The Morality of Freedom*, pt I.
10. Rawls, *A Theory of Justice*, p. 194.
11. See Grofman and Feld, 'Rousseau's General Will: A Condorcetian Perspective', *American Political Science Review*, 82 (1988), 567–76. Of course, the jury theorem implies that autocracy is preferable to democracy from the point of view of realizing an independently just outcome if independent voters are, on average, more likely than not to hold mistaken views of justice. Thus, the use of this theorem to defend democratic institutions depends on the existence of a relatively competent electorate.
12. Rawls, *A Theory of Justice*, p. 315.

13. Christiano, 'The Authority of Democracy', *The Journal of Political Philosophy*, 12 (2004), 266–90.
14. For commentary on Rawls's complex argument for this position, see Joshua Cohen, 'For a Democratic Society', in Samuel Freeman (ed.), *The Cambridge Companion to Rawls* (Cambridge: Cambridge University Press, 2003), pp. 86–139, esp. pp. 91–111.
15. See Dworkin, *Sovereign Virtue*, pp. 5–7.
16. Rawls, *Political Liberalism*, pp. xlviii, 223; 'The Idea of Public Reason Revisited', pp. 581–2.
17. Rawls, 'The Idea of Public Reason Revisited', pp. 578.
18. This problem of how to reconcile autonomy as self-government with the need for political constraints to protect autonomy goes back at least to Rousseau. For discussion of Rousseau's distinction between moral and civil freedom, on which my discussion in this paragraph trades, see Neuhouser, 'Freedom, Dependence and the General Will', *Philosophical Review*, 102 (1993), 363–95.
19. This is consistent with two positions: that an autonomously chosen unjust life is (*a*) no better for an individual or (*b*) that it is worse for her. Dworkin holds the first view: see *Sovereign Virtue*, pp. 263–8 and, for commentary, see Clayton, 'A Puzzle about Ethics, Justice, and the Sacred', in Justine Burley (ed.), *Dworkin and His Critics* (Oxford: Blackwell, 2004), pp. 102–4. The second view is consistent with Raz's view of the value of personal autonomy: see *The Morality of Freedom*, pp. 378–81.
20. Here, I assume the impossibility of certain relationships extensively discussed by Frankfurt in the context of different questions concerning moral responsibility. In Frankfurt's cases, we allow individuals to decide a course of action for themselves unless we judge that they are about to take a wrong course, in which case we intervene to ensure that they take the right course. In these cases we maximize the chances of the individual taking the right course of actions off her own bat, while still ensuring that the right course of action is taken. See Frankfurt, 'Alternate Possibilities and Moral Responsibility', in *The Importance of What We Care About* (Cambridge: Cambridge University Press 1988). While such intervention is compatible with the view adopted here, there are obvious epistemic difficulties in prescribing it as a public rule.
21. For a defence of the view that children's development of the capacities and habits required for citizenship are not secure without citizenship education in schools, see Kymlicka, 'Education for Citizenship', in *Politics in the Vernacular: Nationalism, Multiculturalism, and Citizenship* (Oxford: Oxford University Press, 2001), pp. 300–3.

22. Burke, 'Speech at Mr. Burke's Arrival in Bristol', in Isaac Kramnick (ed.), *The Portable Burke* (Harmondsworth: Pengiun Books, 1999), p. 156.
23. Indeed, the deliberative conception need not be democratic. It is quite possible for a deliberative citizenry to exist alongside a decent consultation hierarchy, as Rawls describes it. See, *The Law of Peoples*, pp. 71–8. Of course, the desirability of such a political arrangement is another matter.
24. See Rawls, *Political Liberalism*, pp. 220–1.
25. See Waldron, 'Mill and the Value of Moral Distress', in his *Liberal Rights*, ch. 5.
26. Rawls, *Political Liberalism*, p. 217.
27. For the idea of holding one's ethical values in a liberal spirit, see Waldron, 'Theoretical Foundations of Liberalism', in *Liberal Rights*, ch. 2.
28. See Raz, *The Morality of Freedom*, pp. 401–7.
29. There are interesting questions about the contours of the distinction between political and non-political restraint that require further exploration. For example, may an association exclude black people or women if it sincerely believes their inclusion is contrary to the basic tenets of its grounding faith? I do not think it may, but then what is the distinction between the exclusion of black people or women on the one hand and gays on the other?
30. Nozick, *Anarchy, State and Utopia* (Oxford: Blackwell, 1974).
31. See Rawls, *Political Liberalism*, lect. VII.
32. Ibid. pp. lviii–lix.
33. Of course, certain *left*-libertarian conceptions might, at least in practice, satisfy the threshold of decency in social and economic justice as specified by the reciprocity criterion. For a version of left-libertarianism, see Otsuka, *Libertarianism without Inequality*, esp. ch. 1.
34. Simmons, *Moral Principles and Political Obligations* (Princeton, NJ: Princeton University Press, 1979), pp. 147–52.
35. Raz, *The Morality of Freedom*, p. 57; 'Facing Up: A Reply', 1180–3.
36. For further discussion of Simmons's case, see Waldron, 'Special Ties and Natural Duties', *Philosophy and Public Affairs*, 22 (1993), 3–30, esp. 29–30.
37. See Rawls, *A Theory of Justice*, secs. 53–9.
38. If it is optional, participation may remain praiseworthy. The optionality of participation does not imply that liberals are committed to taking no stand on its value.
39. See *Political Liberalism*, pp. 205–6. Earlier in lect. V, Rawls asserts the good of political society in enabling citizens to develop and exercise their sense of justice. It might be thought that participation in political affairs is intrinsically valuable for individuals as free and equal persons without having to assert the claim that such participation is good for them from the point of

view of their well-being, all things considered. See ibid. pp. 201–4. This is an intriguing idea, but it succumbs to the general problem I noted in Section 1.3, which besets Rawls's political conception of our interests. Why should one who rejects the holding of influence or authority over others as valuable in one's non-public life affirm it as in one's interest in the political domain? To be sure, one has an interest in being recognized as having the status of a free and equal person and, therefore, in having the right to participate politically should one so desire, but this does not imply that one's life is lacking in some respect if one does not exercise that right.

40. Miller, *On Nationality* (Oxford: Clarendon Press, 1995), p. 27, and ch. 2 for further elaboration on each of these features of nationality.
41. Ibid. pp. 18–19, 22–3.
42. Ibid. pp. 71–2.
43. Ibid. p. 65.
44. Williams, 'Review of *On Nationality*', *Mind*, 110 (2001), 515.
45. In fact Williams distinguishes two questions. First, would it be permissible for the nationalist faction to exclude non-members from the most productive resources? Second, would it be impermissible for the non-members, who are excluded, to take back an equal share of the most productive resources without the consent of individuals in the nationalist faction. Williams claims that many will answer both questions negatively, and there would be a more widespread rejection of the nationalists' entitlement to the resources they enjoy, when this correlates with a duty on the part of others not to take back an equal share of resources.
46. The modest claim is made by White, 'Education and Nationality', *Journal of Philosophy of Education*, 30 (1996), 327–43; 'Patriotism without Obligation', *Journal of Philosophy of Education*, 35 (2001), 141–51.
47. In addition to the modest instrumental defence of nationality, that it can be a vehicle of realizing justice, White offers the argument that even if it is possible to be committed to liberal principles directly, it is less desirable than being committed to liberal justice because we have affective ties to others. As he writes:

    Is a community bound together only by attachment to principles conceivable? Perhaps. But for many people, including myself, it would not be an attractive one. I would not like to be a younger member of a family bonded in a similar principle-orientated way, aware that my parents were attentive to my needs not out of affection but only because they saw this as a parental duty. Neither, I suggest, would virtually anyone else. Similarly, like most people I would feel more comfortable in a wider community where people felt a more immediate sympathy for each other. A national community can provide this more spontaneous, less intellectualized kind of attachment, thus strengthening the bonds at the civic level. (White, 'Education and Nationality', 332)

This particular analogy between the family and the polity is, however, contested. True, individuals standardly have affective ties to fellow family members, but many do not exhibit such attachments or sympathy to individuals within the same political jurisdiction. From a liberal point of view, White and others should be free to pursue their comfort within a larger sympathetic community, but that is possible within an arrangement in which citizens are committed to the principles and institutions by which they are governed, whether or not they feel any particular sympathy towards their fellow citizens.

48. Mason, 'Political Community, Liberal-Nationalism, and the Ethics of Assimilation', *Ethics*, 109 (1999), 272. This notion of belonging to a polity seems compatible with the account of liberal legitimacy I offered above, which consists in a commitment to do one's fair share in supporting the salient legitimate institutions that apply to one and to acknowledge other political obligations to the polity. For further discussion of how natural duties can generate special obligations to one's fellow citizens, see Waldron, 'Special Ties and Natural Duties'.
49. Pogge, 'Relational Conceptions of Justice: Responsibilities for Health Outcomes', in Sudhir Anand, Fabienne Peter, and Amartya Sen (eds.), *Public Health, Ethics, and Equity* (Oxford: Oxford University Press, 2004), pp. 135–61.
50. I do not broach the related issues of political education with respect to future generations and the environment, important though these are.
51. I take these figures, which are collated from figures published by a variety of international organizations, including the UN Development Program, UNESCO, and the International Labour Organization, from Pogge's recent paper, 'Recognized and Violated by International Law: The Human Rights of the Global Poor', *Leiden Journal of International Law*, 18 (2005), 719. For further discussion of these figures see his *World Poverty and Human Rights*.
52. Pogge, *World Poverty and Human Rights*, p. 99.
53. The distinction between social and cosmopolitan liberals is drawn by Beitz, 'Rawls's Law of Peoples', *Ethics*, 110 (2000), 669–96. See also Nagel, 'The Problem of Global Justice', *Philosophy and Public Affairs*, 33 (2005), 113–47.
54. Rawls, *The Law of Peoples*, p. 37.
55. Dworkin, *Sovereign Virtue*, p. 6.
56. Nagel, 'The Problem of Global Justice'.

57. Pogge, 'Relational Conceptions of Justice: Responsibilities for Health Outcomes'.
58. See, for example, Singer's classic paper, 'Famine, Affluence and Morality', *Philosophy and Public Affairs*, 1 (1972), 229–43, which has generated a sizeable literature on the demandingness of morality.
59. Pogge, 'World Poverty and Human Rights', *Ethics and International Affairs*, 19 (2005), 1.
60. See Pogge, *World Poverty and Human Rights*, pp. 130–9 and ch. 8. Rawls's account of the law of peoples is a liberal account in this sense. Included within the law of peoples are a principle of free trade among peoples and the need to exclude outlaw states, which violate human rights. The participation of countries in rules which deny free trade and extend borrowing privileges to outlaw states makes them partly responsible for the harm that other peoples suffer.
61. Friere, *Pedagogy of the Oppressed* (Harmondsworth: Penguin Books, 1972), p. 41.
62. Ibid.
63. The Government also produced non-statutory guidance on primary level (5–11) citizenship as part of personal, social, and health Education.
64. Qualifications and Curriculum Authority (QCA), *Education for Citizenship and the Teaching of Democracy in Schools: Final Report of the Advisory Group on Citizenship* (London: QCA, 1998).
65. For a full statement of the Crick Report's proposed outcomes of citizenship education by the end of compulsory schooling, see ibid. p. 44.
66. See Department for Education and Employment/QCA, *The National Curriculum for England: Citizenship Key Stages 3–4* (London: HMSO, 1999), pp. 14–16.
67. Tooley, *Reclaiming Education* (London: Cassell, 2000), pp. 147–53.
68. QCA, *Education for Citizenship*, p. 16.
69. Evaluating whether political competence is related to age is difficult. For an assessment see Chan and Clayton, 'Should the Voting Age be Lowered to 16? Normative and Empirical Considerations', Working Paper, no. 2004–6, Department of Sociology, University of Oxford, November 2004 (http://www.sociology.ox.ac.uk/swps/2004–06.html), 1–33, esp. 12–26. Nevertheless, the data cited there indicate that there is some age effect in respect of political competence and that there are grounds for believing that the low levels of political literacy and participation in young people that worry the Advisory Group are problems that diminish with age.
70. QCA, *Education for Citizenship*, p. 17.
71. Tooley, *Reclaiming Education*, p. 145.

72. See McLaughlin, 'Citizenship Education in England: The Crick Report and Beyond', *Journal of Philosophy of Education*, 34 (2000), 549–54; QCA, *Education for Citizenship*, pp. 56–61.
73. On this issue see, for example, Elster, *Sour Grapes*, ch. 4.
74. Tooley, *Reclaiming Education*, p. 145. Similar claims about the inevitability of left-wing bias, given the nature of the teaching profession in Britain, are offered by Flew, *Education for Citizenship* (London: Institute of Economic Affairs, 2000).
75. Wollheim, *Socialism and Culture* (London: Fabian Society, 1961), p. 32.
76. Ibid. p. 35.
77. One argument for the long-standing feminist concern to reform the family and workplace to reduce the inequalities that exist between men and women is that this would facilitate education for justice. Despite the profound importance of this issue, I do not discuss the family as a seedbed of justice. The conception of these matters that best complements the liberal account of education for justice outlined in this chapter is defended by Okin, *Justice, Gender and the Family*, esp. chs. 1, 7–8.

5

The Age of Majority

It is natural, finally, to turn to questions of justice with respect to determining the *end* of childhood. Here, our central questions concern justice with respect to the acquisition of legal rights that are normally enjoyed by adults but denied to children. Should there be a so-called age of majority and, if so, at what age should it be set?

No one denies that it is sometimes just to distinguish between individuals and allocate legal rights to some but not to others. Yet some claim that *age-based* discrimination is unjustified or unjust. Others accept the justice of age-based qualifying conditions for certain rights, but disagree over the particular age at which the law should recognize that individuals have those rights.

One way of proceeding is to discuss the age of majority in general terms, on the assumption that the development of individuals is such that if they qualify for one legal right normally enjoyed by adults, they qualify for all such rights. However, this approach seems unlikely to succeed, because different legal rights serve different interests and ends and, consequently, it is not obvious that the same qualifying conditions apply in the case of each legal right. For example, the legal right to drive serves people's interests in being mobile and safe whilst travelling. A trade-off is effected between these interests and suitable thresholds of driving competence are set for the allocation of the right to drive more or less dangerous vehicles. By contrast, the legal right to fight in the armed forces is sensitive to a very different set of interests—the interests of the public in being protected from external aggression and in providing peacekeeping services to other countries, and the interests of individuals in not being killed or traumatized by participating in armed conflict. Because they serve quite different interests, there is no reason to assume that the qualifying conditions for the rights to drive and to fight should be similar.

A more promising strategy is to assess the issue of the age of majority on a case-by-case basis, in a manner that is sensitive to the particular reasons for conferring the particular right in question. Nonetheless, this case-by-case approach to the age of majority rests on the view that age-based discrimination is, in principle, justified, which some have disputed. Thus, in this chapter, I defend the justice of age-based discrimination in principle, and then turn briefly to discuss the age of majority in the case of one of the most significant rights from the point of view of political morality: the right to vote.

5.1 EQUALITY AND AGE-BASED DISCRIMINATION

Is it ever permissible to distinguish between individuals on the basis of age? If it is not, several practices common to different kinds of society stand condemned at the bar of justice. For example, in virtually every society there are minimum age requirements for the rights to drive, marry, have sex, live independently of one's parents, vote, as well as be held legally responsible for one's actions. Are such practices that discriminate on the basis of age objectionable in the same way as discrimination on the basis of sex or race is?

It is not acceptable simply to argue for the permissibility of age-based discrimination on the grounds that it is a universal practice among humankind, because that would be to make an invalid inference. We cannot infer the normative conclusion that a practice is just or legitimate from the factual premise that it is widespread, or widely held to be justified. To take a well-known example, many object to the horrific treatment of animals in factory farms or medical experiments, even though these kinds of treatment are common to virtually every society and widely believed to be permissible. Indeed, the appeal to widely held beliefs would not provide a robust critique of racism or sexism, once we recall that historically these practices were customary aspects of many communities, and continue to be so in certain parts of the world. Considerations of justice and legitimacy are ideals to which we appeal to criticize prevalent social practices and shared understandings, rather than ones that simply mirror them.[1]

In order to assess whether age-based discrimination is on a moral par with racism or sexism, we must ask what is unjust about the latter and gauge whether there is a parallel case for the injustice of age-based discrimination.

Singer, who propounds a parallel case argument with respect to the treatment of animals offers an account of unjust discrimination on the basis of an ideal of equal consideration of individuals' interests. Unjust discrimination, he claims, consists in attaching unequal importance to the interests of different individuals in virtue of their membership of different groups.

> The racist violates the principle of equality by giving greater weight to the interests of members of his own race, when there is a clash between their interests and the interests of those of another race. Similarly the speciesist allows the interests of his own species to override the greater interests of members of other species.[2]

Thus, if two individuals have the capacity to feel pleasure or pain, it is plausible to believe that each has an interest in not having avoidable pain inflicted upon them. And this remains the case, Singer claims, whether the individuals in question are of the same race or of different races. Similarly, the argument extends to condemn speciesism. A chimp and a child have similar interests in being free of physical pain and, therefore, it is unjust, he argues, always to select the chimp to undergo medical experiments if conducting such experiments is justified.

However, this argument does not provide support for making rights typically enjoyed by adults available to children. There is a well-known distinction between equal treatment and treatment as an equal.[3] While the former asserts that each individual should receive the same distribution of an item, the latter requires that each individual be treated with the same level of concern and respect as anyone else. So, for example, positive discrimination in favour of women in the workplace or education, say, violates equal treatment because particular jobs or university places are not available on equal terms to men and women. However, it might be argued that this unequal treatment is justified in the name of treating men and women with equal concern and respect if positive discrimination is a suitable means of reducing the incidence of traditional sexism in hiring or within the workplace, in which women are not treated as equals.[4]

Moreover, in the case of certain rights it is inappropriate to require the right in question to be held by everyone. The right to abortion, for example, is sometimes defended as a right that provides women with equal opportunity for self-defence and self-determination. But even though it is defended on the basis of a principle of equal consideration, the right to abortion is not a right from which men can benefit.

In the same way, denying children the right to live independently might be consistent with treating them as equals. Locke's distinction between being born *in* and being born *to* equality expresses a similar view:

> Children, I confess are not born in this full state of Equality [which consists of the equal right to natural freedom], though they are born to it. Their Parents have a sort of Rule and Jurisdiction over them when they come into the World, and for some time after, but 'tis but a temporary one. The Bonds of this Subjection are like the Swadling Cloths they are wrapt up in, and supported by, in the weakness of their Infancy. Age and Reason as they grow up, loosen them till at length they drop quite off, and leave a Man at his own free Disposal.[5]

Children have different interests compared to adults, principally because they have developmental interests with respect to which they are not the best judge.[6] Because they have different interests, equal consideration of their interests supports different treatment to that enjoyed by adults. Children benefit from having legal rights that are tailored to the specific interests they have, rather than by being offered rights that serve the interests of adults.

One objection to the egalitarian case for excluding children from the enjoyment of certain rights draws a distinction between the *enjoyment* of rights and their *exercise*. Consider John Holt's proposal 'that the rights, privileges, duties, responsibilities of adult citizens be made *available* to any young person, of whatever age, who wants to make use of them'.[7] In this view, it will often be the case that the inevitable consequence of children having different capabilities and interests is that they will not use the rights that are available to them, because most children will not form a desire to participate in politics or choose to form their own home. Thus the lives of children and adults respectively will have a very different shape, but this is consistent with the availability of adult rights to everyone.

Holt's proposal suffers from two related problems.[8] First, it jeopardizes the good of paternalism. Children's interests are often served by others *overriding* their desires and wishes, forcing them to attend school, to avoid attractive but hazardous items, or to take unpalatable medicine. Holt is too sanguine in his assumption that children will not take up the freedom of choice extended to adults if that freedom does not serve their interests. There are countless instances in which even very young children would, if it were available to them, take up the right to manage their own education, say, by absenting themselves from school.

Now Holt might accept that this would be in one way bad, but nevertheless insist that this bad is outweighed by the good of changing the relationship between adults and children which the availability of adult rights to children would produce. This, it seems, is part of the rationale for his proposal:

> I have come to feel that the fact of being a 'child,' of being wholly subservient and dependent, of being seen by older people as a mixture of expensive nuisance, slave, and superpet, does most young people more harm than good.[9]

Yet his proposal is a clumsy tool with which to challenge such harmful relationships. The proposal is certainly not sufficient, because it fails to challenge various unjust, manipulative, or oppressive practices that adults might inflict on children within families and other institutions. True, if children who suffer in these ways form a desire to escape from such burdens, the availability of the right to enter different relationships as they choose may benefit them. However, this fails to deal with injustices that also cause children to acquire malformed beliefs or desires. An oppressive relationship might lead to children becoming resigned to their condition, in which case they may never form a desire to escape from their oppression. In addition, the availability of adult rights is not necessary to produce healthy adult–child relationships, because there are many alternative ways of changing these relationships, which operate through different mechanisms. Holt is surely right to campaign for the elimination of the conception of children as 'superpets' or 'slaves', but that campaign is better served by initiatives that challenge those views directly rather than by providing children with opportunities to exit from family relationships as they wish.

The second related problem with Holt's proposal is that it fails to recognize that the enjoyment of a right should be sensitive to the interests of others. This is particularly relevant in the case of the right to vote, for example, which gives individuals the power to influence decisions that affect the lives of others as well as their own. I say this is a related problem, for, as I have argued, one important interest we have as free and equal persons is to honour our duty of justice, i.e. to treat others in accordance with a reasonable conception of justice. If this is accepted, then each of us has an interest in having the opportunity to influence social decisions only if we can reasonably be expected to use that opportunity with sufficient maturity. In other words, an individual's interest in bringing her sense of justice to bear on political decisions does not support an extension of the franchise to those who merely *want* to vote.

Thus, our provisional conclusion is that treating individuals as equals is compatible with unequal treatment and, in particular, the denial of certain rights to particular individuals. Furthermore, one ground for justifying such an inequality of rights, which applies in the case of certain rights, such as the right to vote, relates to individuals' competence. Certain rights protect interests that depend upon an individual's maturity in a particular field. We do not have an interest in driving, but an interest in driving safely. We do not have an interest in registering a vote, but an interest in bringing our sense of justice to bear on social issues. Consequently, whether or not a particular individual should enjoy a particular legal right should sometimes depend upon whether the individual would be competent in exercising that right.[10]

But we have not yet justified age-based discrimination. Although the argument above rebuts proposals for the universal availability of legal rights and supports the view that rights possession may sometimes vary in line with competence, it has not established that rights possession may vary with age. To press the analogy with sexism once more, while many accept the permissibility of hiring the best qualified candidate for the job, they insist that it is unjust if women are excluded from competing for it, or if they are not treated on the basis of their own individual merits. Similarly, considerations of competence support restrictions on who qualifies for a driving licence, but this is consistent with the rejection of a minimum age below which one is not legally permitted to take a driving test.

Similarly, with respect to voting rights, John Harris has claimed that 'if full political status is to be granted only to the competent, then a large and significant proportion of children must be granted full political status and a very great number of adults must be disenfranchised'.[11] In the context of voting, what matters fundamentally is the possession of certain capacities, motivations, and understanding, which are relevant to the act of voting. Harris's argument is that a minimum age requirement for the franchise arbitrarily discriminates against young people who possess such capacities, motivation, and understanding to a higher degree than some older people do.

In reply, notice first that it is a mistake to assume that the discriminations we make in law or policy should always be guided by what is fundamentally important. Suppose that age is not a *fundamental* consideration in judging qualifying conditions for the vote. Nevertheless, age might be a valuable *proxy* for what is fundamental. The distribution of capacities that we decide are fundamental might be correlated with age, albeit imperfectly. Consequently, age-based discrimination might be an effective way of tracking those capacities that are fundamentally important. This is merely an instance of the rationality of employing action-guiding rules. As in other contexts, we seek, among other things, an effective way of discriminating between competent and incompetent individuals. In selecting for university places, for example, admissions tutors aim, other things equal, to select those who will perform well in the course applied for. Qualifications already achieved clearly do not matter fundamentally in such a selection process, but they might serve as a useful, albeit imperfect, indicator of academic potential.[12] Similar claims might be made with respect to age as a proxy for identifying competent voters.

Let us now turn to the issue of justice. Suppose age is an effective proxy in discriminating between the competent and incompetent. Some claim that age-based discrimination is, nevertheless, unjust. When we are allocating rights and duties to individuals, they claim, like cases should be treated alike. It is unjust to deprive a sixteen-year-old of the vote when an older individual enjoys the vote without possessing any more political competence.

This anti-ageist argument condemns the use of any rule that excludes any competent sixteen-year-old from the vote. But it overlooks our concern to exclude the incompetent. Yet we have good reasons of justice to prevent the incompetent from voting, since their votes might impact negatively not merely on themselves but also on the legal rights and duties enjoyed by others. Following the anti-ageist principle might inhibit our pursuit of justice, all things considered.

The anti-ageist might reply that we should test for competence directly and license individuals as voters, in the same way as individuals take a test to qualify for the right to drive.[13] However, there are various kinds of costs and difficulties in identifying competence on an individual-by-individual basis. First, it might be too costly to make available an accurate test to screen for political competence; for example, it is doubtful that the kinds of judgement required from voters in the political process are amenable to being tested in the relatively costless manner that screening for driving competence is. Second, such a test might have certain undesirable consequences, which we ought to avoid. Those who are denied the franchise on grounds of incompetence might suffer a loss of self-esteem that would impact detrimentally on various aspects of their lives. Such problems are avoided by an age-based rule rather than a competence-based rule, because an age-based rule that tracks competence does not make claims about the relative competence of different individuals.[14]

Some might remain unconvinced by the argument for age-based discrimination. They might point out that we would reject similar arguments in the case of sex- or race-based discrimination. For example, even if it were established that sex is a fairly accurate proxy indicator of competence with respect to a particular job, it would be unjust to exclude women from the competition. Instead, each should be assessed on the basis of her own individual merits, rather than by reference to these proxy indicators. If this claim is accepted, why should this kind of individualized meritocracy not also be applied in criticism of age-based discrimination?

In reply, we might question the assertion that statistical discrimination, which employs group-differentiated indicators as the basis for discriminating between individuals, is necessarily unjust. The rationale for this kind of discrimination is that without it the good of hiring appropriate individuals may be jeopardized, because individualized merit tests are unreliable, or because perfecting the reliability of such tests would be too costly. Plainly, if the proxy indicators used are imperfect, it follows that certain individuals are deprived of opportunities to which they might otherwise be legally entitled. But it is not obvious why the costs to the excluded who are competent outweigh the costs that others would have to bear in the absence of the use of statistical discrimination.[15]

Statistical discrimination is unlike other kinds of discrimination, such as discrimination that is motivated by hatred, or a belief in the moral inferiority of particular groups, or erroneous factual beliefs about the average competence of different groups. Instead, it is compatible with an equal concern for the interests of each individual which supports an allocation of certain rights in a manner that makes effective and efficient discriminations between individuals taking each person's interests into account. For example, statistical discrimination is employed when women choose to be treated by a female doctor in the belief that they are more likely to receive treatment that is effective and with which they feel comfortable. Plainly, it is not the case that treatment by a male doctor will always be worse: there may be some male doctors who provide better care than many women doctors. Moreover, statistical discrimination may make it harder for some male doctors to work in branches of medicine that disproportionately attend to women's health. But that diminution of opportunity, it is argued, is a small price worth paying for the good of providing effective and agreeable medical care to women.

Thus, statistical discrimination seems capable of justification in general when, for example, it is not motivated by hatred or contempt and when the costs it imposes on those who would benefit from an individualized assessment of people's merits are small.[16] Applying this view to the issue of voting rights generates further support for age-based discrimination. If age is an effective proxy indicator of political maturity, and there are reasons to set the voting at eighteen, say, then the objection under discussion asserts that it is unjust to exclude competent individuals who happen to be seventeen. The reply is that given the desirability of having a competent electorate, having a minimum voting age is an effective means of achieving this end, *and* the costs imposed on competent seventeen-year-olds are relatively small. After all, they are excluded for only a few hundred days at most.

Age-based discrimination with respect to the young is, other things equal, less objectionable compared to race- and sex-based discrimination, because sex and race are permanent features of people's lives while, in the course of a normal life, everyone makes the transition from childhood to adulthood. Thus, there are two relevant differences in the normal case. First, age-based discrimination excludes everyone as children, while sex- and race-based discrimination include some and exclude others for potentially their entire lives. Consequently, age-based discrimination is capable of satisfying the egalitarian's envy test, which requires that no one should prefer to have what someone else has. Since the rights they enjoy across their lives are identical, age-based discriminations are not susceptible to objections from comparative disadvantage in the way that sex- and race-based discriminations are. And, second, because childhood is temporary, the costs of exclusion are likely to be less than those involved in discrimination on grounds of race or sex, which may well be permanent and, therefore, more significant.

However, some will remind me that my argument in Section 4.1 insisted that the ideal of legitimacy requires the law to be sufficiently just *and* democratically determined. And they might insist that there are democratic arguments for extending the franchise to those younger than eighteen. One argument of this kind raises the following dilemma. *Either* voting rights should vary in line with political competence, in which case many groups of adults should be denied the vote or some groups should enjoy more votes compared to others; *or* voting rights may not vary with political competence, in which case voting rights should be extended to age groups that display a capacity to understand the act of voting.[17]

The dilemma can be avoided because the inference on which its first horn rests is invalid. It does not follow from the fact that voting rights should track political competence that many adults should be denied the franchise or that certain more competent adults should enjoy plural votes. It is coherent to argue that voting rights can justly be withheld from teenagers if it is shown that their political competence fails to meet a relevant threshold, while at the same time resist the view that, above the threshold, variations in political competence should not produce variations in voting entitlement. Notice that I do not claim that variations in political impact should not vary with competence. It is compatible with liberal democracy for judges and other civil servants to exercise more impact with respect to law and policy through issuing legal judgements or by contributing to the framing of legislation. We cannot deal with the complexity of modern politics without the presence of unequal impact of this kind. Nevertheless, judges and civil servants are not entitled to more votes than others just in virtue of their greater political competence. Because the enjoyment of equal votes is a symbolic declaration of equal standing, absent some justification that supports a deviation from this rule, for those who enjoy the franchise there is a strong case for equal votes.[18]

When we think about the democratic credentials of excluding the young from the franchise, we must distinguish between individuals' status as free and equal persons in a democratic society and the equal right to participate in the law-making process through the casting of votes. As free and equal persons each is owed equal concern and respect. The content of this requirement has received some discussion in previous chapters and need not detain us here. Our pivotal question concerns the relationship between the right to participate in the law-making body and equal concern and respect that is owed to each individual. Now perhaps, as Dworkin argues, this relationship admits different possibilities depending on historical contingencies:

> Our own history is such that no deviation from equal impact within a district—no deviation, that is, from equal vote—is tolerable for us. That strict requirement would not necessarily hold in a community whose history showed that unequal voting did not itself display contempt or disregard. We can imagine, for example, a society in which people gain votes as they grow older, or in which people acquire more votes by pursuing a course of study genuinely open to everyone, or something of that sort. But in a society like our own, in which the vote has traditionally been an emblem of responsibility, weight, and stake, any violation of equal vote would reflect a denial of the symbolic attachment equal vote confirms. That is why loss of vote has so often been used as one of the consequences of a criminal conviction.[19]

Dworkin's argument explains why arguments that seek to establish a connection between excluding the young and excluding other groups are not likely to succeed. Suppose social class is a proxy indicator for political competence, on the basis of which some might argue that social classes that are, on average, less competent should be excluded from the franchise. Perhaps we can imagine a society in which such an exclusion is not treated as disrespectful to, or contemptuous of, the excluded social classes. But such imaginary societies are not ours. Our society is marked by a protracted and ongoing struggle for equal standing between different social classes. Any exclusion from the franchise would, in the light of that history, inevitably be treated as insulting, contemptuous, or pitying. Yet that symbolism of exclusion from the franchise does not extend to the case of the young, partly because of the reasons advanced above. The excluded young will in due course qualify for the vote. Their temporary exclusion cuts across every other social classification, such as race, sex, class, and religion. One's standing as an equal citizen is secured by one's understanding that one will enjoy an equal vote regardless of one's particular political competence. Thus, the democratic challenge to the exclusion of the young can be rebutted without embracing the radical conclusion that other social groups should be excluded from the franchise, or the conclusion that plural voting should be adopted.

In conclusion, then, acknowledging the freedom and equality of individuals is compatible with upholding an inequality of legal rights. Moreover, in some cases, where right possession ought to vary with competence, setting a minimum age condition for the enjoyment of rights may be efficient and just.

5.2 THE VOTING AGE

If the setting of a minimum age for the enjoyment of particular rights is justifiable, then we must consider how the appropriate ages should be set. Here I discuss this issue by assessing in more detail the issue of the age of electoral majority. First, I describe and reject a popular approach to the setting of the minimum voting age that appeals to the ideal of consistency between different rights and duties. Thereafter, I briefly review some evidence relating to the political maturity of different age groups, which is the pivotal consideration with respect to setting an appropriate age of electoral majority.

In many Western democracies, the minimum voting age is set at eighteen. However, the exclusion of sixteen- and seventeen-year-olds has been challenged by a number of political and youth organizations. One prominent argument against the exclusion of sixteen- and seventeen-year-olds appeals to the view that there should be consistency between the ages at which different legal rights and duties are enjoyed. For instance, although it does not argue for a common age of majority at which all legal rights enjoyed by adults become available, Votes at 16, the principal coalition campaigning for the reduction of the voting age in the UK, claims that the right to vote is akin to other rights enjoyed at sixteen, such as the right to have a full-time job, to have sex and beget children, and so on.[20] Here, the parallel might be drawn with Mill's wry comment in the mid nineteenth century that if women are competent to choose their lifelong domestic rulers (husbands), they are surely sufficiently mature to select their temporary political rulers (MPs).[21] In the present context, the claim might be made that if sixteen-year-olds are judged sufficiently mature freely to make the momentous decision to beget children, they should also have the right to influence less momentous decisions about political matters.

Yet these kinds of argument often suffer from inattention to the complex reasons that guide the allocation of legal rights. For example, the argument for consistency between the rights to beget and to vote might be rebutted with the observation that granting the right to have sex to sixteen-year-olds might be an acknowledgement not of the sexual maturity of that age group, but of the difficulty of prohibiting sex. We might not think that sixteen-year-olds have a moral entitlement to beget at sixteen, but accept that it would require too much surveillance or interference in people's lives to prevent them from doing so. Such enforceability problems do not translate to the exclusion of sixteen-year-olds from the franchise. In the voting case, interference or surveillance is not required to prevent these individuals from voting; their names can simply be left off the electoral register.

Another related set of arguments asserts that it is inconsistent to hold individuals to certain legal duties without extending the franchise to them. The most familiar version of this view is the slogan 'no taxation without representation', but some substitute 'taxation' with 'conscription', or other duties. Yet arguments of this kind ignore the countless ways in which the negative freedom of those without the franchise—very young children or tourists, for example—may legitimately be constrained. For example, like others, adolescents are legitimately subject to the restrictions laid down by the criminal law in relation to the life and liberty of others; and the young are taxed in the form of tax on the purchase of several kinds of item. The legitimacy of such constraints is not diminished by the fact that adolescents do not have a voice in the process by which the laws are enacted. As we have seen, the natural duty of justice supports compliance with laws that are sufficiently just.[22]

Nevertheless, at least two claims for consistency between different rights do retain force. First, there are certain cases in which the attributes sufficient to generate a valid claim for one right are also sufficient for other rights. Mill's argument for women's political emancipation from consistency in the treatment of marriage and political rights was, in his day, forceful and well judged. Second, the enjoyment of a certain right supports the enjoyment of other legal rights when the latter are preconditions of the former. For example, it is widely held that the freedom to hear others' views is a precondition of democratic choice. So there is a case for consistency between the voting age and the age at which censorship laws are relaxed, such that when an individual has the vote she might be as informed as any other voter. It would be odd to allow sixteen-year-olds the vote while retaining eighteen certificates for films. But notice that neither of these valid claims for consistency supports sixteen, rather than eighteen, as the age of majority.

A better basis for setting an appropriate age of electoral majority is one that is informed by evidence of relevant differences in the average political maturity of different age groups. Political maturity so understood includes both a *willingness* and an *ability* to engage in democratic choice. Democracies require voters who understand the political system and the pertinent social and economic issues that are the subject of public deliberation. In addition, it is desirable for voters to hold convictions that are internally consistent and that hang together in the sense that they are the product of an appreciation of the relevant reasons that connect different political questions. Moreover, we want political beliefs to be ones that are held responsibly, beliefs that are not subject to revision on a whim but are held on the basis of examined conviction. In addition, given the account of citizenship offered above (Sections 4.2 and 4.3), the ability to engage in mature democratic choice depends upon a sufficient appreciation of the substantive requirements and constraints of public reason and, in particular, the duties of civility and reciprocity.

It is notable that the issue of whether there is indeed an age effect with respect to political maturity is rarely addressed in a rigorous manner. Nevertheless, there is some evidence supporting such an age effect. In our paper, 'Should the Voting Age Be Lowered to 16?', Tak Wing Chan and I review certain relevant data from the British Household Panel Survey concerning the interest of individuals of different ages in politics (which, we argue, is a proxy indicator of willingness to engage politically), individuals' understanding of politics, and the consistency of their political beliefs. Such indicators offer only incomplete and preliminary data with respect to the fundamental features of political maturity that are relevant to setting an appropriate voting age. In particular, they do not provide information about individuals' appreciation of the norms of public reason. Nevertheless, the data indicate that, on average, teenagers display less interest in politics compared to older age groups. Significantly, they also show a greater *gain* in political interest over time, which suggests that teenage is a period of political awakening. Moreover, with respect to people's understanding of politics and the consistency of their political beliefs, the survey data show teenagers to be less politically mature than older age groups.[23]

Now we cannot simply read off an appropriate age of electoral majority from these kinds of evidence. The setting of a voting age must be a complex piece of argument that integrates normative and empirical considerations. Here, I can do no more than make some suggestions about how that argument might run.

The first thing to note is that when setting a suitable voting age, we should not attend to the relative competence of neighbouring age groups, such as the competence gap between seventeen- and eighteen-year-olds. We should reject a flawed argument for lowering the voting age to seventeen, say, which runs as follows: '18-year-olds should have the vote. The competence of 17-year-olds is only insignificantly lower than that of 18-year-olds. Therefore, 17-year-olds should have the vote.'

The evidence does suggest that the age effect with respect to political maturity is indeed a gradual one and, therefore, the maturity gap between seventeen- and eighteen-year-olds is not a significant one. Even if it were significant, we could diminish that gap by selecting closer age points, between, say, eighteen-year-olds and those who will be eighteen in a month or a week. In cases like these, in which there is a gradual development of maturity it is possible to select age points between which there exists only an insignificant or imperceptible difference.

Yet to lower the voting age because of the insignificant differences between eighteen- and seventeen-year-olds would be irrational, as Quinn explains in his case of the self-torturer.[24] Quinn describes an imaginary device that inflicts pain on a person through an electrical current. The distinctive feature of the device is that a person may select an incremental increase in the current that is so small that the difference in pain is imperceptible. Now Quinn wants to question a conception of rationality, which asserts that one should maximize one's advantage at each decision point. He asks us to consider an individual who is offered $100 each day in return for a permanent incremental increase in the current. Because the increments are set so low the individual does not perceive any difference in pain compared to the previous day. According to the conception of rationality that prescribes maximization at each decision point, it is rational for the self-torturer continually to take the daily offer of $100 in return for an imperceptible increase in the current. The consequence of operating with this conception of rationality, however, is that the individual becomes a millionaire who suffers extreme pain, because although the increase in the current is imperceptible between days, it produces significant differences in pain when compared across years or decades.

A similar problem arises in the case of the voting age. If we ask whether the voting age should be eighteen or the week before one's 18th birthday, the difference in political maturity will be insignificant. Indeed, this is likely to be true of all week-long gaps along the age spectrum. Thus, setting the voting age by assessing competence between age groups separated by merely weeks is likely to lead us to enfranchising ten-year-olds, which would clearly be damaging to the quality of political decisions. A sequence of imperceptible or insignificant changes can add up to a significant change.[25] In both the self-torturer case and the voting age case, we ought, following Quinn's alternative conception of rationality, to identify a *reasonable* cut-off point. In the case of the self-torturer there may be an argument for the person to take some minor pain in return for income, but he or she needs to make that choice by considering what it would be rational to do if the current settings are sufficiently far apart rather than on a daily basis. Similarly, with respect to the voting age we must identify a reasonable cut-off point, which will enfranchise age groups that would maintain the quality of democratic decisions without jeopardizing that good by continuing incrementally to lower the voting age. Quinn teaches us that it is not irrational to identify a reasonable cut-off point even if there would be no significant loss of political competence from lowering the age of electoral majority still further.

Identifying a reasonable age threshold for the franchise is no easy task. Theoretical considerations can take us only so far and, ultimately, we must rely on straightforward moral argument and judgement. In the real world, of course, there are existing practices with respect to the voting age that we may use as baselines to judge alternatives. We might operate on the basis of an evaluation of the level of political competence displayed by the existing electorate and ask whether it is more than sufficient or not sufficiently high. For example, should we be sanguine or concerned about the level of political competence displayed by the existing UK electorate? If one is sanguine, an extension to the franchise to sixteen-year-olds might be justified. Alternatively, if one is appalled at the low level of political competence displayed on average by the present electorate, it is difficult to see how one could justify lowering the voting age given the lower absolute level of political competence exhibited by teenagers.[26] But I shall not pursue these complex matters any further.[27] For our purposes it is sufficient to provide the structure within which the discussion of the age of electoral majority should proceed.

Finally, any reasonable age threshold for the right to vote will inevitably exclude some from the franchise, and this raises further questions in relation to the protective function of democracy. In the absence of the franchise for children, the political system must fashion mechanisms that recognize and give due weight to the status and interests of children. A number of mechanisms have been proposed for doing this including the institution of a Children's Commission or Ombudsman, a Children's Parliament, and plural votes for parents.[28] It is likely that different sets of institutional mechanisms will prove effective in different political contexts. However, as I have been at pains to emphasize throughout, institutional choice should be guided by the ideals of justice and legitimacy and the principles of upbringing that these ideals support.

NOTES

1. For a statement of this view see Dworkin, 'What Justice Isn't', in *A Matter of Principle* (Oxford: Oxford University Press, 1985).
2. Singer, 'All Animals are Equal', in Singer (ed.), *Applied Ethics* (Oxford: Oxford University Press, 1986), p. 222.
3. See Dworkin, *Taking Rights Seriously* (London: Duckworth, 1977), p. 227.

4. For a discussion, see Sumner, 'Positive Sexism', *Social Philosophy and Policy*, 5 (1987), 204–22.
5. Locke, *Two Treatises of Government*, II, sect. 55.
6. Notice that adults also have developmental interests, but the assumption is that typically they are the best judge of their developmental interests.
7. Holt, 'Liberate Children', in William Aiken and Hugh LaFollette (eds.), *Whose Child? Children's Rights, Parental Authority, and State Power* (Totowa: Rowman & Littlefield, 1980), pp. 84–5.
8. There are further problems that we need not explore. One is that he suggests that children should be able to pick and choose which of the adult rights and duties they take up. For example, one might use the right to vote but refuse legal responsibility for one's life and acts. But this position is blind to the problems concerning justice in the distribution of benefits and burdens in society. However, this bizarre position held by Holt can be avoided if a certain set of adult rights are made available to children as a package. Since Holt's position can be revised in this way, this problem does not threaten his central proposal.
9. Holt, 'Liberate Children', p. 84.
10. Plainly, this is not true of all rights. Here we are discussing certain *agency* interests, or the interests we have in acting in a particular way. But we have other interests that do not make reference to how we act. We have an interest in being free of avoidable pain. The right to be free of torture or physical harm is not a right the possession of which depends on considerations of maturity, because the interests this right protects does not prescribe any conduct.
11. Harris, 'The Political Status of Children', in Keith Graham (ed.), *Contemporary Political Philosophy: Radical Studies* (Cambridge: Cambridge University Press, 1982), p. 36.
12. Of course, given the imperfect correlation between qualifications and potential, admissions tutors might seek to improve their selection procedures with the use of other indicators, such as information about the extent to which individuals from different kinds of school tend to progress once at university.
13. Notice that the analogy with driving is not a particularly good one, because although the right to drive a car without supervision is conditional upon passing a test, there is a minimum age requirement for a provisional licence, the possession of which is required to take the test.
14. For related and further objections to direct competence tests, see Archard, *Children, Family and the State*, p. 25.
15. Here, we need only discuss the costs to *competent* individuals who are excluded compared to the costs that everyone would have to bear in the

absence of statistical discrimination. For we are discussing the choice between direct competence tests and using age-based discrimination as a proxy indicator of competence. Since the incompetent, by hypothesis, have no moral claim to the right in question, their exclusion by either mechanism is not a cost. The only costs that age-based discrimination imposes fall on the competent who are excluded.

16. Here I follow the argument of Arneson, 'Against Rawlsian Equality of Opportunity', esp. 83–93.
17. This dilemma is suggested by Schrag's argument in 'Children and Democracy: Theory and Policy', *Politics, Philosophy and Economics*, 3 (2004), 365–79.
18. See Dworkin, *Sovereign Virtue*, pp. 200–1.
19. Ibid. p. 201.
20. Votes at 16, 'Submission to the Electoral Commission's Review of Voting Age "How Old is Old Enough" ', available at www.votesat16.org.uk.
21. Mill, *The Subjection of Women*, ch. 3, par. 2.
22. For further criticism of consistency arguments for lowering the voting age, including those that rest on the slogan of 'no taxation without representation' see Cowley and Denver, 'Votes at 16? The Case Against', *Representation*, 41 (2004), 57–62; Archard, *Children: Rights and Childhood*, 2nd edn. (London: Routledge, 2004), pp. 99–100.
23. Here I summarize the findings in Chan and Clayton, 'Should the Voting Age be Lowered to 16? Normative and Empirical Considerations', esp. 12–26.
24. Quinn, 'The Puzzle of the Self-Torturer', in *Morality and Action* (Cambridge: Cambridge University Press, 1993), pp. 198–209.
25. For further discussion of this problem and its implications for moral theory, see Glover, 'It Makes No Difference Whether or Not I Do It', in Peter Singer (ed.), *Applied Ethics*; Parfit, *Reasons and Persons* (Oxford: Oxford University Press, 1984), ch. 3.
26. Notice, however, that the setting of a voting age may depend upon existing arrangements, in virtue of the symbolic significance of the franchise as outlined earlier. The survey data mentioned above indicate that, like sixteen- and seventeen-year-olds, eighteen- and nineteen-year-olds are significantly less politically mature compared to older age groups. But we might be reluctant to take the vote away from eighteen- and nineteen-year-olds even if this is accepted and they are no more competent than sixteen- and seventeen-year-olds, and even if they are slightly less competent. A loss of rights presently enjoyed can carry greater significance for individuals compared to their not being offered rights they have never possessed. A loss of rights can symbolize a loss of status and can impact negatively on one's self-esteem. To be sure, the non-enjoyment of rights can have similar significance,

as it does when there exists continuing racist or sexist discrimination with respect to rights. Nevertheless, there are countless instances in which it is worse to deprive someone of a good she currently possesses compared to failing to provide her with that good which she currently lacks. One instance is noted above in Dworkin's remarks on equal votes: the loss of voting rights that a criminal suffers in many societies is regarded as a significant harm to her and reflects her lesser social standing compared to sixteen-year-olds, even though the latter do not enjoy the right to vote either. Therefore, there are relevant differences between establishing an age of electoral majority from scratch and taking the vote away from individuals who presently enjoy it.

27. A more detailed examination, and qualified rejection, of proposals to lower the voting age in the UK to sixteen is provided in Chan and Clayton, 'Should the Voting Age Be Lowered to 16? Normative and Empirical Considerations'.
28. For discussion of some of these ideas see Van Parijs, 'The Disenfranchisement of the Elderly, and Other Attempts to Secure Intergenerational Justice', *Philosophy and Public Affairs*, 27 (1998), 292–333; Schrag, 'Children and Democracy: Theory and Policy', 376–8.

Bibliography

Ackerman, Bruce, 'Political Liberalisms', *The Journal of Philosophy*, 91 (1994), 364–86.

Archard, David, 'What's Blood Got to Do With It? The Significance of Natural Parenthood', *Res Publica*, 1 (1995), 91–106.

—— *Children, Family and the State* (Aldershot: Ashgate, 2003).

—— *Children: Rights and Childhood*, 2nd edn. (London: Routledge, 2004).

—— and Colin Macleod (eds.), *The Moral and Political Status of Children* (Oxford: Oxford University Press, 2002).

Archbishops' Council of the Church of England, *Common Worship* (London: Church House Publishing, 2000).

Arneson, Richard, 'Liberalism, Distributive Subjectivism, and Equal Opportunity for Welfare', *Philosophy and Public Affairs*, 19 (1990), 77–93.

—— 'Against Rawlsian Equality of Opportunity', *Philosophical Studies*, 93 (1999), 77–112.

—— 'Democracy is Not Intrinsically Just', in Keith Dowding, Robert E. Goodin, and Carole Pateman (eds.), *Justice and Democracy: Essays for Brian Barry* (Cambridge: Cambridge University Press, 2004).

Beitz, Charles, 'Rawls's Law of Peoples', *Ethics*, 110 (2000), 669–96.

Brighouse, Harry, 'Civic Education and Liberal Legitimacy', *Ethics* 108 (1998), 719–45.

—— *School Choice and Social Justice* (Oxford: Oxford University Press, 2000).

—— and Adam Swift, 'Parents' Rights and the Value of the Family' (unpublished paper, 2005).

Burke, Edmund, 'Speech at Mr. Burke's Arrival in Bristol', in Isaac Kramnick (ed.), *The Portable Burke* (Harmondsworth: Pengiun Books, 1999).

Callan, Eamonn, *Creating Citizens: Political Education and Liberal Democracy* (Oxford: Clarendon Press, 1997).

—— 'Liberal Legitimacy, Justice, and Civic Education', *Ethics*, 111 (2000), 141–55.

Caney, Simon, 'Anti-perfectionism and Rawlsian Liberalism', *Political Studies*, 43 (1995), 248–64.

Casal, Paula and Andrew Williams, 'Equality of Resources and Procreative Justice', in Justine Burley (ed.), *Dworkin and His Critics* (Oxford: Blackwell, 2004).

Chan, Tak Wing and Matthew Clayton, 'Should the Voting Age be Lowered to 16? Normative and Empirical Considerations', Working Paper, no. 2004–6, Department of Sociology, University of Oxford, November 2004 (http://www.sociology.ox.ac.uk/swps/2004-0, 1–33).

Christiano, Thomas, 'The Authority of Democracy', *The Journal of Political Philosophy*, 12 (2004), 266–90.

Church of England, *The Book of Common Prayer* (Oxford: Oxford University Press, 1969).

Clayton, Matthew, 'Political Liberalism, Disagreement, and Sectarianism', *Polis: Revistă de Ştiinţe Politice*, 6 (1999), 71–92.

—— 'The Resources of Liberal Equality', *Imprints*, 9 (2000), 63–84.

—— 'Rawls and Natural Aristocracy', *Croatian Journal of Philosophy*, 1 (2001), 239–59.

—— 'Individual Autonomy and Genetic Choice', in Justine Burley and John Harris (eds.), *A Companion to Genethics* (Oxford: Blackwell, 2002).

—— 'Liberal Equality and Ethics', *Ethics*, 113 (2002), 8–22.

—— 'A Puzzle about Ethics, Justice, and the Sacred', in Justine Burley (ed.), *Dworkin and His Critics* (Oxford: Blackwell, 2004).

—— and David Stevens, 'School Choice and the Burdens of Justice', *Theory and Research in Education*, 2 (2004), 111–26.

Cohen, G. A., *Karl Marx's Theory of History: A Defence* (Oxford: Oxford University Press, 1978).

—— 'On the Currency of Egalitarian Justice', *Ethics*, 99 (1989), 906–44.

—— 'Incentives, Inequality, and Community', in Stephen Darwall (ed.), *Equal Freedom* (Ann Arbor, MI: University of Michigan Press, 1995).

—— 'The Pareto Argument for Inequality', *Social Philosophy and Policy*, 12 (1995), 160–85.

—— 'Where the Action Is: On the Site of Distributive Justice', *Philosophy and Public Affairs*, 26 (1997), 3–30.

—— *If You're an Egalitarian, How Come You're So Rich?* (Cambridge, MA: Harvard University Press, 2000).

—— 'Expensive Taste Rides Again', in Justine Burley (ed.), *Dworkin and His Critics* (Oxford: Blackwell, 2004).

Cohen, Joshua, 'Reflections on Rousseau: Autonomy and Democracy', *Philosophy and Public Affairs*, 15 (1986), 275–97.

—— 'The Economic Basis of Deliberative Democracy', *Social Philosophy and Policy*, 6 (1989), 25–50.

—— 'Moral Pluralism and Political Consensus', in David Copp, Jean Hampton, and John Roemer (eds.), *The Idea Of Democracy* (Cambridge: Cambridge University Press, 1993).

—— 'A More Democratic Liberalism', *Michigan Law Review*, 92 (1994), 1503–46.
—— 'Pluralism and Proceduralism', *Chicago-Kent Law Review*, 69 (1994), 589–618.
—— 'Procedure and Substance in Deliberative Democracy', in Seyla Benhabib (ed.), *Democracy and Difference: Contesting the Boundaries of the Political* (Princeton, NJ: Princeton University Press, 1996).
—— 'For a Democratic Society', in Samuel Freeman (ed.), *The Cambridge Companion to Rawls* (Cambridge: Cambridge University Press, 2003).
Cowley, Philip, and David Denver, 'Votes at 16? The Case Against', *Representation*, 41 (2004), 57–62.
Daniels, Norman, *Just Health Care* (Cambridge: Cambridge University Press, 1985).
—— *Am I My Parents' Keeper? An Essay on Justice between the Young and Old* (New York: Oxford University Press, 1988).
—— 'Equality of What: Welfare, Resources, or Capabilities?' in *Justice and Justification: Reflective Equilibrium in Theory and Practice* (Cambridge: Cambridge University Press, 1996).
Department for Education and Employment/Qualifications and Curriculum Authority, *The National Curriculum for England: Citizenship Key Stages 3–4* (London: HMSO, 1999).
Doppelt, Gerald, 'Is Rawls's Kantian Liberalism Coherent and Defensible?' *Ethics*, 99 (1989), 815–51.
Dorkenoo, Efua, *Cutting the Rose—Female Genital Mutilation: The Practice and Its Prevention* (London: Minority Rights Publications, 1995).
Dworkin, Ronald, *Taking Rights Seriously* (London: Duckworth, 1977).
—— *A Matter of Principle* (Oxford: Oxford University Press, 1985).
—— *Law's Empire* (London: Fontana Press, 1986).
—— 'Foundations of Liberal Equality', in Grethe Peterson (ed.), *The Tanner Lectures on Human Values*, vol. XI (Salt Lake City, UT: University of Utah Press, 1990).
—— *Sovereign Virtue: The Theory and Practice of Equality* (Cambridge, MA: Harvard University Press, 2000).
—— 'Justice in the Distribution of Health Care', in Matthew Clayton and Andrew Williams (eds.), *The Ideal of Equality* (London: Palgrave, 2002).
—— '*Sovereign Virtue* Revisited', *Ethics*, 113 (2002), 106–43.
—— 'Ronald Dworkin Replies', in Justine Burley (ed.), *Dworkin and His Critics* (Oxford: Blackwell, 2004).
Dwyer, James, *Religious Schools v. Children's Rights* (Ithaca, NY: Cornell University Press, 1998).

Elster, Jon, *Sour Grapes: Studies in the Subversion of Rationality* (Cambridge: Cambridge University Press, 1983).

Feinberg, Joel, *Harm to Self* (New York: Oxford University Press, 1986).

—— 'The Child's Right to an Open Future', in *Freedom and Fulfilment: Philosophical Essays* (Princeton, NJ: Princeton University Press, 1992).

Fleurbaey, Marc, 'Equality of Resources Revisited', *Ethics*, 113 (2002), 82–105.

Flew, Antony, *Education for Citizenship* (London: Institute of Economic Affairs, 2000).

Frankfurt, Harry G., 'Alternate Possibilities and Moral Responsibility', in *The Importance of What We Care About* (Cambridge: Cambridge University Press, 1988).

Friere, Paulo, *Pedagogy of the Oppressed* (Harmondsworth: Penguin Books, 1972).

Galston, William A., *Liberal Pluralism: The Implications of Value Pluralism for Political Theory and Practice* (Cambridge: Cambridge University Press, 2002).

Glover, Jonathan, *Causing Death and Saving Lives* (Harmondsworth: Penguin Books, 1977).

—— 'It Makes No Difference Whether or Not I Do It', in Peter Singer (ed.), *Applied Ethics* (Oxford: Oxford University Press, 1986).

Gray, John, *Mill on Liberty: A Defence* (London: Routledge, 1983).

Green, Leslie, 'Internal Minorities and Their Rights', in Will Kymlicka (ed.), *The Rights of Minority Cultures* (Oxford: Oxford University Press, 1995).

—— 'Associative Obligations and the State', in Justine Burley (ed.), *Dworkin and His Critics* (Oxford: Blackwell, 2004).

Grofman, Bernard and Scott Feld, 'Rousseau's General Will: A Condorcetian Perspective', *American Political Science Review*, 82 (1988), 567–76.

Gutmann, Amy, 'Children, Paternalism, and Education: A Liberal Argument', *Philosophy and Public Affairs*, 9 (1980), 338–58.

Harris, John, 'The Political Status of Children', in Keith Graham (ed.), *Contemporary Political Philosophy: Radical Studies* (Cambridge: Cambridge University Press, 1982).

Hobbes, Thomas, *Leviathan*, ed. Richard Tuck (Cambridge: Cambridge University Press, 1991).

Holt, John, 'Liberate Children', in William Aiken and Hugh LaFollette (eds.), *Whose Child? Children's Rights, Parental Authority, and State Power* (Totowa: Rowman & Littlefield, 1980).

Hubin, Donald, 'From Children's Rights to Parents' Rights' (unpublished paper, 2000).

Hume, David, *An Enquiry Concerning the Principles of Morals*, eds. L. A. Selby-Bigge and P. H. Nidditch (Oxford: Clarendon Press, 1975).

—— *A Treatise of Human Nature*, eds. L. A. Selby-Bigge and P. H. Nidditch (Oxford: Clarendon Press, 1978).

—— 'On Suicide' in Stephen Copley and Andrew Edgar (eds.), *Selected Writings* (Oxford: Oxford University Press, 1993).

Kagan, Shelly, *The Limits of Morality* (Oxford: Clarendon Press, 1989).

Kymlicka, Will, *Liberalism, Community and Culture* (Oxford: Clarendon Press, 1989).

—— 'Education for Citizenship', in *Politics in the Vernacular: Nationalism, Multiculturalism, and Citizenship* (Oxford: Oxford University Press, 2001).

Larmore, Charles, 'Political Liberalism', *Political Theory*, 18 (1990), 339–60.

Levinson, Meira, *The Demands of Liberal Education* (Oxford: Oxford University Press, 1999).

Locke, John, *Two Treatises of Government*, ed. Peter Laslett (Cambridge: Cambridge University Press, 1988).

McLaughlin, T. H., 'Parental Rights and the Religious Upbringing of Children', *Journal of Philosophy of Education*, 18 (1984), 75–82.

—— 'Citizenship Education in England: The Crick Report and Beyond', *Journal of Philosophy of Education*, 34 (2000), 541–70.

Macleod, Colin, 'Conceptions of Parental Autonomy', *Politics and Society*, 25 (1997), 117–40.

—— *Liberalism, Justice, and Markets: A Critique of Liberal Equality* (Oxford: Oxford University Press, 1998).

Mason, Andrew 'Political Community, Liberal-Nationalism, and the Ethics of Assimilation', *Ethics*, 109 (1999), 261–86.

—— *Community, Solidarity and Belonging: Levels of Community and their Normative Significance* (Cambridge: Cambridge University Press, 2000).

Mill, J. S., *On Liberty*, in John Gray (ed.), *On Liberty and Other Essays* (Oxford: Oxford University Press, 1991).

—— *The Subjection of Women*, in John Gray (ed.), *On Liberty and Other Essays*, (Oxford: Oxford University Press, 1991).

Miller, David, *On Nationality* (Oxford: Clarendon Press, 1995).

Mulhall, Stephen and Adam Swift, *Liberals and Communitarians*, 2nd edn. (Oxford: Blackwell, 1996).

Nagel, Thomas 'Moral Conflict and Political Legitimacy', *Philosophy and Public Affairs*, 16 (1987), 215–40.

—— 'Rawls on Justice', in Norman Daniels (ed.), *Reading Rawls: Critical Studies on Rawls' 'A Theory of Justice'* (Stanford, CA: Stanford University Press, 1989).

—— *Equality and Partiality* (New York: Oxford University Press, 1991).

—— 'Justice and Nature', in *Concealment and Exposure: And Other Essays* (New York: Oxford University Press, 2002).

—— 'The Problem of Global Justice', *Philosophy and Public Affairs*, 33 (2005), 113–47.

Neuhouser, Frederick, 'Freedom, Dependence and the General Will', *Philosophical Review*, 102 (1993), 363–95.

Nozick, Robert, *Anarchy, State, and Utopia* (Oxford: Blackwell, 1974).

Okin, Susan Moller, *Justice, Gender, and the Family* (New York: Basic Books, 1989).

Otsuka, Michael, 'Luck, Insurance, and Equality', *Ethics*, 113 (2002), 40–54.

—— *Libertarianism without Inequality* (Oxford: Oxford University Press, 2003).

Parfit, Derek, *Reasons and Persons* (Oxford: Oxford University Press, 1984).

Pierce, John and John Webster, 'USDA Estimates Child Rearing Costs', (Washington, DC: United States Department of Agriculture Press Release No. 0097, 2001).

Pogge, Thomas, *Realizing Rawls* (Ithaca, NY: Cornell University Press, 1989).

—— *World Poverty and Human Rights* (Cambridge: Polity Press, 2002).

—— 'Relational Conceptions of Justice: Responsibilities for Health Outcomes', in Sudhir Anand, Fabienne Peter, and Amartya Sen (eds.), *Public Health, Ethics, and Equality* (Oxford: Oxford University Press, 2004).

—— 'World Poverty and Human Rights', *Ethics and International Affairs*, 19 (2005), 1–7.

—— 'Recognized and Violated by International Law: The Human Rights of the Global Poor', *Leiden Journal of International Law*, 18 (2005), 717–45.

Qualifications and Curriculum Authority, *Education for Citizenship and the Teaching of Democracy in Schools: Final Report of the Advisory Group on Citizenship* (London: Qualifications and Curriculum Authority, 1998).

Quinn, Warren, 'The Puzzle of the Self-Torturer', in *Morality and Action* (Cambridge: Cambridge University Press, 1993).

Rawls, John, 'Reply to Habermas', *Journal of Philosophy*, 92 (1995), 132–80.

—— *Political Liberalism*, paperback edn. (New York: Columbia University Press, 1996).

—— *A Theory of Justice*, rev. edn. (Cambridge, MA: The Belknap Press of Harvard University Press, 1999).

—— 'The Idea of an Overlapping Consensus', in *Collected Papers* (Cambridge, MA: Harvard University Press, 1999).

—— 'The Idea of Public Reason Revisited', in *Collected Papers* (Cambridge, MA: Harvard University Press, 1999).

—— *The Law of Peoples* (Cambridge, MA: Harvard University Press, 1999).

—— *Justice as Fairness: A Restatement* (Cambridge, MA: The Belknap Press of Harvard University Press, 2001).

Raz, Joseph, *The Morality of Freedom* (Oxford: Clarendon Press, 1986).

—— *Practical Reason and Norms* (Princeton, NJ: Princeton University Press, 1990).

—— 'Facing Up: A Reply', *Southern California Law Review*, 62 (1989), 1153–235.

Rousseau, Jean-Jacques, *On the Social Contract*, ed. Roger Masters, trans. Judith Masters (New York: St Martin's Press, 1978).

Sandel, Michael, *Liberalism and the Limits of Justice* (Cambridge: Cambridge University Press, 1982).

—— 'Review of *Political Liberalism*', *Harvard Law Review*, 107 (1994), 1765–94.

Scanlon, T. M., 'The Moral Basis of Interpersonal Comparisons', in Jon Elster and John Roemer (eds.), *Interpersonal Comparisons of Well-Being* (Cambridge: Cambridge University Press, 1991).

—— *What We Owe to Each Other* (Cambridge, MA: The Belknap Press of Harvard University Press, 1998).

Schrag, Francis, 'Justice and the Family', *Inquiry*, 19 (1976), 193–208.

—— 'Children and Democracy: Theory and Policy', *Politics, Philosophy and Economics*, 3 (2004), 365–79.

Simmons, A. John, *Moral Principles and Political Obligations* (Princeton, NJ: Princeton University Press, 1979).

—— *The Lockean Theory of Rights* (Princeton, NJ: Princeton University Press, 1992).

—— 'Justification and Legitimacy', *Ethics*, 109 (1999), 739–71.

Singer, Peter, (ed.), 'All Animals are Equal', in *Applied Ethics* (Oxford: Oxford University Press, 1986).

Smith, Michael, *The Moral Problem* (Oxford: Blackwell, 1994).

Sumner, L. W., 'Positive Sexism', *Social Philosophy and Policy*, 5 (1987), 204–22.

Swift, Adam, *How Not to Be a Hypocrite: School Choice for the Morally Perplexed Parent* (London: Routledge, 2003).

Temkin, Larry, 'Equality, Priority, and the Levelling Down Objection', in Matthew Clayton and Andrew Williams (eds.), *The Ideal of Equality* (London: Palgrave, 2002).

Tooley, James, *Reclaiming Education* (London: Cassell, 2000).

Vallentyne, Peter, 'Equality and the Duty of Procreators' in David Archard and Colin Macleod (eds.), *The Moral and Political Status of Children* (Oxford: Oxford University Press, 2002).

—— 'The Rights and Duties of Childrearing', *William and Mary Bill of Rights Journal*, 44 (2003), 991–1010.

Van Parijs, Philippe, 'The Disenfranchisement of the Elderly, and Other Attempts to Secure Intergenerational Justice', *Philosophy and Public Affairs*, 27 (1998), 292–333.

Votes at 16 'Submission to the Electoral Commission's Review of Voting Age "How Old is Old Enough" ' (London: Votes at 16, 2003).

Waldron, Jeremy, 'Legislation and Moral Neutrality', in R. E. Goodin and Andrew Reeve (eds.), *Liberal Neutrality* (London: Routledge, 1989).

—— 'Justice Revisited (A Review of *Political Liberalism*)', *Times Literary Supplement* (18 June 1993), 5–6.

—— 'Mill and the Value of Moral Distress', in *Liberal Rights: Collected Papers 1981–1991* (Cambridge: Cambridge University Press, 1993).

—— 'Special Ties and Natural Duties', *Philosophy and Public Affairs*, 22 (1993), 3–30.

—— 'Theoretical Foundations of Liberalism', in *Liberal Rights: Collected Papers 1981–1991* (Cambridge: Cambridge University Press, 1993).

—— 'Disagreements about Justice', *Pacific Philosophical Quarterly*, 75 (1994), 372–87.

White, John, 'Education and Nationality', *Journal of Philosophy of Education*, 30 (1996), 327–43.

—— 'Patriotism without Obligation', *Journal of Philosophy of Education*, 35 (2001), 141–51.

Williams, Andrew, 'John Rawls, Communitarian' (unpublished paper, 1992).

—— 'Incentives, Inequality, and Publicity', *Philosophy and Public Affairs*, 27 (1998), 225–47.

—— 'The Rejection of Perfectionism' (unpublished typescript, 2000).

—— 'Review of *On Nationality*', *Mind*, 110 (2001), 512–16.

—— 'Equality for the Ambitious', *The Philosophical Quarterly*, 52 (2002), 377–89.

—— 'Equality, Ambition, and Insurance', *Aristotelian Society Supplementary Volume*, 78 (2004), 131–50.

Wollheim, Richard, *Socialism and Culture* (London: Fabian Society, 1962).

Wollstonecraft, Mary, *A Vindication of the Rights of Woman*, in Janet Todd (ed.), *Political Writings* (Oxford: Oxford University Press, 1994).

Index

CPSIA information can be obtained
at www.ICGtesting.com
Printed in the USA
BVOW06*1425071216
469194BV00029B/43/P

9 780199 268948